Re-Imagining Relationships in Education

Re-Imagining Relationships in Education

Ethics, Politics and Practices

Edited by
**Morwenna Griffiths,
Marit Honerød Hoveid,
Sharon Todd and Christine Winter**

WILEY Blackwell

This edition first published 2015
Originally published as Volume 48, Issue 2 of *The Journal of Philosophy of Education*
Chapters © 2015 The Authors
Editorial organization © 2015 Philosophy of Education Society of Great Britain
Blackwell Publishing was acquired by John Wiley & Sons in February 2007. Blackwell's
publishing program has been merged with Wiley's global Scientific, Technical, and
Medical business to form Wiley-Blackwell.

Registered Office
John Wiley & Sons Ltd, The Atrium, Southern Gate, Chichester, West Sussex, PO19 8SQ,
United Kingdom

Editorial Offices
350 Main Street, Malden, MA 02148-5020, USA
9600 Garsington Road, Oxford, OX4 2DQ, UK
The Atrium, Southern Gate, Chichester, West Sussex, PO19 8SQ, UK

For details of our global editorial offices, for customer services, and for information about
how to apply for permission to reuse the copyright material in this book please see our
website at www.wiley.com/wiley-blackwell.

The rights of Morwenna Griffiths, Marit Honerød Hoveid, Sharon Todd and Christine
Winter to be identified as the authors of the editorial material in this work has been
asserted in accordance with the Copyright, Designs and Patents Act 1988.

Wiley also publishes its books in a variety of electronic formats. Some content that
appears in print may not be available in electronic books.

Designations used by companies to distinguish their products are often claimed as
trademarks. All brand names and product names used in this book are trade names,
service marks, trademarks or registered trademarks of their respective owners. The
publisher is not associated with any product or vendor mentioned in this book. This
publication is designed to provide accurate and authoritative information in regard to the
subject matter covered. It is sold on the understanding that the publisher is not engaged in
rendering professional services. If professional advice or other expert assistance is
required, the services of a competent professional should be sought.

Library of Congress Cataloging-in-Publication data is available for this book.

ISBN: 9781118944738 (paperback)

A catalogue record for this book is available from the British Library.

Front cover image: Photo of an art-work created by Dr Khudu-Petersen and her teacher
education students in the University of Botswana, copyright Andreas Gessner.

Set in 11.25 on 12 pt Times by Toppan Best-set Premedia Limited

Printed in Singapore by C.O.S. Printers Pte Ltd

01   2015

Contents

Notes on Contributors

Rebecca Adami Department of Education, Stockholm University, Frescativägen 54, Stockholm, SE-10691, Sweden

Ruth Cigman Department of Humanities and Social Sciences, Institute of Education, 20 BedfordWay, London WC1 OAL, UK

Arnhild Finne Department of Education, Norwegian University of Science and Technology, Loholt Alle, NTNU, Trondheim, NO-7491, Norway

Heather Greenhalgh-Spencer Department of Curriculum and Instruction, College of Education, Texas Tech University, Box 41071, Lubbock, TX 79409-1071

Morwenna Griffiths Moray House School of Education, University of Edinburgh, Thomson's Land, Holyrood Road, Edinburgh EH8 8AQ, Scotland, UK

Marit Honerød Hoveid Department of Education, Norwegian University of Science and Technology, Loholt Alle, NTNU, Trondheim, NO-7491, Norway

Rachel Jones Department of Philosophy, George Mason University, Robinson Hall B, GMU, Fairfax, VA-22030, USA

Aislinn O'Donnell Faculty of Education, Mary Immaculate College, University of Limerick, South Circular Road, Limerick, Ireland

Amy Shuffelton Cultural and Educational Policy Studies, Loyola University Chicago, 820 N Michigan Ave, Chicago, IL-60611, USA

Sharon Todd Department of Education, National University of Ireland, Maynooth, County Kildare, Ireland

Caroline Wilson Duoda, Women's Research Centre, University of Barcelona; Postal address: 57 High Street North, Crail, KY10 3RA, Fife, Scotland, UK

Christine Winter Department of Education, University of Sheffield, 388 Glossop Road, Sheffield S10 4BJ, UK

Introduction

Work in philosophy of education has, especially since the late 1980s, turned to the study of relationships in its espousal of the idea that education is or ought to be something other than a faceless enterprise bent solely on social reproduction and the sterile transmission of knowledge. A broad spectrum of theorists who embrace a range of philosophical outlooks—pragmatism, hermeneutics, psychoanalysis, Levinasian ethics, feminism and posthumanism, to name the most influential—speak of the connections, attachments and affiliations between people as essential features of any education worthy of its name. Although there is wide variation in terms of characterizing relation as that which occurs between individuals, persons, subjects, beings, or psyches, this strand of educational thought has crystallized around the idea that being with others in relation is a primary condition of our educational life. Such ideas set themselves against any account of education that is bereft of the 'human' element, and they specifically speak against the new technocracy ushered in by what some see as a neo-liberal agenda, or market-driven interests.

What this book brings to the table is a re-imagining of relationships in education that both draws upon and extends earlier work in the field while also bringing new theoretical insights to bear on contemporary practices in education. It focuses on conceiving not only the dyadic aspects of the teacher-student relation, but reframes the idea of relationships as being intrinsically linked with the ethical and political nature of education itself. It also extends our conceptions of relationships beyond the humanist enterprise. Thus, the relationships discussed here simultaneously deal with both the micro-level of educational interaction and the macro-level of what meaning such relationships have within the context of wider society.

Aside from this major unifying point, one of the striking characteristics of this book is the diversity represented by the chapters as a whole. On one level such diversity reveals itself in terms of the different philosophical perspectives explored in relation to our common theme of educational relationships. In this regard, the chapters range across the philosophical thought of Hannah Arendt, Samuel Beckett, Jacques Derrida, Félix Guattari, Luce Irigaray, Emmanuel Levinas, Jean-François Lyotard, Luisa Muraro, Plato, Jean-Jacques Rousseau, and Mary Wollstonecraft, to name a few. On another level, diversity appears in the very rendering of what 'relationships' mean, and further what makes them 'educational'. The relationships between school-community, curriculum knowledge and subjectivity, human and nature, and bodies and experience are some of the ways in which relationships are depicted as being linked to views of education that are not only about formal settings, but about questions of life, existence, and change. This indicates to us that there is a perceptibly felt need to broaden and extend the scope of what constitutes relationships, and particularly what meaning they can have for, in and through education. On yet another level, 'diversity' itself operates as a philosophical idea or assumption in many of the essays. Attention is granted to the plurality of meaning, for instance, generated through our actions, our narratives, and our encounters with literature, nature, and other human subjects, all of which are always already relational. Moreover, since relationships themselves are presented here as being both plural and diverse, traditional conceptions of autonomy, singularity, unity and failure are reconsidered as embodying complex dynamics, connections and affiliations. Such diversity demonstrates that the purpose of re-imagining relationships is thus not about offering a single, unified response to complex educational questions, but to open up a landscape of thought, where new kinds of questions can be raised.

The background for the group of women authors in this book is the annual Women in Philosophy of Education symposium, sponsored by PESBG. A way of philosophizing has developed over the course of these seminars which we argue is pivotal to a development of philosophical thought in education. The working format, enabling both the individual and the collective approach to philosophizing is something we have pursued in this book. For example, in the events leading up to this book, we held discussion-based seminars. There, we all presented our works in progress, which had been read in advance by everyone, and then we critically discussed with the authors how to extend and strengthen their work. The seminars were where the idea for this book was generated. Over the course of the past year we have had not only the usual extensive e-mail contact, but two face-to-face meetings—one in Limerick, the other in Stockholm—to comment and work on each other's texts. This was in many ways a time-consuming process, but it was rewarding in terms of building good professional relations and developing our scholarly work. Through respect, listening, and much laughter we have created an environment where everyone committed and continually recommitted themselves to the work we started off a little over a year ago. Such commitment, we venture, was only possible through the collaborative community created by this process. This is for all of us—editors and authors included—a wonderful accomplishment and stands testament to the idea that collaboration lies at the heart of seeking excellence in our academic work.

Morwenna Griffiths
Marit Honerød Hoveid
Sharon Todd
Christine Winter

1
Re-reading Diotima: Resources for a Relational Pedagogy

RACHEL JONES

My starting point in this chapter is one of the earliest texts in the Western tradition to explore the relations between philosophy and pedagogy, Plato's *Symposium*. In this text, love (or more properly, *eros*) plays the mediating role, turning a love of wisdom into a pedagogical erotics that enables a journey of enlightenment. *Symposium* thus seems a promising resource, both for reflecting on the specifically relational aspects of the educative process, and for the collective project of reimagining the ethics and practices of pedagogical relationships. As I will go on to show, however, things are not so simple. At a key moment in the text, Plato's metaphysical trajectory pulls away from a fully relational dynamic and leads instead towards a more solipsistic journey. This journey ends by valorising the reproduction of the same rather than the generation of the new, surprising or unexpected. In many ways one thus has to read against the explicit direction of the text to recover the resources for a generative, relational pedagogy that, I will argue, are still to be found there.

To help generate such readings, I will turn to the work of more recent thinkers, including Hannah Arendt, Jean-François Lyotard and Luce Irigaray as well as David Halperin, Christine Battersby, Bell Hooks, Richard Smith and Morwenna Griffiths. My suggestion is that by approaching *Symposium* through their work, this text can yield insights that are helpful for contemplating the educational process in a more contemporary context, and in particular, for thinking about the nature of pedagogical relations in ways that contribute to the specific aims of this book.[1] On the one hand, *Symposium* affirms that, as the editors of this book put it, 'being with others in relation is a primary condition of our educational life and therefore demands our serious attention, both as teachers and as theorists.' By bringing together a group of friends to discourse about love, *Symposium* performatively confirms that education is a fundamentally *shared* engagement. This is

Re-Imagining Relationships in Education: Ethics, Politics and Practices, First Edition. Edited by Morwenna Griffiths, Marit Honerød Hoveid, Sharon Todd and Christine Winter. Chapters © 2015 The Authors. Editorial organization © 2015 Philosophy of Education Society of Great Britain. Published 2015 by John Wiley & Sons Ltd.

reinforced both by its dialogical form and by the content of a number of key passages that focus specifically on *eros'* role in pedagogical relations (both philosophical and civic). In keeping with Plato's suspicions about the written word (*Phaedrus* 274b-278e), *Symposium* presents this engagement as one primarily shared between living human beings (and only indirectly with us, the readers of the text). Its sustained examination of *eros* can provide insights into the kinds of dynamics that are conducive to generative encounters between students and teachers, as well as to genuinely transformative learning and teaching.

On the other hand, the shared discursive space staged by *Symposium* is constituted by a number of exclusions: most explicitly, when the flute-girl is asked to leave and withdraw to women's quarters (*Symposium* 176e),[2] but also implicitly because, as Athenian convention would demand, the discoursing company is formed of only free men (and not slaves). Plato's text might thereby prompt us to ask whose exclusion is constitutive of our own discursive and educative spaces. In *Symposium*, the initial expulsion of the flute-girl is undercut by Diotima's later inclusion as an apparently privileged female voice. As we will see, however, Diotima's status is far from straightforward and points to a deeper issue in the text (and Plato's philosophy more generally) concerning the place of difference and the privileging of sameness. Indeed, it is Plato's commitment to a particular metaphysics—I will argue—that compromises the pedagogical potential of his own text. To be fully useful to the project of reimagining relationships in education, key elements of *Symposium* need to be disentangled from this metaphysical frame, as well as from the hom-(m)osociality that reflects the Platonic idealisation of sameness. The critical lens provided by the work of more recent thinkers helps us to undertake this disentangling. More specifically, Lyotard, Irigaray and the other thinkers I will draw on here help us to select those aspects of *Symposium* that are most conducive to re-thinking pedagogical relations with an attentiveness to bodies, differences, and generative dependencies. Together, these texts and thinkers point us towards a relational pedagogy that would complement the recent turn to a relational self through which feminist philosophers have sought to displace the dominant Western model of the autonomous individual subject.[3]

Such a pedagogy has three key features. First, relations are not seen simply as a means to an end—necessary to allow a teacher to impart information effectively, for example, or the student to acquire a particular skill set—but as the constitutive and always embodied site of education understood as an ongoing and open-ended process. Second, the multiple relations that constitute the educative process (including relations to previous educative encounters) do not rely on fixed or pre-existing roles, but simultaneously constitute its participants as 'learners' and 'teachers'—or perhaps better, as 'learning' and 'teaching', understood as always relational (and never mutually exclusive) activities. And third, the focus of such a pedagogy is thus on the relations that constitute the educative process and the encounters that foster them, rather than on outcomes or individual participants considered as wholly independent of those relations.

I INTRODUCING DIOTIMA

The tension between the metaphysical trajectory of *Symposium* and the relational resources that I am suggesting are also to be found there is most dramatically evident in the section of the text with which I will be concerned here. In this section, Socrates reports the conversations in which a wise woman of Mantineia once taught him about love (*eros*) (*Symposium* 201d-212b). 'Diotima's speech' (as it is often known, despite its dialogical structure) is intriguing for many reasons, not least because it is the only place in Plato's known oeuvre where a woman takes on the part of the philosopher.[4] This leads to the obvious question: 'Why is Diotima a Woman?'—though as David Halperin shows, there is far from an obvious answer.

Halperin's extended essay on this topic (1990) aids my suggestion that *Symposium* may contain resources for a relational pedagogy. In its original Athenian context, Halperin argues, Diotima's speech was already transgressive due to its portrayal of the erotic relations that should characterise properly philosophical encounters. Diotima conforms to Athenian convention by aligning the most ideal erotic relations with those between male lovers. However, Halperin shows how Plato's presentation of Diotima appropriates key elements of what was culturally constructed as 'feminine' in ways that depart from the traditional Athenian model of male erotic relations (which still recognisably informs some of the earlier speeches in *Symposium*). Such relations were carefully structured to support what was considered the proper transition from boy to man, and hence, active citizenship. The standard model of the lover (*erastes*) / beloved (*eromenos*) relation was strongly hierarchical. The older, male lover actively took pleasure in his younger beloved, who could accept but crucially should not take pleasure in his passive, receptive position: the male citizen-to-be should not learn to like the feminine, submissive role (Halperin 1990, pp. 30–36).

Halperin argues that Plato subverts this hierarchical norm in two ways. First, in both *Symposium* and *Phaedrus*, Plato develops a model in which the beloved feels a kind of active counter-*eros*. While at odds with Athenian convention, philosophically this is crucial, as it means the beloved actively participates in the journey towards wisdom that (for Plato) ought to be the shared goal of both lover and beloved (pp. 129–37). Second, Diotima's 'correct pederasty' (p. 113, quoting *Symposium* 211b) involves shifting the conception of erotic desire from acquisitive to procreative. As Halperin notes, this shift is reflected directly in the text as Diotima rejects Socrates' initial view that *eros* is a desire to possess the beautiful and instead teaches that *eros* is a desire 'for birth and procreation in the beautiful' (p. 137, quoting *Symposium* 204d and 206e), in a generative encounter that releases the creative energies of both participants, as emphasised by the multiple metaphors of birth and begetting that infuse Diotima's teaching (including, most notably, the image of male pregnancy).[5]

Halperin is suspicious of just how 'feminine' these features of reciprocity and generation really are (as reflected in the fact that, in Plato's text, the part of Diotima is voiced by Socrates and written by Plato). He argues that the identification of the feminine with a reciprocity that undoes the active/passive binary, as well as in terms of procreation, is a construction of female 'difference' that already takes both the physiology and the cultural representation of male bodies and desires as the norm.[6] The feminine is aligned with a lack of masculinity (i.e. the desire to dominate in hierarchical relations) or with what masculinity lacks (i.e. the capacity to give birth) (pp. 143–5). Even more importantly, these 'feminine' (i.e. non-masculine) qualities of reciprocity and birth are figured via Diotima in ways that allow them to be re-appropriated as intrinsic to the *male* philosopher's erotic journey, while holding their femininity at a protective distance through the mask of a female speaker: 'The essential element in Plato's staging of "femininity" . . . is a mimetic transvestitism' (p. 146).[7]

I am sympathetic to Halperin's claim that 'when Diotima speaks, she does not speak for women: she silences them' (p. 145). But I am also concerned that to read *Symposium's* references to female generative powers as *only* a masculine textual construction risks silencing women in another way.[8] Feminist thinkers have argued that the generative capacities manifest in pregnancy and birth provide us with potential models of self and relation that contest the dominant modern ideal of the autonomous individual. Such an individual is both archetypally male and characterised by its constitutive independence from others. In contrast, Battersby has argued, to be positioned as *female* in

Western modernity has been to be aligned with 'a body that births'. Such a body makes relations of dependency the norm and allows otherness to be sustained within a (thoroughly fleshy and bodily) self (Battersby, 1998, pp. 38–9). Insofar as it entails deviating from the modern ideal of autonomous selfhood, 'being female' has meant being 'allocated to a non-privileged position in a social and conceptual nexus of power' (Battersby, 1994, p. 137). But reflecting on the female body understood specifically as a 'body that births' can also provide resources for re-conceptualising the self, as well as its relations to otherness (Battersby, 1998, 2007). Thus, despite Halperin's (justified) suspicions about the ways in which *Symposium* appropriates the feminine to serve the male philosopher's ends, we can also read Diotima's emphasis on reciprocity and generation as pointing to a different philosophical perspective. This perspective comes into view once the figures of pregnancy and birth are seen not *just* as reflecting appropriative male fantasies about reproduction, but *also* as offering alternative ways of thinking about bodies, desires, and relations that open up if (like Battersby) we take a different (distinctively female) body as the norm.

I will return to the pedagogical implications of Battersby's position in the final section of this chapter. First, however, I will explore a series of responses to Diotima by drawing on Arendt, Lyotard, and Irigaray. Through their work, I hope to tease out the transformative pedagogical potential contained in Diotima's teachings. Each of the responses I trace can be seen as developing key aspects of Halperin's reading. Thus, I will argue that the model of pedagogical *eros* as generative rather than possessive can be extended and deepened through Arendt's reflections on natality and Lyotard's on infancy. In turn, both reciprocity and generative becoming are privileged in Irigaray's subversive re-appropriation of Plato's original text. As shown by Marit Hoveid and Arnhild Finne, Sharon Todd, and Caroline Wilson (Chapters 5, 4, and 2 of this book, respectively), Irigaray's philosophy of sexuate difference is a fruitful source for a relational approach to education.[9] Like Battersby, Irigaray also returns us to pregnancy and birth as belonging to a specifically female body.[10] However, if Irigaray's refiguring of the erotic encounter generates an image of pedagogical relations as reciprocally transformative and open to difference, Battersby's reflections on a 'body that births' are more helpful for thinking about the asymmetrical dependencies and unequal power relations that typically characterise the pedagogical scene. As both Griffiths and Amy Shuffelton show (Chapters 11 and 3, respectively), the devaluation of dependencies remains a critical issue in education, in both historical and contemporary contexts, and particularly in relation to gender. Thus, in the final section I conjoin Battersby with Smith, Griffiths and Hooks to resituate Diotima's teaching in relation to pedagogical issues of autonomy and dependency.

II DIOTIMA, ARENDT AND NATALITY

Diotima's teaching of Socrates begins by emphasising love's intermediary nature: if love desires what it lacks, and love loves the beautiful and good, love cannot itself *be* beautiful and good. Instead, love is *in between* the beautiful and good and the bad and ugly; hence the pedagogical role of *eros*, as the mediating force which carries those who lack, yet still desire wisdom, along the difficult path between ignorance and understanding.

Diotima proceeds to describe love as a 'begetting in beauty, in respect to both the body and the soul' (*Symposium* 206b). Human beings are pregnant or fecund, she explains, full of potentiality which they long to release; love of another's beauty allows them to bring forth what they bear (206c–d). Such engendering is initially presented as 'an immortal element' in mortal human creatures. However, as Diotima's speech progresses, a crucial division occurs. *Eros* is divided into love of physical beauty, which engenders merely physical (hence mortal) offspring, and love of beautiful souls, which generates offspring that come closer to immortality in the form of beautiful discourse or ideas (208e–209e). This hierarchy is reinforced by Diotima's concluding lesson, where she explains how one who is pregnant in soul—providing they are properly educated—will pass from love of a particular body, to love of appearances in general, to the higher beauty of souls, and then of laws and knowledge, until finally they are turned towards an encounter with Beauty itself (210a–212a). Unlike the transient beauty of the flesh, Beauty itself neither comes to be nor perishes, neither grows nor diminishes. Only in encountering such transcendent and eternal beauty is the loving soul inspired to give birth to true virtue, the closest a human being can come to immortality.

Approached through the work of Arendt, Diotima's speech can be seen as embodying a crucial shift in perspective. According to Arendt, the Western philosophical tradition turns away from an originary Greek concern with *immortality*, and reorients itself towards the *eternal* in ways that devalue the plurality of singular lives that take shape in the transient earthly realm (Arendt, 1958, pp. 17–21). Insofar as Diotima's speech begins with a celebration of immortality generated through erotic encounters involving both body and soul, and moves towards a hierarchy in which the highest form of love leads away from particular bodies and towards the eternal form of Beauty itself, it can be seen as dramatising this shift.

Arendt's concern is with the way this orientation towards the eternal turns politics into a question of law and order, of how best to rule the unruly realm of appearances. The political is thereby removed from its proper domain, which is characterised by action: the capacity to initiate new and unpredictable chains of events through words and deeds in the public realm (Arendt, 1958, pp. 175–247). Such a capacity is rooted in the fact that, while human beings may be destined to die, they begin in birth, and are hence characterised not only by mortality, but also by natality, as a capacity for new beginnings (pp. 176–8, 246–7). It is natality whose value is displaced in the final part of Diotima's teaching, despite the metaphors of birth that pervade the text. This displacement has pedagogical as well as political implications, for according to Diotima's final words, true virtue is produced not through the birth of new thoughts, but only to the extent that the lover is able to replicate a vision of eternal beauty. The questioning journey of the Platonic student of *eros* turns out not to be genuinely open and unpredictable; instead, its pre-determined end is located in an eternal ideality where beginnings would be neither possible nor necessary.

Nonetheless, reading Diotima through Arendt generates not only a critical response but also a productive one. Her emphasis on natality points us back to the earlier part of Diotima's speech where all humans are described as pregnant 'both in body and in soul', and where *eros* animates an encounter that allows those who are 'bursting with life' to give birth in a state of 'great excitement' (*Symposium*, 206c–e). Such aspects of the text might helpfully return us to a conception of the educative process as involving both bodies and minds, as well as to a model of pedagogical encounters as generative and 'natal', able to initiate new beginnings—new ways of thinking and being—in all their 'startling unexpectedness' (Arendt, 1958, p. 178).[11]

Arendt also provides two helpful counterparts to the educative process understood as generative and natal, for as she shows, such processes are always fragile and risky, and their full effects are irreversible without being entirely predictable. These unavoidable risks are mitigated, first, by a capacity to make (and keep) promises, which offsets the uncertainty of the future by setting up 'islands of security' that allow for continuity in human relations; and second, by forgiveness, which releases us 'from the predicament of irreversibility—of being unable to undo what one has done', even though one can never fully know or predict the consequences of one's actions (p. 237).

Translated into a pedagogical context, these capacities speak to the trust that must be cultivated and the forgiveness that must be promised for real (risky, natal) learning to begin: the promise (implicit or explicit) that each will engage in the process constructively, that mistakes will be an occasion for learning not punishment or humiliation, and that unexpected and unintended harm will be forgiven. Promising and forgiving are essentially relational capacities, belonging to the plural site of human existence and action. They find their home in the educative process as an always-relational site of exposure and care. Thus understood, education might not only be natal, but a privileged site for the cultivation of natality, that capacity for new beginnings which reminds us that 'men, though they must die, are not born in order to die but in order to begin' (p. 246).

III DIOTIMA, LYOTARD AND INFANCY

Arendt's concern with the reduction of politics and philosophy to regimes of law and mastery is shared by Lyotard, who uses Diotima's speech to suggest that Plato's metaphysics scapegoats women by making them the representatives of the unruly realm of appearances. Through her alignment with corporeal desire and (merely) physical reproduction, woman is identified with the 'poverty' of the transient realm of becoming 'through which, people say, we must pass to attain timeless truth.' (Lyotard, 1993b, p. 71) Against this 'timeless truth' that denies the value of becoming and difference, Lyotard sides with the poverty of the feminine (p. 70, p. 114). Such poverty engenders a resourceful inventiveness that escapes the (metaphysical) law of the masters and allows thinking to emerge in the midst of life.

Despite Lyotard's positive re-valorisation of the phenomenal world of (unmasterable) becoming, we might well suspect that his alliance with the feminine constitutes another example of the appropriative logic Halperin critiques, whereby the feminine is constructed to serve the interests of the male subject (here, in escaping metaphysical mastery), especially as Lyotard explicitly assimilates the feminine to his own concept of the pagan (p. 114). Happily, as we will see, Lyotard's engagement with Diotima's presentation of *Eros* is linked to another, less problematic figure in his work, one that will also be aligned with the inventiveness poverty demands: namely, that of infancy. On Lyotard's approach, Diotima becomes a figure divided against herself. In the later part of her teaching, she seems to become one of those 'people' who advocate passing through appearances to attain timeless beauty and truth. But in an earlier passage, she dramatises the alliance of poverty and resourcefulness that Lyotard himself values. In Diotima's account of the birth of *Eros*, Plenty (*Poros*) partakes in too much wine on Aphrodite's birthday and is discovered in a drunken stupor by Poverty (*Penia*) (*Symposium*, 203b–e). Here their roles switch, for poverty shows considerable resourcefulness in taking advantage of Plenty's defenceless state to conceive *Eros*, who inherits qualities from both parents. Thanks to his mother, he is poor, unkempt, shoeless and homeless, a wanderer who sleeps under the stars; thanks to his father, he is inventive, bold, always weaving some stratagem, a sophist and a sorcerer.

In his essay, 'On the Strength of the Weak', Lyotard draws explicitly on Diotima's mythic tale to counter metaphysics with the sophistic metamorphoses of *Eros*, who he sees as 'the opposite of a master' (1993b, p. 71). However, despite the way he also associates the subversive 'strength of the weak' with the feminine (ibid., pp. 70, 93, 108–114), Lyotard emphasises that the qualities of *Eros* that elude the logic of the masters are inherited from his father (p. 70). Rather than reading this as a simple dismissal of *Eros'* mother (it is the philosopher-masters who are guilty of identifying women with lack, according to Lyotard), we might instead see this double alignment of *Eros*—with the feminine power of dissimulation as well as the resourcefulness of *Poros*—as recalling Diotima's original description, in which *Eros* inherits qualities from both his father *and* his mother.[12] *Eros* thereby subverts the philosophical project of mastery by crossing *between* the qualities (masculinity and femininity, plenitude and lack, even life and death) on whose opposition and mutual exclusion the mastery of truth depends.[13]

Rather than being aligned with the feminine, the subversive combination of powerless vulnerability and obstinate inventiveness that characterises the infant *Eros* comes to be associated in Lyotard's writings with infancy per se (see 1993b, p. 149), understood not as a chronological stage of life but an existential condition that can be renewed at any age (1993b, p. 149; 1993a, pp. 99–107). For Lyotard, infancy is the state of exposure that results when the certainties of the subject are undone, when we are returned to an indeterminacy for which we are unprepared, and when a searching curiosity is all that is left to us, prompting a questioning that has to proceed without ready-made criteria. Infancy is the impoverishment that demands we judge in the absence of the law, and the inventiveness that makes it possible to do so.[14] Thus, infancy is the condition of genuine learning and—because it allows the search for wisdom to be indefinitely renewed—the condition of philosophy.

In contrast to the Platonic model, the philosophical education made possible by infancy does not lead to a vision of timeless ideals that govern the proper path of thought. Rather, infancy makes it possible to begin to think again, to initiate thought, without knowing in advance where it will lead. Infancy sustains the 'work of recommencement' (Lyotard, 1993a, p. 102): it makes possible the judgements without criteria that break open accepted truths and call into question past values and future destinations, setting our thoughts and our imaginations in motion. Infancy is thus also the condition of *teaching* philosophy, which cannot be reduced to the application of a method or technique. Instead, it means showing someone what is involved in exposing oneself to the vagaries of thought: 'You cannot open up a question without leaving yourself open to it. You cannot scrutinize a "subject" . . . without being scrutinized by it. You cannot do any of these things without renewing ties with the season of childhood, the season of the mind's possibilities' (p. 100). Lyotard, like Christine Winter (Chapter 7), values the time spent on sideroads that throw one off the accepted course; like Aislinn O'Donnell (Chapter 6), his work calls for a re-evaluation of failure. For one can learn nothing from others 'unless they themselves learn to unlearn' (Lyotard, 1993a, p. 101): unless they enter the classroom without having made up their minds in advance—unless they are willing to be cast adrift, and allow themselves to be returned to infancy.

Just as Arendt aligns the capacity for beginnings with natality, so for Lyotard, infancy's questioning inventiveness repays a debt to birth by re-affirming the possibility of beginning anew. Yet in both Arendt's reflections on natality, and Lyotard's on infancy, the figure of the mother is for the most part curiously absent. In Arendt's case, this is because of the way she distinguishes natality as a power for beginning manifest in action from physical birth, which—in a troubling echo of Diotima's hierarchical teaching—is relegated to the sphere of labour and biological necessity. For his part, Lyotard insists that birth is 'not merely the biological fact of parturition', but 'the event of a possible radical alteration in the course compelling things to repeat the same': it is birth as *event* which is ontologically significant, rather than actual birth, in which the radicality of the event is both revealed and concealed (1993b, p. 151). This abstraction of birth from the body of the mother into the figure of the event also finds echoes in Plato's philosophy, where birth and pregnancy are metaphorically appropriated to affirm the generative power (and hence, the ontological significance) of the non-corporeal life of the soul and (above all) the Forms. Thus, in displacing the role of the mother, both Lyotard and Arendt inadvertently reinscribe traces of the very metaphysical tradition they seek to challenge. In this regard, it is telling that both thinkers continue to invoke the Greek figure that presents human existence as a coming from and returning to nothingness (see for example Lyotard, 1993b, p. 146; Arendt, 1978, p. 19). In contrast, Irigaray will insist that birth is not a 'coming from nothing', but a passage into the world through the body of a woman.

IV DIOTIMA, IRIGARAY AND THE GENERATIVE ENCOUNTER

Making birth the starting point for an account of human existence means beginning with the relation of each singular being to the flesh and blood m/other from whom he or she comes. Human existence is thereby seen as both constitutively sexuate, and constitutively rela-tional. Again, this ontological reorientation has significant pedagogi-cal implications (as Todd and Wilson also explore). For Lyotard, philosophy is 'an exercise in discomposure' which is 'first and fore-most an *autodidactic* activity' (1993a, pp. 100–1; my emphasis). In ways that reflect his distancing of infancy as event from the originary corporeal relation to the mother, the real work of philosophy takes place when thought unravels and the thinking subject becomes other to itself, rather than in relations *between* ourselves and actual others (whether those others are encountered as textual voices, or flesh and blood interlocutors).[15] By contrast, Irigaray's emphasis on the onto-logical primacy of the maternal relation holds open the promise of a more thoroughly relational model of the self, and hence, the peda-gogical process. This is not to deny that learning and growth involve becoming other to ourselves in the unsettling ways Lyotard describes. Rather, it is to remember that the condition of such processes of becoming other to ourselves are the relations with those actual others that allow us to come into being (and into language) in the first place, just as it is our ongoing encounters with others that will unsettle us and make us think again.

Further resources for a relational pedagogy emerge in Irigaray's own re-reading of Diotima's speech, 'Sorcerer Love' (Irigaray, 1994).[16] Like Arendt, Irigaray is uneasy about the final trajectory of Diotima's teaching. To counter this, she directs us back to the earlier passage in *Symposium* where Diotima tells Socrates that:

> All men [human beings] are pregnant in respect to both the body and the soul, [. . .] and when they reach a certain age, our nature desires to beget. It cannot beget in ugliness, but only in beauty. The intercourse [*sunousia*, lit. being with] of man and woman is

a begetting [or giving birth]. This is a divine thing, and pregnancy and procreation are an immortal element in the mortal
living creature (206c).[17]

For Irigaray, this passage (206c–e) reinforces love's role as intermediary: it is love that brings lovers together, in such a way that their being
with one another allows them to release what they bear in a joyful
engendering. It also helps Irigaray develop an account of the erotic
encounter based on a model of birth and gestation as generative rather
than merely reproductive. Whereas later, Diotima will emphasise the
desire to secure immortality via one's offspring (i.e. via reproduction),
in this earlier passage, the erotic encounter simply *is* a bearing or
begetting: intercourse, or more literally, being with another in love, is
generative in and of itself. Whether or not a child is born, love
engenders a being-with one another which is a rebirth of the lovers
themselves, in a continual process of regeneration and growth.[18] In
turn, this mutual re-engendering constitutes a 'passage to immortality': not because it turns mortals into immortal *beings*, but because it
manifests immortality as a perpetual *becoming*, and thus a 'perpetual
becoming-immortal' that takes place within mortal life (Irigaray,
1994, pp. 187–9).

   Despite the ways in which, for Diotima, *eros* animates the ideal
pedagogical relation, Irigaray does not unpack the specifically pedagogical implications of her re-reading of this text. However, if we map
the dynamics of her rendering of the erotic encounter back onto a
pedagogical context, several key points emerge. First, and most obviously, the pedagogical encounter is also a site for releasing the potential for growth in processes of becoming and change; thus, the
pedagogical encounter can also be a way of affirming the possibilities
for perpetual becoming harboured within mortal life, and hence
*re*affirming the promise of birth. Here again it is vital that Irigaray
conceives of birth as generative rather than merely reproductive: likewise, the educative encounters capable of renewing the promise of
birth will consist not in the passive reproduction of received ideas, but
the generation of thought and the imagining of possibilities, as well
as new capacities and connections. Second, because on Irigaray's
reading, the natal promise that Diotima discerns in all human beings
is reaffirmed in a thoroughly relational scene, so the pedagogical
process can also be resituated within a fully relational context: not in
the auto-affective unravelling of the subject, but in the space *between*
singular beings who encounter one another in their difference(s) (see
also Todd and Hoveid and Finne, Chapters 4 and 5, respectively).

Third, in recovering the explicitly relational nature of Diotima's original teaching (in contrast to the final solitary encounter with Beauty itself), Irigaray displaces another well-known Platonic image for the pedagogical process: that of the Socratic midwife. This image presents the teacher as one who helps others give birth to ideas while being barren and past child-bearing age themselves (*Theaetetus*, 149a–151d). Irigaray's reading of Diotima's erotic pedagogy, like Halperin's, offers a more reciprocal model of the educative process as an encounter in which both student and teacher are transformed. Here the good teacher would be a pregnant midwife, ready to learn as they teach. However, because Irigaray argues that it is only in the later sections of Diotima's speech that the lovers' encounter is mediated by a third, *external* goal (the production of a child, the attainment of truth), and that, in earlier passages, love needs no external outcome but is expressed in the generative becomings of the encounter itself,[19] her reading allows for greater emphasis on the way that each of those engaged in the encounter are *differently* transformed. In this way, she reminds us that reciprocity does not have to entail sameness or even equivalence: it can involve the return of one gesture (a smile) with another quite different (a welcoming wave), and can occur between those of a different sex, race, age or ethnicity, where what might be reciprocated is an attentiveness to one another's differences without the desire to assimilate or appropriate. On this model, fertile peda-gogical relations would be those allowing differing potentials to be realised in differing ways.

Fourth, on Irigaray's reading, the erotic encounter becomes a process of giving birth (*un enfantement*) in which what is reborn is the lovers themselves, who are thereby returned to infancy (*l'enfance*).[20] Love therefore creates the conditions for its own renewal: those returned to infancy can begin all over again. Similarly, a pedagogical encounter that allows latent potential to be released and new capacities to develop simultaneously regenerates the conditions for future learn-ing and growth. Positive learning experiences also renew our openness to others, reminding us that such openness can lead to pleasurable and exciting journeys of transformation. Thus one might say that infancy itself is what is engendered anew in the pedagogical encounter: not as a *lack* of adult capacities, but as new beginnings and renewed poten-tialities. This means that 'infancy' is not here understood as a state of immaturity equated with deficiency, but rather as Dewey conceives it: as 'a force positively present—the *ability* to develop . . . the *power* to grow.' (Dewey, 2004, pp. 40–1) It is this positive power that makes adults mourn the loss of immaturity (ibid), and that is re-affirmed in both Lyotard's notion of infancy and Irigaray's re-reading of the erotic encounter. On this model, learning is not a matter of passively absorbing knowledge to fill a gap or lack, but an active, ongoing, relational process of exploring diverse powers and capacities.

V RE-THINKING DEPENDENCIES AND POWER RELATIONS

At this point, I would like to recall the vulnerability that Lyotard reminds us is constitutive of infancy, and thus, the manifold ways in which the pedagogical relation can be distorted or abused. As Smith notes, it is in an effort to refuse or overcome our vulnerability that we seek to deny the attachments and dependencies that bind us to others, particularly through love. Smith turns to Diotima to make this point, reworking the final part of her speech as follows:

My attachment to particular things and particular people exposes me to the possibility of their loss. If I love an heirloom vase, say, for its sentimental value as well as its intrinsic beauty, then my feelings are bound up with and dependent upon its fortunes. It might be safer to become a connoisseur of vases in general, since then there are other candidates for my interest and affection if one is damaged. Safest of all is to become a connoisseur of the quality or qualities for which I loved the vases: to become a lover of beauty in general (Griffiths and Smith, 1989, p. 283).

If things are risky enough with vases, they are worse with other human beings, who 'change, or move away, or grow up, or die. Our loved ones are hostages to fortune, as the phrase has it. Emotional dependence upon them can only end in grief' (ibid.). Smith thus offers an implicit critique of Diotima's climactic lesson that is different from but complementary to Irigaray's. On Smith's reading, the underlying motivation for loving not particular others, but beauty in general is to protect us from the vulnerability we fear will result from attachment. This means we sacrifice a love of others 'for their otherness, their unique, irreplaceable particularity'—the kind of otherness that fecundates the encounter Irigaray describes—and instead love them 'for their similarity to ourselves' or to a general ideal, and thereby for a 'repeatable quality' which ensures that 'substitutes can in principle be found' (ibid.).

At one point Smith suggests that the fact that 'independence is seen as automatically a more desirable state than dependence has much to do with the natural human dislike of risk and vulnerability' (ibid.). However, in the fuller discussion to which his reference to Diotima is a prelude, he and Griffiths show how this dislike is dramatically intensified by the Western Enlightenment tradition, whose emphasis on a distinctive and highly individualistic conception of autonomy starkly devalues both dependencies and attachments along with the vulnerabilities that accompany them. Rather than seeing a fear of vulnerability as entirely natural, I would suggest that this tradition thereby contributes to the naturalisation of such fears (not least through the sublime; see Griffiths, Chapter 11). At the same time, its insistence on the value of entirely self-determining individuals (at least as an ideal) represses the fact that, if vulnerability is indeed natural to human beings, it is natural to us as constitutively *relational* beings. As Judith Butler movingly writes, 'We're undone by each other. And if we're not, we're missing something' (2004, p. 23): what we are missing are the very relations that make us who we are.

If dependencies are constitutive of identities as intrinsically relational, then as Griffiths and Smith emphasise, 'dependence is not something we ought to accept *for the sake of* autonomy, as if it were a stage to go through and pass beyond to proper adult independence or as if dependence were a continual but sometimes inconvenient need' (1989, p. 291). Rather, we urgently need ways of thinking—and educating—that cease to devalue the dependencies, attachments and vulnerabilities that are not just unavoidable, but a generative and constitutive part of what Griffiths elsewhere calls the 'web of identity' (1995).[21] One starting point for redressing the balance might be to strategically reverse the image of attachments and dependencies as weakening an otherwise invulnerable self, and instead to imagine a self that becomes ever thinner, more brittle and fragile as well as more impoverished, as the net of relations that constitute it are withdrawn. However, as Smith and Griffiths also note, in a Western context informed by the ideal of the modern liberal individual, 'The rhetoric of independence and autonomy is so powerful that it sounds paradoxical to assert the value of dependence'. Thus, 'Perhaps, in the end, we must simply accept that some things can no longer be said' (p. 292).

Griffiths and Smith turn to art to *show* 'what it has become virtually impossible to *say*' (p. 292). Literature can provide counter-narratives of the self that show how dependencies might be valued while complicating and expanding our understandings of what might be meant by 'autonomy' or 'independence'. We could also turn to the theoretical resources developed by some feminist philosophers, including Griffiths' own discussion of women's often paradoxical relations to the modern, individualist concept of autonomy. As she shows, these apparent paradoxes tend to dissolve if we learn to listen to the different notions of independence and autonomy—as woven through with dependencies and emerging within webs of relations—that women's stories have to offer (Griffiths, 1995).

Battersby reinforces Griffiths' view that in Western modernity, women tend to find themselves in a paradoxical position, caught between conflicting ideals of autonomy and care (Battersby, 2007, pp. 136–7). She also agrees that this position need not be seen as wholly negative—a trap women are powerless to resist—but can become a site from which alternative conceptions of self and identity can be worked out (Battersby, 1998, 2007). In her development of an account of the self that takes the female body that births as the norm, Battersby emphasises that one of the features of such an account will be that unequal power relations and dependencies—such as exist between a mother and a foetus or infant—will also be seen as the norm (1998, pp. 8, 38). This approach to the self provides a distinct alternative to the modern conception of ideally equal, fully self-determining individuals. It puts us in a better position to deal with the fact that in the classroom, as in the wider social contexts within which classrooms are always situated, 'the dependencies that we have are not an interdependency of equals, of a free association of equal people, who will stand by each other in mutual support. They are the mutual dependencies of non-equals' (Griffiths, 1995, p. 30; see also Shuffelton, Chapter 3).

By re-conceptualising dependencies and unequal power relations as a normal and constitutive part of relational identities, Battersby enables us to enquire into their role in shaping educational relations without assuming that they are necessarily a bad thing, to be eliminated wherever possible. Instead, we might investigate the ways in which inequalities can be productive differences that hold open the space for generative encounters, while dependencies can be embodied in relations that not only enable flourishing, but that can also become the site of an embodied ethical education in how to relate to otherness and difference.

This is not to say that differences and unequal power relations do not *also* house opportunities for exploitation and abuse, particularly when they are oppositionally or hierarchically organised. When I teach Kant's *Critique of Pure Reason*, my familiarity with the text and philosophical training give me a power that I can certainly choose to use to belittle or silence, but that I can also deploy to help others find their way into the text, learn to navigate it, and begin to develop their own responses. Neither is it to say that all dependencies are good. For Nietzsche, it is a sign of cultural degeneration to value reason over the senses in a totalising manner, rather than being able to discriminate between the differing values of different sensible experiences for different types of life (Nietzsche, 1990, pp. 39–45). Similarly, we might think it a sign of social and cultural weakness not to be able to discriminate between dependencies in terms of the extent to which they help or hinder different modes of flourishing. The ideal of equality (including the equalisation of all dependencies as not just 'bad', but bad for everyone in the same way) too often disguises an ideal of sameness that is itself oppressive, insofar as it allows no space for differences to be registered and valued. But as Bell Hooks emphasises, describing her own experiences of the feminist classroom, differences—in embodiment, experience, perspective or values—are a key site of learning, providing we do not too quickly shut them down and instead learn to live with the discomfort they may bring: 'Confronting one another across differences means that we must change ideas about how we learn; rather than fearing conflict we have to find ways to use it as a catalyst for new thinking, for growth' (Hooks, 1994, p. 113).

Hooks is a helpful voice to put alongside Griffiths and Battersby. In *Teaching to Transgress* (1994), a collection that includes her own reflections on 'Eros, Eroticism and the Pedagogical Process', she writes:

> When I enter the classroom at the beginning of the semester the weight is on me to establish that our purpose is to be, for however brief a time, a community of learners *together*. It positions me as a learner. But I'm also not suggesting that I don't have more power. And I'm not trying to say we're all equal here. I'm trying to say that we are all equal here *to the extent that* we are equally committed to creating a learning context (Hooks, 1994, p. 153; second emphasis mine).

Hooks' approach points to the dependency of teachers on their students as much as the reverse. This dependency impinges on the affective life of the teacher as well as their sense of identity. If a group of students fails to read, engage, or take any responsibility for the classroom experience, this is not akin to a breach of contract that simply means the teacher will not be able to deliver the lesson they set out to give. It is a breakdown of relations and commitment that, as Hooks describes (pp. 8–9, 158–9), will often manifest in the anxiety and affective distress of the teacher. Conversely, as Hooks also notes, our interactions with our students can (and should) empower us (p. 152). When, in a class on the philosophy of art, a student who was also a sculptor wrote an essay on the active material encounters involved in working with different kinds of metals, I learnt from him in unanticipated ways that informed my research as well as my future ability to teach the material we were discussing; though it remained the case that I got to grade his papers, not he mine.

Cultivating the dynamics in which it is possible to productively confront one another across differences as Hooks suggests is something for which teachers bear a special but never a sole responsibility. In a discussion of collecting, cultural artefacts and colonialism, one of my students spoke passionately and articulately from his perspective as one who had recently moved to the US from Iraq. His comments provided a cross-cultural perspective that was challenging for some of the students in the class, and found strong support from others. This was a galvanising teaching moment that made me deeply aware of my dependence on my students: on the courage of the Iraqi student in speaking up and being prepared to be directly critical of the US (and by implication Western colonial powers more generally); and on the readiness of my other students (who themselves embodied a range of different ethnicities and nationalities) to listen to different, and perhaps challenging, viewpoints and engage with them constructively. Our discussions were critically enriched by his intervention, which showed how the issues we were addressing were not some abstract problem cooked up by academics to make people's heads hurt, but bear on real lives and real cultural and political struggles.

Finally, an attentiveness to the ways in which dependencies can be enabling, rather than simply constraining, also equips us better to deal with situations where power and position are abused in an educational context. Such problems arise not only where the classroom is used 'to enact rituals of control that [are] about domination and the unjust exercise of power' (Hooks, 1994, p. 5), but also (and perhaps more often?) where there is a refusal to recognise or take responsibility for the dependencies (and inter-dependencies) that teaching involves, and that need to be handled with care if they are not to become simply repressive or damaging. To return again to Hooks, 'the classroom should be a space where we're all in power in different ways.' (p. 152) That our students empower us—by teaching us new things, as my sculptor student did, or how to be better, braver teachers, as my student from Iraq did—is another sign of the depth and complexity of our dependence on them, even as we retain power over them in certain respects.

CONCLUSION

In this chapter, I hope to have shown that taking a turn back through Diotima, whose teachings come to us from the beginnings of the

Western philosophical tradition, is still valuable for those of us think-ing about teaching today. The differing responses to Diotima charted here—by turns both sympathetic and critical—point towards an approach attentive to the generative and mutually transformative potential of the pedagogical encounter, as well as to the importance of allowing oneself to be undone in such relations rather than seeking to master otherness and difference. Between them, the diverse think-ers considered provide us with resources for a relational pedagogy in which educational encounters require both the cultivation of differences and the possibility of failure, and whose inherent but desirable riskiness is offset via the cultivation of both trust and forgiveness. Such encounters re-affirm our natal capacity for initia-tion, for forging new beginnings both for ourselves and for—and with—others.

In the final section, I argued that unequal power relations and the asymmetrical patterns of dependency they imply are a constitutive and often enabling aspect of the relational context of learning. As Griffiths and Smith show in their thoughtful exploration of the very different ways in which 'independence' is invoked in the classroom, our choices are not only between, on the one hand, hierarchical relations of dominance versus submission, activity versus passive receptivity; and on the other, 'flat' structures in which all participants are suppos-edly equal. Rather, our models of both social and pedagogical rela-tions can (and should) involve much more nuanced appreciations of the patterns of dependence and independence that result from power relations that are typically *un*equal.

This does not mean simply discounting the importance of autonomy and independence. At a time when we are faced with an ever-increasing circulation and regurgitation of information, Kant's call to have the courage to think for oneself begins to look distinctly radical at times. But it does mean paying more attention to the kinds of dependency that make independence possible: when I think *about* Irigaray or Kant, I also think *with* and *thanks to* them, even when I am critical of them. And as this example suggests, it also means attending to the ways in which we stand to gain more autonomy, not less, from nurturing our relations, particularly where those relations involve the kinds of encounters with difference and even conflict that Irigaray and Hooks teach us to value. If we are constitutively relational selves, welcoming difference into the relations that constitute us can increase the possibilities for weaving together differing perspectives in ways that afford new beginnings for thought and action, paths into the future that emerge *from* our relations to others without simply being deter-mined *by* any one of them.

In the end, such an approach would necessitate a rethinking of the very concept of autonomy in ways that go beyond the scope of this chapter.[22] But at the very least, it suggests that the goal of education should not be to cultivate individual autonomy understood on the modern (broadly Kantian) model as a capacity to govern oneself through reason alone in ways that systematically devalue dependency and make us less rather than more able to live with vulnerability and difference. Rather, the goal of a relational pedagogy should be to cultivate capacities that enable one to attend to and take responsibility for the relations that make one who one is, in ways that include critical reflection, emotional intelligence, and a willingness for action where required.[23]

NOTES

1. In this chapter I shift quite loosely between the 'pedagogical' and the 'educational'; for a helpful differentiation, see Sharon Todd (Chapter 4), whose chapter also links the pedagogical to becoming, birth and infancy.
2. I draw on translations of *Symposium* by both Allen (Plato, 1991) and Cobb (Plato, 1993); references use the standard Stephanus system.
3. In addition to Irigaray's work, see for example Battersby, 1998; Cavarero, 2000; and Griffiths, 1995.
4. Though note that in *Menexenus*, Socrates refers to Aspasia (a real, Milesian woman and the mistress of Pericles) as his teacher in rhetoric; on Aspasia and Diotima, see Halperin, 1990.
5. For an excellent discussion of these images that assesses key previous interpretations, see Sandford, 2010.
6. Halperin argues that Plato (via Diotima) presents female desire as inextricably combining pleasure and reproduction. But as it is in fact in the male body that 'reproductive function cannot be isolated from sexual pleasure', Plato's text performs a 'double movement': feminine pleasure is first modelled on male physiology, and then re-appropriated by male philosophical lovers via the teachings of a 'feminine' character (Halperin, 1990, p. 142).
7. See also Cavarero 1995, pp. 91–107. Given the importance of Halperin's work on queering and queerness, this critique of 'mimetic transvestitism' might seem surprising, for such rhetorical and performative manoeuvres can trouble the alleged 'naturalness' of both gender and sexuality (as shown by Judith Butler). I take it that Halperin's point here is that what is being mimed in Diotima's speech is femininity *as constructed in relation to men and male desire*, in ways that echo Irigaray's critique of the feminine as the 'other' of the male subject.
8. To be fair, Halperin is refreshingly self-critical about the risks of reinscribing the feminine as a male author in ways that silence women while perpetuating the concerns of men; see Halperin, 1990, p. 114, p. 149.
9. As Wilson notes, the name chosen by a group of Italian feminists inspired by Irigaray's work was 'Diotima'.
10. On the pedagogical potential of Irigaray's retrieval of the maternal body see Todd on the 'placental economy', Chapter 4.
11. See both Todd and Greenhalgh-Spencer (Chapters 4 and 10, respectively) on pedagogies that foster the unpredictable and new.

12. See also the essay 'The Survivor' (Lyotard, 1993b), where Lyotard's characterisation of infancy strongly echoes the way that Diotima's *Eros* combines qualities from *both* his mother and his father. Elsewhere, in order to counter the role of lack in Western metaphysics, Lyotard sides firmly with 'an Eros that is all *Poros*' (1993b, p. 86), though this *Eros* is still aligned with the subversive humour of the pagan and the feminine.
13. Thus read as a 'queer' figure of 'crossing', *Eros* points to productive resonances between Lyotard and Halperin; for Lyotard, the feminine and the pagan 'transsexualize the social body' (1993b, p. 114).
14. On these points, see especially: 'The Subject of the Course of Philosophy' (Lyotard, 1993a); 'The Survivor' (1993b), and the volume from which it is drawn (not yet fully translated into English) *Lectures d'enfance* (Lyotard, 1991).
15. For Lyotard, 'becoming other to oneself' is not a fundamental alienation that needs to be resolved; rather it is in this undoing of the subject that thinking happens and an ethical relation with alterity can emerge. For Irigaray, emphasising the constitutive role of lived, embodied relations with actual others aids in the cultivation of a relational ontology no longer dependent on a sacrificial and matricidal logic.
16. This essay was originally published in English in *An Ethics of Sexual Difference* (Irigaray, 1993); unfortunately (perhaps for copyright reasons) one of the long quotations from *Symposium* that appeared in Irigaray's French original is curtailed in this version; hence, I am using the alternative Kuykendall translation (Irigaray, 1994).
17. The Greek word for 'intercourse' here (*sunousia*) can signal intercourse in either a sexual or a social sense. The word for 'begetting', *tiktein*, can apply to both sexes and can also be translated as 'giving birth'.
18. Irigaray's project is often seen as inimical or even hostile to queer theory. But her refiguring of the erotic as a non-teleological and generative (rather than reproductive) encounter opens up the possibility of a critical alliance with Halperin and other queer theorists, who have also subjected the reproductive imperative to critique.
19. See Todd on how Irigaray's 'placental economy' also figures the mediation between self and other as a 'threshold of becoming'.
20. Love, Irigaray says, gives birth to lovers—'*enfanter des amants*'—or more literally, love makes infants of lovers (Irigaray, 1984, p. 33).
21. As Griffiths notes: 'My dependent close relationships feel as though they increase freedom more than they diminish it. I can live my life more as I would want to when I have dependent close relationships with a range of other people. . . . My freedom to do some things is increased if I do not have to consider others. But my freedom to be myself is bound by those others and our ways of leading a life together.' (1995, p. 30)
22. For a sustained re-thinking of autonomy and independence in terms of an always relational project of self-creation, see Griffiths, 1995.
23. My thanks to the book editors and anonymous readers for their extremely helpful comments.

REFERENCES

Arendt, H. (1958) *The Human Condition* (Chicago, IL, University of Chicago Press).
Arendt, H. (1978) *The Life of the Mind* (New York, Harcourt).
Battersby, C. (1994) Unblocking the Oedipal: Karoline von Günderode and the Female Sublime, in: S. Ledger, J. McDonagh and J. Spencer (eds) *Political Gender: Texts and Contexts* (London, Harvester Wheatsheaf).
Battersby, C. (1998) *The Phenomenal Woman: Feminist Metaphysics and the Patterns of Identity* (Cambridge, Polity).

Battersby, C. (2007) *The Sublime, Terror and Human Difference* (London, Routledge).
Butler, J. (2004) *Precarious Life: The Powers of Mourning and Violence* (New York, Verso).
Cavarero, A. (1995) *In Spite of Plato: A Feminist Rewriting of Ancient Philosophy*, S. Anderlini-D'Onofrio and Á. O'Healy, trans. (Cambridge, Polity).
Cavarero, A. (2000) *Relating Narratives: Storytelling and Selfhood*, P. A Kottman, trans. (London, Routledge).
Dewey, J. (2004) *Democracy and Education* (New York, Dover Press).
Griffiths, M. (1995) *Feminisms and the Self: The Web of Identity* (London, New York, Routledge).
Griffiths, M. and Smith, R. (1989) Standing Alone: Dependence, Independence and Interdependence in the Practice of Education, *Journal of Philosophy of Education*, 23.2, pp. 283–94.
Halperin, D. M. (1990) Why Is Diotima a Woman?, in: *One Hundred Years of Homosexuality* (New York, London, Routledge).
Hooks, B. (1994) *Teaching to Transgress: Education as the Practice of Freedom* (New York, London, Routledge).
Irigaray, L. (1984) *Éthique de la différence sexuelle* (Paris, Éditions de Minuit).
Irigaray, L. (1993) *An Ethics of Sexual Difference*, C. Burke and G. Gill, trans. (London, Athlone).
Irigaray, L. (1994) Sorcerer Love, E. Kuykendall, trans., in: N. Tuana (ed.) *Feminist Interpretations of Plato* (University Park, PA, Penn State University Press).
Lyotard, J-F. (1991) *Lectures d'enfance* (Paris, Galilée).
Lyotard, J-F. (1993a) *The Postmodern Explained*, J. Pefanis and M. Thomas, eds (Minneapolis, MN, University of Minnesota Press).
Lyotard, J-F. (1993b) *Toward the Postmodern*, R. Harvey and M. Roberts, eds (New York, Humanity Books).
Nietzsche, F. (1990) *Twilight of the Idols/The Anti-Christ*, R. J. Hollingdale, trans. (Harmondsworth, Penguin).
Plato (1991) *The Symposium*, R. E. Allen, trans. (New Haven, CT, Yale University Press).
Plato (1993) *Symposium, in The Symposium and the Phaedrus: Plato's Erotic Dialogues*, W. S. Cobb, trans. (New York, State University of New York Press).
Sandford, S. (2010) *Plato and Sex* (Cambridge, Polity).

2
Towards a Thinking and Practice of Sexual Difference: Putting the Practice of Relationship at the Centre

CAROLINE WILSON

INTRODUCTION—EQUALITY IS NOT ENOUGH: BRINGING THE PRACTICE OF RELATIONSHIP INTO THE FOREGROUND

In the last centuries, in the Western world, educational systems and beliefs have undergone considerable changes. There has been a huge shift with respect to 'gender' equality due to the politics and thinking that argued for the inclusion of girls and women in formal education in absolutely the same conditions as boys and men. This goal has, in many ways, been achieved.

When we hear of horrendous situations for girls and women in other, more distant countries, it seems only natural to believe and support the idea that what would make life better for them would be to fight for educational rights such as Western children and youth now enjoy.[1]

The underlying assumption is that an equal opportunity to education implies a direct relationship with personal and social freedom. However, this assumption has been problematised in recent decades. It is a difficult subject to unpack and tackle because there is so much of value in the Western history of education as a whole, and so much work, courage and passion has gone into bringing about the present educational possibilities for both sexes. And yet, issues concerning equality remain. We are challenged frequently with the idea that girls are presently attaining at a higher level than boys at school. Indeed, in some European countries now, girls outnumber boys in university classrooms. Newspapers and research reports multiply, assessing the situation and discussing the implications for boys, as a quick Google search will demonstrate, bringing up many studies and reports in the last year alone which attempt to explain *why* this is the case and why it is a matter for concern. It is as if, having situated girls as the victims

Re-Imagining Relationships in Education: Ethics, Politics and Practices, First Edition. Edited by Morwenna Griffiths, Marit Honerød Hoveid, Sharon Todd and Christine Winter. Chapters © 2015 The Authors. Editorial organization © 2015 Philosophy of Education Society of Great Britain. Published 2015 by John Wiley & Sons Ltd.

of an unfair situation for centuries, and fighting for them to be included on equal terms in the classroom, we now have a situation whereby the pendulum has swung the other way to turn boys into the victims. This is a logical argument following on from one of the main aims of feminist movements to ensure an equality of opportunity for women and men at all levels of society. As long as our tools and paradigms for measuring the behaviour and performance of boys and girls remain anchored in the belief that the logical and just outcome should be one where neither sex outperforms the other, it is likely that we will continue to see questions such as this arising.[2]

It is difficult to go beyond this paradigm given that an influential feminist endeavour of the past few hundred years in the West has been to fight very hard for the right to inclusion in the public world on the same terms as the male sex. However, as we shall see below, a considerable amount of work has taken place in the last half century, put in motion by the question of Luce Irigaray 'Égales à qui? [Equal to Who?]', which invites us to start asking questions emphasising the signifier of sexual difference. These questions might enable us to go beyond the concern that boys and girls should perform to the same standards and produce the same results. Bringing the signifier of sexual difference into play means that we cannot take for granted that the same achievement (or not) in tests and exams is a reliable measure of children's flourishing.

If we consider Irigaray's idea that becoming equal to men might not be the clear path to female freedom that has been supposed and that sexual difference could reveal itself to be a signifier that releases the human potential of *both* sexes, then what constitutes equal education? In the same way as we might apply the signifier of sexual difference to the learning of girls and boys, we can also ask whether this signifier might be applied to male and female educators and begin to ask questions from a fresh perspective. What is taught? How is it taught? Who is it taught by? Is it possible that much of the substance of what is taught depends on a historically *male* version of what is important and a *male* interpretation of how the world works? How to change this to reflect a teaching environment whereby both sexes are free to flourish and bring their difference into the classroom?

At the same time, we have to ask questions about the way that the *relationships* between those who teach and those who are taught have been conceived in what is recognised by many as a patriarchal symbolic order that recognised male authority above all. Has the massive incorporation of the female sex in education changed this substance or method? The answers to this are far from clear, but it seems important to ask the questions (e.g. see Riddell *et al.*, 2005; Griffiths, 2006).

LUCE IRIGARAY AND THE IMPLICATIONS IN EDUCATION OF HER CHALLENGE TO RETHINK THE WORLD

Luce Irigaray (1974) has presented us with a political as well as a philosophical challenge. Following Heidegger's idea that each age has something to think through anew, she suggests that sexual difference is that 'something' for our current era; in her view, Western philosophy and culture have been based on the experience and interpretation of only one of the sexes and this one sex has utilised and usurped the experience and meaning of the other, 'different', sex. In her opinion, the female sex has not yet signified itself in a free way. In fact, neither has the male sex done so, given its history of dominance, usurpation, elimination or subjugation of that which was different from itself. So, for her, the feminist project to establish and ensure equality for women and men has developed into a more sophisticated questioning of whether this project was in fact sufficient for the true flourishing of both sexes.[3]

To signify, or to name, is to make symbolic order.[4] Irigaray intimates that our symbolic order is biased, *out* of order, and proposed that we apply the signifier of sexual difference to it. That is, to reconsider how we might signify ourselves and our world, through the prism of sexual difference.

If we accept this challenge, no aspect of our world and the junctures at which our lives connect and interrelate to it remain the same. Education, in all its dimensions, is clearly at the heart of this challenge. Our educational systems and activities cannot help but be a reflection of the beliefs and values that underlie those of our symbolic order. Even more, we might contemplate that through educational structures an intensification of the transmission of the existing symbolic order is facilitated. What is being transmitted and the way in which this transmission takes place through the hierarchies of relationships mark the organisation of educational structures on every level, from the relationships between politicians of education, managers of education, teachers themselves and parents, particularly mothers, given the latter are, generally and to date those most involved with each child's formation from the very first. Thus, if Irigaray is correct and our symbolic order is seriously biased, this educational process may require serious interrogation. It is a symbolic order that has historically left women out in terms of recognising them as the first and ongoing teachers of children in their capacity as mothers, that has been late to incorporate women as formal teachers and philosophers of education, and that seems still to pay little attention to relationships of power and authority that may still be operating negatively in the politics of how education is organised. Further, the current symbolic order is unlikely to be one which happily recognises and works with female authority and the order that comes into being through the maternal relationship with an infant as soon as or even before it is born.

In Italy and Spain, groups of teachers and lecturers have been working on these issues for the past 40 years (see Puissi, 2013). The work of these educators shares aspects with educational theorists who seek to realign the close intersections between relationship and the educational enterprise—of which the chapters in this book are a strong sample—but they are unique in grounding themselves in what has been called the politics of the symbolic or the politics of sexual difference. In this politics, we are asked to re-think ourselves as *sexuate* human beings, born of and brought into the world of shared meaning and language by a woman—our mother or the one in her place—and always relating to the world through this sexuate self. The practice of relationship itself is seen to be the central vehicle through which human beings learn and understand themselves, others, and the world around them.

This idea of a sexuate self has tremendous implications for theories and practices of education. This is particularly so given a historically dominant model of educational philosophy that has seen the mother and the work she does in the first years of an infant's life as peripheral, both in terms of the influence that this work has on a human being and understanding it as the first main model of how learning takes place: that is, learning is always contingent upon relationship.[5] As a child grows older and passes through different educational phases, the idea that relationships are key to how learning transpires do not receive much attention. There is a strong recognition that teachers make a difference to learning[6] but not that *relationship* is the central and vital vehicle that ensures the transmission of knowledge.

The connection between this disregard of the centrality of relationship and a patriarchal order that did not tend to recognise female authority—and certainly did not consider women in terms of development of the mind or as producers of great knowledge—is not an innocent one. The work of Irigaray and then others, particularly Luisa Muraro, first opens up questions about what this means for formal education, and second, brings women back on to the central stage for a new discussion about the potential for the meaning of sexual difference at all levels of education, formal and otherwise. A feminism that seeks equality with men can only do this to a certain extent, since the underlying male model remains strong and may resist the free movement of sexuate difference, thus generating a lot of tension and confusion. One of the paradoxes when it comes to applying a theory of equality is that it allows little room for the reality of evident non-equality in the relationships between human beings. The truth is that nearly all human relationships, let alone those between women and men, are asymmetrical; there are moments of total dependence on the other, partial dependence and relative independence or interdependence. If we consider the arena of education, we see that framing relationships in terms of equality will not get us very far. A thinking that takes on fully the importance, on both a philosophical and practical level, of the centrality of relationship to education may prove more fruitful at this stage.

SEXUAL DIFFERENCE AS POLITICAL STRATEGY

Irigaray's context at the time of writing *Speculum of the Other Woman* (1974/1985) was both that of an exciting, rapidly developing women's movement but also that of a woman who had enjoyed access to an extensive level of education in a previously male-dominated intellectual world, a woman who had received the fruits of what women for various centuries had been striving for. It was from this position, however, that her *experience* entered into conflict with what must have seemed, in principle, the chance to enjoy privileges and apparent freedoms that previous women could only have dreamed of. *Speculum of the Other Woman* is perhaps the result of that collision between theory and experience, and, through that collision, a new theory is forged.

   Was it, then, precisely this collision, between a woman (one of many of her generation) permitted finally to access areas of life that seemingly represented freedom, (education, for instance) and a symbolic order and intellectual tradition that in fact had little room for her *sexuate* freedom that enabled her to bring forth the mediation that she did?

   That Irigaray's thinking emerges from the feminist context of the late 1960s and early 1970s in the Western world is no accident. This period of women's history has had a huge impact in many places of the globe. I would say that her challenge, that of an urgent need to (re) think sexual difference is deeply rooted in and born out of the women's politics of that time. However, it may be that this has not been fully understood. In particular, there is a lack of recognition of its connections with the particular French-Italian-Spanish feminist movements from which it emerged.

THE MILAN WOMEN'S BOOKSTORE COLLECTIVE AND DIOTIMA: THE PRACTICE OF RELATIONSHIP ITSELF AS A POLITICAL FORM

Irigaray was translated into Italian by Luisa Muraro. Luisa Muraro was one of several women philosophers who, together with women from other spheres, created Diotima, the Women's Philosophical Community at the University of Verona in 1983. Prior to this, much of the philosophical thinking and women's politics referred to here had originated around the Milan Women's Bookstore, whose book, *Non credere di avere dei diritti* (Milan Women's Bookstore Collective, 1987), constitutes almost the only text that exists in an English translation of this history (Milan Women's Bookstore Collective, 1990). Irigaray's incitement to re-think sexual difference had a significant impact on the directions that the above-mentioned Italian women were to take politically and theoretically. The contradictions they observed between feminist struggles in Italy at the time and women's actual experiences inspired them to take sexual difference as a starting point as they explored and invented what they called political figures—the practice of attributing new meaning to old words and concepts, this time including their experience as women seeking greater freedom in the world. In their work and thinking together, they began to formulate the idea that, for sexual difference to come more strongly and freely into being, the practice and naming of relationships between women might in fact be the ground of a new political point of departure:

It is very likely that none of us were taught that we needed to take special care of our relations with other women and to consider them an irreplaceable source of personal strength, originality of mind, and social self-assurance. And it is difficult to have a notion of how necessary this is because in the culture we receive, a few products of female origin have been preserved, but not their symbolic matrix, so that they appear to us as regenerated by male thought (Milan Women's Bookstore Collective, 1990, p. 28).

The women of the Milan Women's Bookstore Collective and Diotima invented a word, *affidamento*, translated into English as entrustment. This particular concept developed into work on the figure of female authority, understanding authority as a relational, circulating, political figure. Authority was perceived as a *relational* quality of symbolic wealth freely available to be used immediately between women: it does not require *a priori* access to echelons of power.

The women of Milan and Diotima saw the relationships between women as of *primary political* importance. They believed that one of the first keys to bringing sexual difference into the world more strongly was to start by giving more significance to relationships between women as a site where sexual difference could be developed and nurtured, then to be made stronger in the shared world.

To illustrate this, they take and rework Virginia Woolf's proposal of a room of one's own (Woolf, 1929). It is not enough, they say, to have a physical, material room, because without a new symbolic placement, we may not know what to do there. If women manage to acquire that room, and the economic means to occupy it, they may, nevertheless, not know how to use it, since it cannot be a question of merely adopting the ways in which men have used similar space:

> Virginia Woolf maintained that in order to do intellectual work, one needs a room of one's own. However, it may be impossible to keep still and apply oneself to work in that room because the texts and their subjects seem like extraneous, oppressive blocks of words and facts through which the mind cannot make its way, paralysed as it is by emotions which have no corresponding terms in language. The room of one's own must be understood differently, then, as a symbolic placement, a space-time furnished with female gendered references, where one goes for meaningful preparation before work, and confirmation after (Milan Women's Bookstore Collective, 1990, p. 26).

According to this idea, however much apparent equality and power in the given world women might achieve, however many laws are passed to protect and guarantee their theoretical freedom, the point remains that without this symbolic placement, rooted and nurtured in the relationships between them, women and girls will continue to be fragile in the world.

THE SYMBOLIC ORDER OF THE MOTHER—LUISA MURARO

Luisa Muraro, in her book *L'ordine simbolico della madre* [*The Symbolic Order of the Mother*] (Muraro, 1991a),[7] sets out to investigate the point of departure of what she calls the free existence of women in the world. As a philosopher at the University of Verona who also participated in Diotima and the Milan Women's Bookstore, she found herself with the problem of having been drawn to the discipline of philosophy only to discover that the philosophy she learned at university was not able to provide her with what she was looking for. She explains in her book:

Philosophy attracted me because I was looking for symbolic independence from given reality. I wanted to never again find myself at the mercy of casual and unforeseen happenings. But I did not achieve it because, as I finally understood, the philosophy that was able to shelter me from the capricious domain of the real, at the same time set me against my mother, whose work I judged, implicitly, to be badly done. I wanted to go to the beginning of things to understand and to understand myself; however, I was going against my mother (1994, p. 8).

That is, Muraro wanted to go back to the 'origins' in order to understand herself and her position in the world and had seen philosophy as the language and discipline that would enable her to do so. However, she discovered that those origins contemplated by philosophical thought made almost no mention of her mother—her mother was conspicuous by her absence. Muraro writes of the importance in philosophy of the starting point, referring back to Plato, Descartes and Husserl, and suggests that they were missing something. They were lacking in something because, as Irigaray suggests, the basis of Western philosophical thinking was predicated on the usurpation of the female sex, not least the work of the mother. So, the starting point had been taken from that work but disguised and presented as something else that excluded the mother. In seeking reference points from those male thinkers, Muraro discovers that she is being asked to go against the work of her mother. What is more, a part of her is attracted to this possibility. The symbolic independence from chance events that she seeks, offered to her by her philosophical predecessors, tempts her to forget that her origins lie in the work of her mother:

Because in me there was, without my knowing it, a dark aversion towards the author of my life, which philosophy came to reanimate in a kind of way, and because between this and that dark feeling a vicious circle had been formed (1994, p. 8).

This is a paradox that, on reflection, is almost inevitable for women educated through a male model of education who have believed for centuries that accessing it and participating in it was their route to freedom. From this new perspective, however, we can see that the issue is more complex and, in terms of sexuate freedom, will inevitably lead to contradictions and distortions. Muraro set to finding a way out of this vicious circle, and this was the lever for her discovery of a new starting point, a founding stone that signalled a 'fresh' place from which to think the self and the world. This founding stone was to be found in the work of the mother, a work of relationship which, in male thought, had barely been symbolised.

Luisa Muraro distinguishes between speaking of the mother as a metaphor and speaking of her symbolically. This is perhaps a fundamental but difficult point. It is possibly this confusion that leads to critiques of this thinking as a kind of idealised matriarchy, an essentialist utopian thinking that clashes clearly with both women and men's experience of real women who are, like men, flawed human beings capable of causing harm as well as good. It is important not to lose sight of the fact that when Muraro brings the term *symbolic order of the mother* into being, she is deeply rooted in the politics of sexual difference and seeks to avoid such idealisations.

She acknowledges herself to be poor in her own knowledge of this symbolic order and unclear at first as to where it might lead, but suggests that one way to explore this is to resort to the real experiences that we have as infants in relation to our mother, or the one in her place. That is, it is not necessary to make of our mothers a metaphor, a romantic idealisation. It is a question of restoring that relationship to a different place, allowing us to unravel the confusion of having started off in that relationship and having received our first philosophical base there, receiving language and meaning through that primary first relationship, to then be introduced through the general culture and formal schooling to the notion that the generation of meaning and the philosophical have little to do with the mother.

In Muraro's training as a philosopher at university the mother had been absent. That her mother was the author, literally, of Muraro's life was of course an undeniable fact. But as the transmitter and creator of meaning through that first relationship via which an infant is brought into the shared world of understanding (the symbolic order), she was absent. So, Muraro is saying, our political task is to symbolise (attribute meaning to/make philosophy of) the process that takes place between mother and infant and understand that this is the starting point of philosophy—for both sexes:

> I will write to say my meaning of mother. But first, I should say that the non-metaphorical symbolism of the mother was not waiting for me to discover it in order to have a place; it already has a place, in fact, and a very strong place, a fortress, in our infancy. . . I entrust, therefore, to the little girl that I was, those with whom I grew up, the little girls and boys that live amongst us, the task of affirming the non-metaphoric symbolism of the mother. I will take on board the task, a secondary one, of translating it into philosophy (1994, p. 20).

We might question the idea that the task of translating this into philosophy is a secondary one. In fact, the endeavour undertaken by Muraro is potentially a radical operation, since, if we accept it, we are challenged to rethink our conceptual framings of the world from an entirely new starting point. That said, the point being made by Muraro is that this symbolic work is already being and has always been done, by mothers or the one in her place. The confusion arises in that what is taught and transmitted as the work and thought of philosophy has been deprived of the recognition of its origins. She says:

> As we know, philosophers have been inspired by the figure and the work of the mother. They, however, inverting the order of the operation carried out, have presented the maternal work as a copy (and many times a bad copy) of the real thing. In this they have been complicit with the patriarchy, which presents the father as the true author of life (1994, p. 20).

She sees her task then to restore this to language, to translate what is in fact already happening in the primary relationship with the infant into the philosophy that circulates in the world.

Dependence, in this case that of an infant on the adults who care for her, is a notion that is crystallising into a 'new' understanding of our conceptualisation of relational structures.[8] The reality of dependence as a necessary element of many relationships acts as a stumbling block when we want to perceive ourselves as autonomous subjects who can be guaranteed protection in that autonomy through law. This dependence on the mother (or the one in her place) presents us with a paradigm then for a different philosophy of relationship. Muraro explains that she is (only) introducing into philosophy that which in reality she was given by her mother:

> I introduce into philosophy what my mother signifies for me, basing myself on what it meant when my need and dependence on her was total. But I should add that it was her who introduced me to philosophy, as she did to everything else that I know. How this happened, I still do not know very well, but it has to be taken literally and not in the manner of the philosophers (1994, p. 20).

In continuation, Muraro writes of the way in which feminism, in its more recent history, had tried to deconstruct the patriarchal system in order to be free of it, an endeavour which has proved to be never ending. Muraro claims that once the vicious circle is broken, through restoring the mother and her work to philosophy, the path to the dismantling of patriarchal systems changes and becomes far less tiring. A free sense of existence will be found, she argues, neither in the philosophical systems which have based their development on the usurpation of the maternal work nor in the arduous attempt to challenge those systems on every level in order to transform them. There is a simpler route. She argues that it is rather gratitude and recognition of that first work of the symbolic order that will open up a place of freedom for both sexes.

To illustrate this operation, she writes of her own experience in relation to her own discipline. Once able to translate the reality of her philosophical origins in her relationship with her mother into symbolic wealth/order (that is, she found a language for it), she discovered a philosophical freedom that liberated her from the need to fight against what she now perceived as false attempts to appropriate those origins. Once she had discovered this new route, she no longer felt that she had to put her energies into arguing against the existing systems of philosophy.

She writes of how, once she had reached this point and named it, the previous ideas, which she had spent years learning and working with, ceased to bother her. It might have been thought that a long process would have had to take place for her to liberate herself. However, this proved not to be so—this apprenticeship to the philosophy that had evolved through a long patriarchal history merely slipped from her. Neither did she need to reject this learning; it seemed to resituate itself into a place that was simply no longer problematic for her:

> I have found the following explanation: it is obvious that anti-maternal contents exist in (my) philosophical culture, but they have not been able to take root profoundly in me for the simple reason that precisely the anti-maternal meaning of a great part of philosophy has prevented me from learning it well. In other words, whilst admitting that the most rigorous feminism may be right about the need to unlearn patriarchal culture, and I accept this, the problem for me is turning out to be very simple, because in my case it is a matter of unlearning something that I never managed to learn (1994, p. 18).

A new operation had taken place, then, one that Muraro and others were to understand and name as an operation of the symbolic. She understood that this operation was vital if the efforts of feminism to break through patriarchy were to take effect, and not, as seen throughout women's history, be partially erased generation after generation. Muraro writes:

Feminism has produced a profound critique of the patriarchy and of the multiple philosophical and religious complicities which have sustained its system of domination. But this work of criticism, although it is vast and precise, will be erased within one or two generations if it does not find its affirmation. Only that can return to society, and above all, to women, the symbolic strength contained in the female relationship to the mother and neutralised by male dominion (1994, p. 21).

QUESTIONS IN EDUCATION

Returning the mother, or rather, the work of the mother,[9] to philosophy, particularly educational philosophy, opens us up to a whole new landscape. One of the paradoxes we are presented with is that a great part of the work of formal education for arguably the most formative years of children's lives is already carried out mostly by women in many cultures. If this work is understood in philosophical terms as a continuation of the work already begun by the mother, if there is not a violent rupture with that order, presumably this transition will be more harmonious.

There are many questions raised by the thinking of Irigaray and Muraro, and little scope to develop them here. If the idea is that change can come about through women authorising one another in their experience as women, as sexuate subjects (and the same applies to the male sexuate difference), bringing change into the classroom would require an *a priori* recognition of this fact. It might lead to a situation in which men and women teachers would understand that embracing this sexuate difference and working *with* it could generate a new awareness of how relationships between them might change. The initial idea would be to transform our rather fearful and conservative need to all be the same, into a journey towards a whole new plethora of possibilities emerging from the idea that the difference between the sexes, as Irigaray had postulated (1974, 1984) may well be an exciting point of departure.

If we acknowledge the historical omission of mothers and women as the first philosophers in their work to bring children into a shared symbolic order, we are able to see that restoring this knowledge to philosophy requires us to look again at every stage of the educational process. As that process continues, more men are introduced as teachers of children. The politics of sexual difference insists that the flourishing of sexuate difference in both women and men, girls and boys, relies, ultimately, on *both* sexes taking up the challenge to rethink themselves and the world.

In terms of education, there is a relative lack of men at earlier stages of children's lives. By the time young people reach further education, however, they may learn with more male teachers than female. There are many issues at stake here if we consider that, by the time of university, until recently, teachers have been predominantly male and transmitting knowledge often still predicated on the usurpation of the maternal work. That is, as education progresses, culture and knowledge is ever more stripped of both the recognition of the symbolic order of the mother, and, until relatively recently, the real presence of women as teachers.

This chapter holds that key concepts already very central to many of those committed to educational philosophy, such as equality, freedom, autonomy, authority, flourishing and the relationship with parents, could well be nourished and enriched through a consideration of the work taking place that as yet is little known in the English language. At the same time, if we refer back to the questions posed in the introduction ('What is taught and learnt? Why is it taught and learnt? How is it taught and learnt? Who is it taught and learnt by?'), we can see that there may be some value in reconsidering these concepts in the light of this work.

Whilst this chapter has sought to show the already existing work attempting to change our symbolic order undertaken by specific groups of women, the fact is that this is a philosophical and political project that ultimately relies on both sexes if it is to prosper. To bring sexuate difference into education in such a way as to enrich and transform cannot be done beyond a certain point unless both women and men agree that it is a fruitful way to go forward. The aim of this chapter has been to try to introduce the work already done and to point to areas for future consideration.

Education, and the right to it, has been and still is, one of the most important tenets of the women's movement. The relationship between education and freedom is evidently very strong, although it could benefit perhaps from deeper questioning at this stage, if we agree that there is a need to consider that the history of educational philosophy was for a long time based on a model taken from the experience of only one sex.

There is not the scope here to go into the question of authority, female or male, despite the fact that it forms part of the areas in which the Italian women referred to previously work very seriously, following on from Hannah Arendt's analysis of a crisis in authority in the Western world (1958). The discussion of authority is therefore a significant missing dimension from this chapter that would contribute in perhaps important ways to enriching the discussion that the author seeks to open up. It is perhaps worth mentioning here that it would be absolutely impossible to cover the enormous body of work undertaken by the authors referred to here over the past forty years. This chapter, thus, is seeking first of all to point to work and thought that for some reason is largely unknown of in the English-speaking world with the desire of opening up discussion. As such, some of the concepts and ideas referred to above may appear, at first sight, difficult.

This chapter has brought several elements to the fore. First, it has explored the emergence of a whole new philosophical idea, brought into being by Luce Irigaray in the context of the women's movements of the 1960s and 1970s in Europe. Second, it outlined how this idea was developed in Italy and Spain to restore the work of the mother to the origins of what we understand as education and philosophy, emphasising the need to bring relationship itself as the vehicle for this process onto centre stage *and keep it there.*

NOTES

1. The complexity of how this plays out is discussed by Rebecca Adami in Chapter 8.
2. In Chapter 7 of this book, Christine Winter shows us how problematic certain current prescriptive stances are when it comes to measuring academic attainment and success, if we care about allowing for and nurturing the otherness of each student.
3. As well as *Speculum*, interested readers who know little of Irigaray's opus might like to start with *Ethique de la différence sexuelle* (Irigaray, 1984), translated into English as *Ethics of Sexual Difference*, (Irigaray, 1993). Also see Hoveid and Finne, and Jones (Chapters 5 and 1, respectively).
4. Readers interested in my usage of the term 'symbolic order' (a term used from Plato through to Lacan with varying interpretations) are referred to the recently published book of the same title (Wilson, 2014).
5. It is important to note that there are exceptions to this and some interesting work does exist which ties in with this idea. Luisa Muraro, whose work we shall consider further on, refers, for example, to the thinking of Winnicott in this area.
6. See, for example, Biesta, 2006. In the UK, both Scottish and English governments focus on the role of teachers as highly significant. In Scotland, see the Donaldson report:http://www.scotland.gov.uk/Resource/Doc/337626/0110852.pdf and in England: https://www.gov.uk/government/publications/the-importance-of-teaching-the-schools-white-paper-2010.
7. As this text is not translated into English, all quotes have been translated by myself, from the Spanish version (Muraro, 1991b).
8. Amy Shuffelton, in Chapter 3, seeks to unravel and explore the reality of dependency in our lives as an ongoing fact.
9. It seems really important to me, especially given common misunderstandings in the interpretation of the thinking of sexual difference such as describing it as essentialist, to clarify that this does not mean an idealised version of woman but a recognition that sexual difference does reveal itself through the two different sexes and has done so historically.

Arguments for gender neutrality and equality may only serve to diminish the potential for symbolic wealth revealed by the idea of the sexuate as signifier.

REFERENCES

Arendt, H. (1958) What Is Authority? (originally published with the title 'What Was Authority?' in C. Friedrich (ed.) *Authority* (Cambridge, MA, Harvard University Press).

Biesta, G. J. J. (2006). *Beyond Learning. Democratic Education for a Human Future* (Boulder, CO, Paradigm Publishers).

Griffiths, M. (2006) The Feminisation of Teaching and the Practice of Teaching: Threat or Opportunity?, *Educational Theory*, 56.4, pp. 387–405.

Irigaray, L. (1974) *Speculum de l'autre femme* (Paris, Éditions de Minuit).

Irigaray, L. [1974] (1985) *Speculum of the Other Woman* (Ithaca, NY, Cornell University Press).

Irigaray, L. (1984) *Ethique de la différence sexuelle* (Paris, Éditions de Minuit).

Irigaray, L. (1993) *An Ethics of Sexual Difference* (London, The Athlone Press).

Milan Women's Bookstore Collective (1987) *Non credere di avere dei diritti* (Turin, Rosenberg i Sellier).

Milan Women's Bookstore Collective (1990) *Sexual Difference* (Bloomington, IN, Indiana University Press).

Muraro, L. (1991a) *L'ordine simbolico della madre* (Rome, Editore Riuniti).

Muraro, L. (1991b) *El orden simbólico de la madre* (Madrid, Cuadernos inacabados, Horas y horas).

Puissi, A. M. (2013) Volver a empezar. Entre vida, política y educación: prácticas de libertad y conflictos fecundos [Starting Again. Between Life, Politics and Education: Practices of Freedom and Fertile Conflicts], *DUODA. Studies of Sexual Difference* 45, University of Barcelona.

Riddell, S. *et al.* (2005) *Insight 24: Gender Balance of the Teaching Workforce in Publicly Funded Schools in Scotland* (Edinburgh, Scottish Executive Education Department). Online at: http://www.scotland.gov.uk/Publications/2005/11/1493519/35199

Wilson, C. (2014) *The Symbolic Order (The Book that Every Woman Should Read and that Every Man Must Read!)* (Crail, Symbolic Order Publishing).

Woolf, V. [1929] (1987) *A Room of One's Own* (London, Grafton Books, www.symbolicorderpublishing.weebly.com).

3
'New Fatherhood' and the Politics of Dependency

AMY SHUFFELTON

To this book's conversation about relationships in education, this chapter contributes an exploration of the devaluation of dependency in the 'new fatherhood' discourses that purport to reinvent familial relationships. Although 'new fatherhood' seems to promise a reconstruction of the domesticity paradigm that has positioned fathers as breadwinners and mothers as caretakers, it maintains the notion that families are self-supporting entities and neglects the extensive interdependence involved in raising children. As a result, it cannot successfully overturn this paradigm and hampers our ability to reimagine relationships along lines that would better serve parents' and children's wellbeing. The chapter raises these issues through an exploration of 'daddy-daughter dances', which manifest new fatherhood discourse as expressed in public schooling. Although the dances are in some ways peculiarly American, they exemplify tensions and inconsistencies around fathers' involvement in child-raising that nag most contemporary Western societies.

The devaluation of dependency, this chapter contends, constrains both intra-familiar and inter-familiar transfigurations of relationship. It limits parents' attempts to reimagine their gendered subjectivities as mothers and fathers, and it sets the terms on which they engage with other families within their communities. Contemporary discourse around maternal, paternal, and parental involvement shifts an increasing share of the responsibility for child-raising onto parents, or so the first section of this chapter contends. Families have always been both private and public, the site of intimate relationships and also a means for the social regulation of reproductive labour—the care of children and their initiation into a common world. As such, families are inevitably sites of contention, as the interests of mothers, fathers, and other members of their social world do not neatly align. Following a brief exposition of the current state of this perpetual power-scuffle, the

Re-Imagining Relationships in Education: Ethics, Politics and Practices, First Edition. Edited by Morwenna Griffiths, Marit Honerød Hoveid, Sharon Todd and Christine Winter. Chapters © 2015 The Authors. Editorial organization © 2015 Philosophy of Education Society of Great Britain. Published 2015 by John Wiley & Sons Ltd.

chapter turns to analysis of daddy-daughter dances. These dances, I argue, both reveal and disguise interdependencies among mothers, fathers, and the wider communities in which children are raised. In the concluding section, I discuss Eva Feder Kittay's notion of 'distributed dependency' as a means of reimagining relationships along lines that recognise (in the double sense of acknowledging and valuing) the interdependence of children and adult citizens, families and the society whose future they procure.

MATERNAL, PATERNAL, AND PARENTAL INVOLVEMENT

In *Maternal Thinking*, Sara Ruddick identifies three demands that define the practice of child-raising. 'Children "demand" that their lives be preserved and their growth fostered. In addition, the primary social groups with which a mother is identified, whether by force, kinship or choice, demand that she raise her children in a manner acceptable to them' (1989, p. 17). For Ruddick, meeting the three demands of 'preservation, growth, and social acceptability' constitutes maternal work. '[T]o be a mother is to be committed to meeting these demands by works of preservative love, nurturance, and training' (ibid.). This chapter explores the efforts of mothers and fathers to meet that set of ineluctable demands, specifically as they do so in relationship with public school. By school, I mean both the families and educators that the school comprises and the public school system as a state institution. Because school represents not only state authority but also a child's chief means of accessing eventual economic and political status, once a child reaches school age, state schooling becomes perhaps the most powerful source of demands for social acceptability. Furthermore, because a child's peers at school are a primary element of his or her social world, parents need concern themselves with those who make up the school community. I find Ruddick's conceptualisation a useful starting point because it reminds us that raising a child involves relationships that reach outside the family as well as within it. Furthermore, these outwards-reaching relationships are not a means of defending private space against state, corporate, and other social intrusion. Rather, they partially constitute a parent's relationship with her child. Because parent-school relationships are inextricable from child-raising, the relationships at the heart of this chapter might best be called parent-school-child relationships.

Schools' expectations of parents are multifarious, inconsistent, and politically contested, but that only makes the practice of raising a child more complicated. As Ruddick recognises, mothers are not free to raise their children entirely in accordance with their own notions of what social acceptability should entail. The fact that public schooling is being simultaneously privatised and centralised, with parents expected to take on the burden of funding core school functions even as federal education policy removes local authority over curriculum and pedagogy, makes the task of negotiating relationships between child and social world all the more dizzying.[1] School districts treat parents both as customers who must be pleased and, at the same time, as obstacles standing between their children and the predetermined ends of the school system. In an age of increasing inequality, parents bear the responsibility of positioning themselves and their children as worthy recipients of the resources needed to achieve success, yet they need to carry this task out with limited authority over educational policy and practice. Reference to parents as 'stakeholders' suggests an erosion of their political agency and its replacement with mere ownership. It would be a mistake, however, to believe that parents are accepting this passive role. Those for whom the practice of child-raising is a primary commitment cannot, by definition, do so.

Parents, that is to say, are *involved* in their children's education. To be a parent, in more than a minimal biological sense, already implies that one is involved in the project of raising a child. It is therefore noteworthy that contemporary policy finds 'parental involvement' a focus of concern.[2] Frequently touting it as a cornerstone of children's school success and exhorting parents to 'get involved', policy rhetoric frames parental involvement as a problem where none might have been thought to exist. The problem framed by this discourse, of course, is in the relationship between family and school, not between parent and child (though 'insufficient' parental involvement in the schooling project is taken by reformers as grounds for state intervention in aspects of child-raising that are otherwise left to the discretion of parents).[3] A parallel discourse of involvement, however, focuses explicitly on one kind of parent/child relationship—*fathers'* relationships with their children. In recent years, fatherhood has become a focus of public anxiety, and the discourse of 'involved fatherhood' presents an idealised resolution. There is no discourse of involved motherhood. By implication, for a mother to be other than involved in raising a child is not to be a mother at all. The closest corresponding rhetoric concerns maternal '*over*-involvement', a term generally used in reference to privileged mothers perceived as overreaching in their efforts to support their children. Anxiety also focuses on 'single-parent families', almost always headed by women, in which mothers are perceived as doubly over-empowered: fathers are absent, and mothers are apt to subordinate the agenda of state schooling to the necessities of maintaining their families. While 'over-involved mother' discourse typically suggests a mother with socio-economic privilege, and 'single-parent family' implies relative poverty, both sets of concerns imply that such mothers hold authority over child-raising that mothers ought not to have. When mothers are perceived as going beyond the expected level of involvement in a praise-worthy way, they are credited as 'involved parents', or perhaps as 'good moms'—not 'involved mothers'. The correlate to concern about paternal neglect of dependent children is concern about maternal authority over their care.[4]

Following reflection on the implications of the words 'mother', 'father', and 'parent', Ruddick selected the word 'mother' to name the practice of 'tak[ing] upon oneself the responsibility of child care, making its work a regular and substantial part of one's working life'. She chose not to use the gender-neutral term 'parent', but explicitly acknowledges that men can be 'mothers', in recognition that the vast majority of those for whom raising a child was central to their working lives were women, yet also to allow for men's eventual shouldering of that work (Ruddick, 1989, pp. 40–51). Since Ruddick published *Maternal Thinking*, expectations of mothers and fathers have changed. So have the demographics and legal interpretations of families, and so has scholarly understanding of gender. The dominant assumption now, in common parlance and in scholarship, seems to be that, because gender is constantly reconfigured through people's choices, child-raising is a position available to persons of any sex and sexuality. To many, it therefore seems more appropriate to call the practice of raising a child 'being a *parent*'. The differential meanings of parental, paternal, and maternal involvement in child-raising, however suggest that what it means to be a parent, to be a father, and to be a mother still varies significantly. The terms demand further consideration.

Caretaking work need not be feminised, nor paid employment and political activity masculinised. Using the term 'parent' to indicate child-raising, however, can suggest that we have already achieved this desirable state of affairs, which is the case neither in practice nor in theory. The ongoing difference between the level of involvement connoted by 'mother', 'father' and 'parent' implies that we have not yet succeeded in reimagining family relationships along lines that promote men's and women's equitable involvement in either child-raising or in political and economic life. 'Parent', the term of choice in important recent work in educational philosophy, is sometimes a suitable word, when it calls attention to what anyone who takes primary responsibility for child-raising does or should do, regardless of gender.[5] Given the persistence of gendered inequities in family life, however, it remains worth focusing some attention on the stubbornly gendered character of parents' experiences. Through an examination of the ideals of involved fatherhood, this chapter argues that the project of reimagining relationships within and between families is hobbled by our inability to reconcile with socio-political equality the dependencies that child-raising entails. Referring to the practice of raising a child as 'being a parent' risks glossing over the philosophical issues these unreconciled aspects of the human condition present. As regards parent-school relationships, unresolved issues of interdependency compromise our ability to create equitable schooling for all families' children.

HONOURING THE MAN WHO PAYS

When the Parent-Teacher Organization (PTO) at my daughter's school instituted a 'daddy-daughter dance' a few years ago, I was baffled. Why would parents and administrators who were in other respects observably committed to girls' equitable achievement celebrate neo-traditional gender ideals in their public school?[6] In their intense fund-raising for the school, in their promotion of arts and sports and academics, parents showed as much enthusiasm for their daughters' school success, and by proxy the career success to which it promises to lead, as for their sons'. Why undercut girls' march into a bright and promising future with a dramatic display of female dependency on male partners? This last question, I came to realise, was a vast oversimplification.

Daddy-daughter dances, frequently hosted by US primary schools, mimic the school prom (which is itself a modernised and democratised version of the elite's debutante ball), but with fathers serving as their daughters' 'dates'.[7] They have some ideological affiliations with the religious right's 'purity balls', at which girls symbolically entrust their sexuality to their fathers, often through a pledge of chastity rewarded with the gift of a ring, but daddy-daughter dances are secular and dodge explicit commentary on sex. Yet, like prom, these dances are sites of contestation through which parents and the state negotiate the meanings of gender, class and sexuality. There are solid grounds for questioning the legitimacy of these gender-stereotyping events within a public school system legally mandated to support gender equity.[8] Paradoxically, though, the dances are also draped in ideals of the 'new fatherhood', a cluster of expectations regarding fathers' actions, affect, and responsibilities that are often attached to the promotion of gender equity. The dances have arisen in the socio-political context of changing families and changing gender expectations for men and women; of neoliberal policies that reduce state support for families and education; and of a rampant, often heavily gendered and sexualised, consumer culture that targets children. This context complicates the meaning of these events. Contemporary fathers are expected to spend more time with their children, to express affection, and to be more involved with their children's schools and social lives—in other words, to take up feminised practices. At the same time, families are expected to be financially self-supporting, which necessitates that either one parent or both commit to full-time work, and this expectation falls more heavily on men (Haney and March, 2003; Wall and Arnold, 2007; Connell, 1995, 2000). As legal scholar Joan Williams emphasises in her research on parents in the workforce, the 'ideal worker' is assumed to be free of obligations to dependents that conflict with his or her commitment to work and therefore remains a masculinised subject position (Williams, 2000; Williams 2010). Neoliberal discourses of 'personal responsibility' reinforce both sets of demands, while neoliberal policies offer little support to fathers attempting to meet them. Daddy-daughter dances provide a window into fathers' and mothers' negotiation of this fraught terrain.

Economic and cultural changes have eroded men's dominance over the family and workplace, putting their relevance to family life into question. 'New fatherhood' discourses respond to these material shifts and the anxieties they provoke. 'New fatherhood' discourse has been little addressed by education philosophy, but a handful of revealing analyses from scholars of public health, social work, and media raise issues that merit philosophers' attention. In their analysis of 'new fatherhood' in the UK and France, Abigail Gregory and Susan Milner identify two distinct strands of fatherhood discourse, which they categorise as 'pessimistic' and 'optimistic.' The pessimistic version, associated with conservative moral panic about divorce and other effects of sexual liberation, laments the decline of patriarchal power (Gregory and Milner, 2011). It 'emphasises the negative effect on children and wider society of lack of paternal presence', Milner and Gregory find, 'in a way which stigmatises fathering behaviors, particularly in certain socioeconomic and racial groups' (ibid., p. 601). In the United States, where the unmooring of impoverished women and children from their few sources of public support has been paralleled by hand-wringing about impoverished fathers, public policy and popular media demand that fathers be held responsible for their children's welfare, usually without questioning the gender norms that devalue fathers whose support of their families is other than financial (Haney and March, 2003).

In contrast to the pessimistic strand's emphasis on pathologised *dependencies*, the 'optimistic' strand of new fatherhood discourse, frequently labelled 'involved fatherhood', emphasises men's and women's new range of *choices*. It celebrates fathers' increased willingness to share housework, their interest in spending more time with their children, and their expressed commitment to women's equality. As Milner and Gregory note, however, this discourse is based on 'optimistic assumptions of change . . . that have not yet proved valid' (Gregory and Milner, 2011 p. 601). The choices available to fathers and mothers are significant, but not as readily available as the discourse implies. This appears to hold, with local variations, across developed Western nations. In the United States, Kathleen Gerson's interviews with young people show, a significant majority of young men and women consider an equitable balance of responsibility for earning money and caring for children to be ideal within a partnership (Gerson, 2010). When they encounter workplace policies that remain stubbornly hostile to such arrangements (and to child-raising in general), however, men are more likely to expect that their female partners will stay home with their children while they take on the primary breadwinner role. Women are less likely to express this preference, but when they face state and workplace policies unsupportive of working mothers, continuing workplace discrimination against mothers' professional advancement, the expectation that mothers bear primarily responsibility for children, and resistant partners, they frequently concede. Gerson's work emphasises the problematic disconnection between young people's ideals and the realities contemporary workplaces create. Whether even the cultural *ideals* have changed as much as some assume is challenged by Glenda Wall and Stephanie Arnold, whose analysis of a parenting column in Canada's *Globe and Mail* newspaper reveals fathers to be presented as secondary caretakers, with those fathers who are primary caretakers presented as exceptional. Even in Scandinavia, the forerunner in gender equity, Thomas Johansson and Roger Klinth find that 'it is still women who take primary responsibility for the children and the home. . . . There is a tendency for men to participate in the "fun" aspects of parenthood, while women are in charge of the rest' (Johansson and Klinth, 2008, p. 60).

In their organization of caretaking, daddy-daughter dances epitomise the aspirations and contradictions of 'involved fatherhood'.[9] Although they purport to reposition men as involved in raising dependent children, the dances reiterate the masculinization of autonomy and the feminization of dependence at material and discursive levels. The language of the Duluth, Minnesota Father-Daughter

Ball 'FAQ' site, for instance, perpetuates the idea that child-care is naturally the province of women. 'We have had many inquiries as to what should be the appropriate age of the daughter(s) attending this event. To answer this, we suggest that the father be comfortable bringing and taking care of his daughter(s) on his own. We do have many female volunteers wearing Logo Badges available to assist the fathers if there is an immediate need' (Father Daughter Ball, 2013). The site does not mention whether those volunteers have experience caring for children or not, merely that they are 'female', thereby reiterating the assumption that women care for children by nature, men by choice. Even those fathers who are taking care of their daughters 'on their own' at the dance are not really on their own. Fathers are excused from the unappealing work of helping young children use the toilet, because female volunteers, the website promises, are also available to escort girls to the washrooms. Care of the body remains gendered work, leaving fathers free to enjoy their dressed-up daughters as objects of appreciation. Through rhetorical sleight of hand, the site 'disappears' these fathers' dependence on women for help with childcare by reimagining it as paternal involvement. Although these examples come from a church-sponsored dance, at my daughter's public school mothers also took nearly all responsibility for the material aspects of hosting a dance for 250 children, from decorating the school gym and arranging tickets to baking over 1000 cupcakes. Mothers' time commitment was erased there as well, as the event was portrayed as a celebration of *fathers'* involvement in their daughters' upbringing.

Accounts of these dances typically lament the limited time fathers have to spend with their daughters but avoid confronting the inconvenient fact that raising children consumes an extraordinary amount of time.[10] What makes the dances valuable, fathers say, is that they provide a *rare* opportunity for a father to spend time with his daughter. 'I don't know about other dads, but for me it is challenging to still find time for those really "great moments" with my daughter', writes Darren Danielson in the magazine *Moms and Dads Today*. 'The Father/Daughter Ball is a valuable opportunity to not only tell our daughters that we love them . . . but to show them' (Danielson, 2012). His language upholds the convention, noted by Johansson and Klinth, that paternal engagement can acceptably be limited to fun activities—to 'great moments'. The claim that he '[doesn't] know about other dads' also speaks to the limited expectation that fathers will do what anthropologists call 'kinship work', i.e., maintain relationships with the other parents who make up their children's community. In contrast, a mother who proffered that she 'didn't know' whether other mothers faced time pressures would immediately discredit herself as a competent parent. Unlike motherhood, which depends upon mothers' relationships within a social world, 'involved fatherhood' is an individualised pursuit.

Like Danielson's, other accounts refer to 'the' daddy-daughter dance, which emphasises the supposed singularity of the occasion. In the *New York Times*, Debra West says of the daddy-daughter dance she attended that 'you would have to be pretty hard-hearted to resist its charms: girls from kindergarten to middle school proudly showing off their dads, while loving fathers dote, as all parents should once in a while, on their lovely daughters.' Here too appears the notion that fathers can dote on their children merely from time to time. The dances' legitimation of 'special occasions' involvement sentimentalises familial relationships without challenging the social arrangements that make it difficult for fathers, and mothers, to combine significant involvement in their children's lives with full-time work. It supports the ideal of a masculinised independent worker, whose job can be his or her primary commitment (only) because the work of raising children (and caring for other dependents) is attended to by an off-stage feminised caretaker.

Daddy-daughter dances are hardly the only manifestation of 'new fatherhood' discourse in public schooling. What makes them especially interesting is that they perform involved fatherhood at a community, as well as an individualised, level. By this, I mean that the dances themselves are, in Butler's sense of 'performativity', performative statements that bring particular subjectivities into being (Butler, 1990). Drawing on John Austin's insight that language can change the material state of affairs (his famous example is the 'I do' of a marriage ceremony [Austin, 1975]), Butler argues that gender itself is an effect of rhetoric. Daddy-daughter dances are a perfect example of Butler's insight that language creates gendered subjectivities. Whether the fathers who attend the dances are deeply involved in raising their children or not, through attending the dance they become, performatively, 'involved fathers.' Notably, the adults attending these dances need not be exclusively fathers living at home with their children. Public schools, especially, often invite girls to bring a substitute daddy if necessary. They have even been held in low-security prisons, allowing fathers whose involvement in childcare is legally minimised to re-subjectify themselves as responsible, involved, fathers (*Inside Edition*, 2013). Returning again to Ruddick's insight that parenting is inextricable from relationships within a particular social world, it should also be recognised that in hosting these dances, the *collective* of parents whose children attend school together become an 'involved community of parents'. Parental involvement, one of the pillars of contemporary educational reform, is grounds for declaring a school to be a 'good school'. When the dances are hosted through school-family partnerships (e.g. the PTO), therefore, the dances function as a performative utterance that claims for the school the status of 'good school'.'

A 1955 *Life* magazine spread on Wellesley College sophomores' 'Big Date With Daddy' unabashedly declares the father-daughter dance to 'honor the man who pays the bills'. Nowadays, the dances appear to celebrate a father's investment of time in his daughter, rather than money, but these dances continue to honour men as earners of paychecks. For one, a father's time is so valuable that it takes a special occasion for him to spend it on his daughter because a father's time is worth money. Mothers volunteer, wearing logo badges or not. Mothers are underpaid at work (with some economists finding nearly all the remaining difference between men's and women's earnings attributable to mothers' decreased pay), and therefore, whether they work full-time or not, their time is, literally, worth less than that of fathers. The work they do raising children is treated as a labour of love, not to be accounted for in economic terms. Secondly, these events honour the man who pays at the level of community. In hosting a daddy-daughter dance, a parent-school partnership declares itself to be (and thereby, performatively, becomes) an 'involved' school community that is taking responsibility, at the family and community level, for its children. It declares that parents are heterosexual and married (regardless of whether they actually are). At a time when marital status strongly correlates with race and socio-economic status, the subjectivity it claims for the school community is also whitened and middle-classed. The school-parent partnership, usually a nearly-all female Parent Teacher Organization, demonstrates itself to be capable of hosting well-attended extracurricular events, which is to say representing a community of 'involved parents.'

This discursive performance has material effects. By declaring itself to be showing proper responsibility for its children, a parent-school community in the age of accountability declares itself worthy of public funding. In an ironic twist, public resources in the neo-liberal era are deemed most appropriate for those persons and communities who have already established themselves as professing independence, shouldering the burden of 'personal responsibility' through work and childcare. Just as welfare policy effects this at the level of families, federal education policy effects it at the level of schools. Those parents at my daughter's school who supported the daddy-daughter dance, in other words, were not undercutting their daughters' march into a bright future. In honouring the man who pays the bills, and thereby claiming public support for their daughters' school, they were supporting it.

DEPENDENCE AND EQUALITY

The consensus that fathers should be more deeply involved in child-raising than they have been in recent generations is widespread and encouraging. That the ideal of involved fatherhood can be logically expressed in the format of neo-traditional courtship dances, however, suggests that our attempts to reimagine familial relationships have not yet broken with the paradigm of domesticity. By domesticity, I mean the idea that adult men are appropriately situated as independent heads of household, whose autonomy in the public sphere depends upon the assignment of caretaking responsibilities to mothers, who are relegated to the private sphere. While the causes of this quintessentially modern organization of personal and political life are surely over-determined, its political rationale was best articulated by Jean-Jacques Rousseau. Whereas other Enlightenment thinkers quick-handedly dismissed caretaking work from political theory, Rousseau's portrayal of Émile and Sophie acknowledges the extent to which dependency, in all its guises, is an ongoing aspect of the human condition that raises serious problems for the Enlightenment ideal of a society constituted by autonomous citizens (Martin, 1985). Rousseau's solution, of course, is to assign dependency to Sophie, i.e. woman-as-mother, in two crucially related ways. First, to Sophie exclusively is assigned the care of dependent children. Second, *because* Sophie is responsible for raising future Émiles and Sophies, she herself must be dependent on both Émile, i.e. man-as-citizen/provider, and on the social approval of those around her. For his embrace of deterministic binaries, Rousseau has been appropriately lambasted, from Mary Wollstonecraft's *Vindication of the Rights of Women* to Morwenna Griffiths's piece in this book. To Rousseau's credit, however, *Émile* (along with both *Discourses*) reveals the extent to which dependency, as both the basis and consequence of real human relationships, throws the Enlightenment political project into question. In contrast with Rousseau, liberal political philosophy, at least in its later configurations, has professed a dedication to women's equality in the public sphere. It continues, however, to exclude dependency from its account of political subjectivity. In treating dependency as an exception to the normal state, or as a state to be overcome, rather than as a core aspect of human existence, it has effectively—if inadvertently—upheld the domesticity paradigm.

In *Love's Labor*, Eva Feder Kittay asks what it would mean for theories of justice to recognise dependency as an elemental characteristic of the human condition. She criticises dependency's sidelining by liberal political philosophy and argues that it needs to be included in any theory of justice that would uphold equality. Her 'dependency critique' of liberal equality makes three major charges. 'First', she contends, 'the conception of society as an association of equals masks the inevitable dependencies and asymmetries that form part of the human condition—those of children, the aging and the ailing—dependencies that often mark the closest human ties' (Kittay, 1999, p. 14). It is important to emphasise that in her account, dependency is neither an exceptional condition nor an entirely regrettable one. Over the course of a human life, there are inevitably periods when we depend upon others, and it is through our dependencies and the care we take of dependents that we forge the relationships that contribute to a flourishing life. Second, 'the presumption of equality obscures the extent to which many of our societal interactions are not between persons symmetrically situated, even when they are between individuals who might otherwise be autonomous' (ibid., p. 15). What a useful theory requires, she says, is 'an appreciation of the inevitable variety of human interactions and a more adequate understanding of what is morally acceptable in asymmetric relations' (ibid., p. 15). Third, 'the equality possible when society is conceived of as an association of equals has trained our gaze on one side of the sexual division of labour: the inclusion of women into the male half' (ibid., p. 15). Policies promoting women's equality in the workforce have indeed advanced the interests of many women, but their success has been achieved by shifting what Kittay calls 'dependency work'—care of children, the ill, and the frail elderly—to paid 'dependency workers'. Because dependency work continues to bring low pay and status, paid dependency workers are generally less well situated than the women thereby enabled to occupy higher status positions. As they are also taking on paid employment, these lower-paid nannies and nursing aides are required to shift care of their own dependents elsewhere, to even lower-paid, lower-status workers. Equality within the family, in other words, is achieved by reinforcing inequalities among families.

Kittay's analysis of dependency work helps make sense of how 'new fatherhood' discourse buttresses inequality rather than resolving it. Young children are prototypically dependent, and the person who makes their care a primary aspect of his or her work is a prototypical dependency worker. Flexible gender roles make it possible for different persons to take up this role—mothers, fathers, or a combination of parents and paid dependency workers. What remains inflexible is that the practice of child-raising makes ineluctable demands that bind the dependency worker to his or her charge. Dependency work thus creates new dependencies, as the dependency worker, in making the needs and interests of the dependent her or his primary concern, cannot attend to her or his *own* needs when they conflict with those of her or his charge. This is true in a strong sense of those who care for very young children, but even when dependents are more able to care for themselves, their needs continue to constrain those who care for them. The person who takes charge of a dependent child is therefore dependent, to an extent that varies depending on the child's neediness, on the support of others. Those who provide for the dependency worker and dependent therefore become, in a sense, secondary dependency workers. Like the needs of dependents, the needs of dependency workers are to a certain extent inflexible, though the farther one gets from the dependent, the greater the apparent 'exit option.' Even the person who takes primary care of a dependent can walk out, but as Kittay points out, most of us consider it morally repugnant to do so except in the most extreme conditions. It is somewhat more acceptable for a secondary dependency worker—e.g. the husband of a stay-at-home mother—to decline the responsibilities of care, but only because the dependency worker, unlike the dependent, has some capacity to seek help elsewhere. Her needs, however, do not disappear; they are merely shifted onto someone else's shoulders—or else neglected.

The 'advanced liberalism' (Rose, 1996) that structures contemporary public policy readily accommodates fathers replacing mothers as primary caretakers, as well as parents paying caretakers to do the portion of child-raising they can not take on due to their own full-time paid employment. It does not accommodate the wider distribution of dependency work that would enable those who make raising a child a primary commitment to have their own needs also met. Dependency is accepted if, *and only if*, it remains within the family—with care either provided by family members or paid for out of the parents' earnings. (In the case of female volunteers, with or without logo badges, dependents are in the hands of *unpaid* dependency workers, which begs the question of who is providing for the needs of those volunteers.) When the bread-winner parent, male or female, is sufficiently well-paid to support a middle class family on one pay-check, a caretaker's choice to become dependent by taking on full-time dependency work is lauded. Less advantaged families, however, who need to turn *outside* the family for secondary dependency work, are stigmatised.

This is true of mothers, as analyses of welfare reform have pointed out. Middle and upper middle class mothers who leave paid employment in order to stay home with children are praised by some, grudgingly accepted by others, and, in a recent slew of popular books lamenting the binds that contemporary workplace, health, and educational policies put them in, treated as objects of compassionate concern. Poor mothers, in contrast, are expected to find alternative care for children as young as infancy so that they can establish financial independence through paid employment. New fatherhood rhetoric is cruelly gender-egalitarian in extending to fathers the same unmeetable set of demands that neo-liberalism has extended to mothers. Pathologising fatherhood rhetoric stigmatises those men who do not or cannot provide primary or secondary dependency work—in the form of childcare or paid employment that covers the costs of childcare— sufficient to keep their families from looking for help. It stigmatises families, that is, who are unable to contain their dependency needs within the family. Involved fatherhood rhetoric, as I have argued, celebrates fathers' fiscal independence alongside their provision of some (not necessarily much) childcare, not the quality of their relationships. The paradigm of domesticity no longer disconnects men and disempowers women along the same strictly gendered lines as it used to, but it has not relaxed its grip in all respects. Fathers, like mothers, find themselves struggling to engage in the fulfilling but demanding work of child-raising while also upholding their obligation to 'pay the bills'. Some men, of course, forego paid employment and depend entirely upon their partners to provide financially, but this is treated as acceptable only as a mirror-image caretaker-breadwinner arrangement, i.e. if the family has sufficient resources to contain its dependencies. New fatherhood has rearranged responsibilities within the family but failed to mobilise the support fathers, alongside mothers and children, really need. Involved fatherhood rhetoric, I would contend, functions as a distraction, not a solution.

Let me add that while I mean to suggest that fathers now find themselves facing perplexities that have previously been mainly the province of mothers (how to live a life that includes raising children, the satisfactions of paid employment, *and* membership in one's social and political communities), I do not mean that fathers and mothers are now in exactly the same circumstances. Men are indeed in a bind. No doubt many of them treasure daddy-daughter dances because they yearn for more time to spend with their children. Yet it would be a mistake to ignore the privileges that continue to attend masculine subjectivity. Because a father's assumption of responsibilities for child-raising is viewed as a freely-made choice, it upholds his claim to be an autonomous subject, in a way that a mother's decision to do so does not. Maternal care is naturalised, and child-raising continues to be treated as naturally a mother's responsibility. Paternal child-raising, in contrast, is seen as a deliberate, often counter-cultural, move that expresses a man's liberation from convention. Because involved fatherhood is treated as a choice that expresses freedom and independence, even fathers who stay home full-time with their children can continue to claim a version of hegemonic masculinity and the rewards it brings.

Kittay offers a better solution to managing our interdependency with her model of 'distributed dependency'. She suggests that care for a needy dependent might be shared among a small number of dependency workers, whose needs in turn are attended to by a wider circle, such that each can expect that in his or her own moments of dependency, care will be reciprocated. 'Incorporating dependency and the dependency relation into social relations', she argues, 'requires a concept of *interdependence* capable of recognizing "nested dependencies." Through a form of reciprocity . . . these nested dependencies link those who need help to those who help, and link the helpers to a set of supports' (1999, p. 132, emphasis added). In challenging the dichotomization of dependence and independence, *Love's Labor* makes the radical suggestion that, rather than shifting the assignment of roles around (with men, or paid nannies, or the state simply filling the role of 'mother'), citizenship be reconceptualised as a position for interdependent human beings.

At its best, public schooling works towards this aim. In supporting public schooling, the wider population of citizens recognises that any society hoping to survive beyond a single generation depends upon its children. When adult relationships with children are considered across time—across a single human life span, with its varying periods of sufficiency and need, and across generations—the eventual dependence of adults upon children who for the moment depend on them comes into focus. Education, in other words, is a nexus of interdependency. Whether contemporary education policy recognises this is quite another matter. 'Personal responsibility' discourse, including the 'new fatherhood' discourses interrogated in this chapter, instead shifts responsibility for educating children onto families. As described above, families are pressed to demonstrate their ability to take care of children 'on their own' in order to qualify for the public funding that is necessary because, *pace* Rousseau, no one can raise a child on his or her own. Like the FAQ website that established the conditions for fathers 'independently' to take care of daughters through dependence on the hushed-up and unpaid labour of female volunteers, contemporary education policy attempts through rhetorical hocus-pocus to transform parent-school-child interdependence into a deal between independent contractors. This is half-effectual magic. New fatherhood discourse cannot fully transform relations of interdependency into relations between independent persons, but neither does it leave relations between men and women, adults and children, families and schools, the privileged and the poor untouched. In trying to turn little girls into princesses and their fathers into kings, it may be turning all of us into frogs. To reject our contemporary transfiguration of parent-school-child relationships, however, is not to deny the importance of reimagining this relationship. With families taking new shapes, and new powers available to men and women alike, transfiguration is called for. Better magic, however, needs to start with the premise of human interdependence.

NOTES

1. This chapter was written from a US perspective. While particulars vary according to national context, privatization and the responsibilisation of individuals and families is happening throughout the developed world, as are profound changes in how gender and family are enacted. See below, for research on new fatherhood in the US, Canada, Britain and France, and Sweden, which finds important discursive similarities in spite of important demographic and political differences.
2. See Robinson and Harris, 2013.
3. See also Shuffelton, 2013.
4. For a deeper consideration of maternal authority, see Wilson (Chapter 2).
5. Cf. Stefan Ramaekers and Judith Suissa, 2011; Suissa, 2006, 2009, 2013; Harry Brighouse and Adam Swift, 2006, 2009.
6. I use the phrase 'neo-traditional' in recognition of the historically documented point that there is no such entity as the 'traditional' family (Coontz, 1992). 'The traditional family' is, instead, a fluid imaginary that responds to present tensions.
7. On school proms, class and gender, see Best, 2000. For an account of related dances that engages more extensively with ethnicity see Alvarez, 2007. These dances are peculiarly American in their hyper-concern about sexuality, their use of the public school as the focus of community social life, and their democratisation of upper class *mores*. I use them here to illustrate aspects of 'new fatherhood' which represent Western ideals much more broadly. I am grateful to Teresa Barton for her assistance researching these dances.
8. As typically held, they violate US federal law, namely Title IX, which mandates that schools providing single-sex extracurricular events must provide a 'reasonably comparable activity' for the other sex. Schools frequently balance the dance with a mother-son sports outing, which reiterates the association of boys with athletics, girls with aesthetics, and is not, therefore, reasonably comparable. The relevant passage of Title IX is at 1681 (a) 8. That the dances also uphold a heterosexist definition of family adds another layer of ethical and legal concern.
9. Because this chapter brings several bodies of scholarship together—feminist theory, other philosophical work on familial relationships, and social scientific research on families—it straddles three sets of terminology: care, child-raising, and caretaking. In my use of these

different terms, I have in most places used a source's own language in discussing it. I have also tried to consistently use 'caretaking' to indicate the practical aspects and 'child-raising' to indicate the ethical and political dimensions of bringing up a child. Because the work of caretaking itself has political and ethical dimensions, as feminist scholars have emphasised, the distinction is imperfect and the difference should not be overstated. Fuller exploration of the differences between what these terms signify would constitute another project. I am grateful to the anonymous reviewer who reminded me to note the varying signification of these terms.

10. Also see Everingham and Bowers, 2006.

REFERENCES

Alvarez, J. (2007) *Once Upon a Quinceañera: Coming of Age in the USA* (New York, Viking).

Austin, J. L. (1975) *How To Do Things With Words* (Cambridge, MA, Harvard University Press).

Best, A. (2000) *Prom Night: Youth, Schools, and Popular Culture* (New York, Routledge).

Brighouse, H. and Swift, A. (2006) Parents' Rights and the Value of the Family, *Ethics*, 117.1, pp. 80–108.

Brighouse, H. and Swift, A. (2009) Legitimate Parental Partiality, *Philosophy & Public Affairs*, 37.1, pp. 43–80.

Butler, J. (1990) *Gender Trouble* (New York, Routledge).

Connell, R. W. (1995) *Masculinities* (Berkeley, CA, University of California Press).

Connell, R. W. (2000) *The Men and the Boys* (Berkeley, CA, University of California Press).

Coontz, S. (1992) *The Way We Never Were: American Families and the Nostalgia Trap* (New York, Basic Books).

Danielson, D. (2012) *Moms and Dads Today*, February-April, pp. 4–5.

Everingham, C. and Bowers, T. (2006) Re-Claiming or Re-Shaping Fatherhood, *Health Sociology Review*, 15.1, pp. 96–103.

Father Daughter Ball (2013) *Frequently Asked Questions of the Father Daughter Ball*. Online at: www.fatherdaughterballduluth.org/?110030

Gerson, K. (2010) *The Unfinished Revolution: How a New Generation Is Reshaping Family, Work and Gender in America* (New York, Oxford University Press).

Gregory, A. and Milner, S. (2011) What Is 'New' about Fatherhood?: The Social Construction of Fatherhood in France and the UK, *Men and Masculinities*, 14.5, pp. 588–606.

Haney, L. and March, M. (2003) Married Fathers and Caring Daddies: Welfare Reform and the Discursive Politics of Paternity, *Social Problems*, 50.4, pp. 461–481.

Inside Edition (2013) Online at: http://on.aol.com/video/father-daughter-dance-for-prison-inmates-517718890#_videoid=517549094

Johansson, T. and Klinth, R. (2008) Caring Fathers, *Men and Masculinities*, 11.1, pp. 42–62.

Kittay, E. F. (1999) *Love's Labor: Essays on Women, Equality, and Dependency* (New York, Routledge).

Martin, J. R. (1985) *Reclaiming a Conversation: The Ideal of the Educated Woman* (New Haven, CT, Yale University Press).

Ramaekers, S. and Suissa, J. (2011) *The Claims of Parenting* (Dordrecht, Springer).

Robinson, K. and Harris, A. (2013) *The Broken Compass* (Cambridge, MA, Harvard University Press).

Rose, N. (1996) Governing 'Advanced' Liberal Democracies, in: A. Barry, T. Osborne and N. S. Rose (eds) *Foucault and Political Reason* (Chicago, IL, University of Chicago Press).

Ruddick, S. (1989) *Maternal Thinking: Toward a Politics of Peace* (Boston, MA, Beacon Press).

Shuffelton, A. (2013) A Matter of Friendship, *Educational Theory*, 63.3, pp. 299–316.

Suissa, J. (2006) Untangling the Mother Knot, *Ethics and Education*, 1.1, pp. 65–77.

Suissa, J. (2009) *Constructions of Parents and Languages of Parenting, Philosophy of Education Yearbook* (Urbana, IL, University of Illinois Press).

Suissa, J. (2013) Tiger Mothers and Praise Junkies: Children, Praise and the Reactive Attitudes, *Journal of Philosophy of Education*, 47.1, pp. 1–19.

Wall, G. and Arnold, S. (2007) How Involved is Involved Fathering? An Exploration of the Contemporary Culture of Fatherhood, *Gender & Society*, 21.4, pp. 508–527.

Williams, J. (2000) *Unbending Gender: Why Family and Work Conflict and What To Do About It* (Oxford, Oxford University Press).

Williams, J. (2010) *Reshaping the Work-Family Debate: Why Men and Class Matter* (Cambridge, MA, Harvard University Press).

4
Between Body and Spirit: The Liminality of Pedagogical Relationships

SHARON TODD

> . . . I hardly exist and if I do exist it's with a delicate care.
> Surrounding the shade is a teeming, sweaty heat. I'm alive. But
> I feel I've not yet reached my limits, bordering on what? Without
> limits, the adventure of a dangerous freedom. But I take the risk,
> I live taking it (Clarice Lispector, *The Stream of Life*).

After our parents and caregivers, the most common relationship that many of us experience is the one with our teachers. From an early age we come into encounters, more or less warm and inviting, severe and distant, with teachers from whom, if we are lucky, we learn not just about what we are, but who we are. Such learning, in my view, occurs not simply through the curriculum, but through moments that punctuate the apparent continuity of classroom routine—small, transformative moments, to use Lispector's words, of 'delicate care' that disrupt the commonplace. It is nothing overt or explicit, nothing that can be articulated fully through words, but a subtlety of presence that allows a bit of life in all its messiness to enter:

> *A teacher standing near, the feeling of goosebumps, a warmness creeping from the centre of my body radiating out to my limbs. I am seven years old and sense, without having to see, my teacher hovering over my shoulder. Wanting to smell her scent, to feel her breath against my cheek and to glimpse the baby-fine hairs on her own, to touch her skin, knowing it would be warm. The nearness of it all—her presence, my awareness—almost painful, yet full of pleasure. It is sudden and I'm a bit frightened of what's happening. No contact, no touching, yet something palpable and close. I do not understand this, I sense it, and I am different.*

Re-Imagining Relationships in Education: Ethics, Politics and Practices, First Edition. Edited by Morwenna Griffiths, Marit Honerød Hoveid, Sharon Todd and Christine Winter. Chapters © 2015 The Authors. Editorial organization © 2015 Philosophy of Education Society of Great Britain. Published 2015 by John Wiley & Sons Ltd.

I have often thought about this moment—and similar ones—over the course of a lifetime in classrooms as both teacher and student. I recollect this here in the context of this book on relationships, for I think there is something profoundly pedagogical in moments such as these. Such moments are pedagogical not because they occur in educational contexts—which they can and do—but these moments also constitute what is 'educational' about life: that through our encounters with others (human and non-human alike) we shift the borders of our self understanding. That we alter and transform in this way is not merely the hope of education, but is the pedagogical act of living *par excellence*.

From the earliest conceptions of education, the transformation of the self was recognised as belonging to an encounter with a teacher (witness the Socratic questioner; the Voltairean gardener; the Deweyan guide. Although much educational philosophy has grappled with the proper image of the teacher in order to bring forth the desired changes in students, I want to shift the focus here in order to highlight the relationship between teacher and student itself as a specifically *pedagogical* one—pedagogical because the relationship occasions transformation and becoming (Castoriadis, 1997).[1] This means that all kinds of relationships are pedagogical—one can speak of the pedagogy of a film or text (Lusted, 1986), just as one might speak of what one becomes in relation to a colleague, pet or friend. However, unlike the pedagogical aspects of a relationship, say, between siblings, friends, colleagues or lovers, the relationship between teacher and student is doubly so, since it rests upon an educational intentionality, or 'demand' for change (Todd, 2003), that these other relationships do not.

In this sense, reimagining educational relationships as specifically pedagogical ones requires moving beyond our intentionality (or at least bracketing it off momentarily), in order to uncover the aspects of relationality that occasion one's becoming. That is, that people change and become is not always dependent upon the intentionality behind the circumstances. Teachers can desire certain changes in their students, but students' lives change in unpredictable ways, outside of these desires. As the recollection above indicates, change can occur in a mixture of disturbance and delight: it disturbs in terms of the unknowingness it opens up, generating feelings of being overwhelmed, and it carries with it an intensity of physical sensation that itself can be unsettling as well as deeply pleasurable and erotic. In this sense, the transformation involved in one's becoming is rarely easy. The quote from Clarice Lispector intimates that living life is about exceeding limits, about living it as a risk. Life resides in mystery and excess: we do not know what awaits. And life is also not what we live in containment, cut off from the senses, but about being exposed to the 'teeming, sweaty heat' by which we know we are alive. In this sense it is bodily and beyond the body simultaneously: it is a sensibility that also gestures toward an unnameable openness beyond our limits. Existence, on this meaning, lies between the corporeal and a sense of limitlessness, or what I here refer to as spirit.[2]

In order to explore this liminal space in between body and spirit, the chapter first outlines a case for why liminality is of educational and not only of pedagogical concern, building on James Conroy's notion of the *liminal imagination* and his emphasis on the importance of metaphor for calling our attention to the ontological spaces that make up educational practice. I then use this metaphor both substantively and methodologically, offering a reading of Clarice Lispector's novel *The Stream of Life* as a performance of the liminal imagination in its attempt to put into focus the embodied and transcendent aspects of becoming, both of which I see are central to defining what is *pedagogical* about human existence. It is here through her literary language that we can begin to approach the subtle, aesthetic quality of one's experiences of becoming. The chapter then turns to developing how different metaphors may be mobilised to signify the particularly *relational* quality of becoming, drawing on Luce Irigaray's work to explore more closely the corporeal and spiritual aspects of becoming *in relation*. I then turn my attention to a more fulsome discussion of the significance of approaching pedagogical relationships in education in this way and what this signifies for the teacher-student encounter in particular.

THE LIMINAL IMAGINATION, METAPHOR AND EDUCATION

There have been many ways of capturing the transformation of the self, and it is no secret that modern education has been built upon the idea that students not only can but ought to change, develop, and progress. Indeed, in a very obvious sense, educational discourses of all philosophical persuasions have used metaphorical language to 'capture' this change in learning. For instance, John Dewey speaks of growth, Jean Piaget and Lawrence Kohlberg of stages, Nel Noddings of flourishing, and Martha Nussbaum of cultivation. Within the current climate of economic efficiency, students' capacities for change are spoken of in terms of outcomes, productivity, and standardisation. Metaphors are akin in this regard to what Deleuze and Guattari (1994) say of a concept:[3] 'it posits itself and its object at the same time as it is created' (p. 22). A concept, on their view, generates a certain landscape of 'reality' in creating new objects of thought. Metaphors, like concepts in this sense, approximate and focus our attention on certain 'things' rather than others, and in fact bring into being certain relationships that would not have been possible before. For example, Dewey's (1969/1938) metaphor of growth calls forth a relation whereby the teacher acts as someone who tends to and guides the student along her path of educative experience; Morwenna Griffiths (Chapter 11) shows how the language of the natural in Rousseau signals a particularly gendered set of relationships; and the economic metaphor of outcomes sets up a quality of relationality whereby the teacher is to focus primarily on the results or products of 'learning' instead of on its processes or its connections to the student herself. In order, then, to bring something into our field of awareness a shift in our metaphorical language is required to initiate new ways of thinking and practicing education. I argue here that exploring the existential dimensions of pedagogical relationships between body and spirit similarly requires a language of in-betweenness, or liminality, that gives full weight to the complex processes of human becoming.

James Conroy (2004) in *Betwixt and Between: The Liminal Imagination, Education and Democracy* makes a case for the importance of liminality for education, and outlines its reliance on metaphor. Writing against the backdrop of what he sees as an impoverishment of educational discourse around actual classroom practice, Conroy seeks to open up classroom space by developing the metaphor of the threshold, or liminality, as a way of discussing the human, existential quality of educational settings. For Conroy, liminality serves to act as a 'heuristic metaphor' 'to delineate particular kinds of ontological spaces in and around the school' (p. 57). As such, the liminal 'operates' in-between categories and spaces that sit 'at the threshold of experience' (pp. 7–8). Although his work is concerned with how these spaces exist on the threshold of social, political, cultural and religious intelligibilities, in pointing to the specifically ontological possibilities that such spaces offer Conroy nonetheless opens up the practice of education to its own role in human becoming. He suggests that with respect to education, the notion of liminality can be deployed in three ways: a liminal education, a liminal disposition, and liminal communities. It is the first two of these that holds particular relevance for the pedagogical relationship between teacher and student and thus I confine my discussion to these.

Conroy argues that a *liminal education* needs to acknowledge the ways in which ontological possibilities are created outside the structuring intentionalities of teaching: '. . . much of human thought, reflection and engagement with the world emerges out of the cracks and fissures of our personal and social relations and not in the wide-open structured spaces' (p. 62). This means that the asymmetrical power dynamics which structure teacher-student relations are some-times disrupted by such liminal spaces. 'In the liminal moment both are equal in the face of this or that encounter with an idea, a creation, comprehension or insight. No longer is there a separation between teacher and student—each learns, each encounters' (p. 62). In what he refers to as his second deployment of the metaphor, he writes of developing a *liminal disposition* of the teacher that can aid in prepar-ing and fashioning possibilities for these moments to happen. 'Prac-tically, this entails the willingness to take chances, the capacity to let things take their own course, the patience to hang back' (p. 65). Conroy suggests that what is required on the part of teachers is a vision for cultivating their own and others' imagination. This is not a call for teachers to live 'in a world of *as if*'—as if their work were not deeply shaped by social, economic and cultural pressures and only needs to embrace an 'ideal' of liminality in order to dispense with them. Eschewing this kind of illusory practice, Conroy instead sug-gests that 'such a vision entails the recognition that the liminal is not, by definition, the main fare of the day, rather that the day is configured in the light of it' (pp. 65–66). The liminal, therefore, acts as a horizon of possibility that guides teachers' educational work.

There are two things particularly worthy of note in this depiction of a liminal education and liminal disposition. First is that Conroy implicitly gestures to the 'momentary' nature of liminal encounters; that is, while they can be enhanced by a certain 'disposition' on the part of the teacher, they rise up of their own accord, in an engagement with texts, ideas, and others in the present. Thus, immanent to the quality of liminality is an understanding of the importance of the here and now for initiating human becoming.[4] Secondly, the separation of teacher and student perhaps does not so much disappear, as Conroy seems to suggest, but is rather, in my view, recast in a new register where the categories of teacher and student are suspended; it is more that the opportunities for becoming—and not the roles as such—become more equal in liminal encounters. Thus, the metaphor of liminality seeks to bring into our field of awareness the deeply per-sonal aspects of becoming which are always connected to our living in the present moment, beyond—or perhaps in spite of—the regulatory roles we occupy in classrooms.

Conroy also avails himself of metaphor in another sense in intro-ducing the liminal imagination. This is not only a metaphor that stands for the whole of his liminal project, it also signals the specifically literary, artistic, and poetical dimensions of human existence. There is a sense here that the way to create better conditions for liminal spaces to emerge in education is for teachers to turn to the qualities of relationality opened up by the arts.[5] Conroy signals out the especial place poetry can occupy in this project: '. . . poetry which draws on its linguistic heartland—metaphor, aphorism, banal and sublime descriptions of the everyday—is never contained by, or reduced to, that heartland since it twists and stretches those very ordinary words so that it persistently pushes at the very edges of communicative possibility' (p. 12). Poetry, on Conroy's meaning, is itself a liminal form of expression whose purpose is not to 'name' but to suggest, intimate, and approach. Metaphor is not confined to syntactical substitution of one word for another, but it 'also plays a semantic role in that it offers us a new way of relating to its object; it enables us to generate new images, new sensations and changes in emotional states' (p. 150). Poetical expression thereby performs the very conditions of meaning that Conroy is seeking to employ in classroom spaces.

With this, the liminal imagination becomes, in my view, both an *orientation* to teaching and education at the same time as it calls forth an *alternative mode of theorising* education. As for the former, liminality reframes our attention to the ontological aspects of education that are bound to our everyday, lived experiences in classrooms. As for the latter, the liminal imagination functions methodologically to delineate an approach that uses literature, poetry and the arts in order to explore the liminal spaces of existence as central to educational thought. It is in the spirit of this methodological sense of the liminal imagination that I turn now to explore Clarice Lispector's *The Stream of Life* in order to explore the experience of existing in its everydayness.

THE PEDAGOGICAL AS AN EVERYDAY EXISTENTIAL EXPERIENCE

Clarice Lispector's (1989/1974) experimental novel, *The Stream of Life*,[6] unfolds in present time; the nameless main character is a disillusioned painter who has recently turned to writing to try to express her 'existence' as it gets created, or creates itself, moment by moment, instant to instant. It is a lyrical, impressionistic work, with no real plot or narrative, and the language is far more poetic in its aim and structure than what is usually associated with the novel form. The narrator (if we may be permitted to call her that) writes the text as a letter of sorts to a past lover, persistently addressing herself to the question of who she is 'in this instant'. What she continually returns to is the ineffable quality of existence and its rootedness in liminal spaces that resist codification. Echoing Conroy's remarks above in relation to poetry, Lispector reveals not simply the limits of language, but the ways in which language pushes us to a point beyond our communicative possibilities.

Lispector uses language as a means for performing existence as a 'coming-into-being' (p. 51) located between the body and what lies beyond it: 'it is subtle, like the most intangible reality' (p. 15) yet it has, as we will see, a tangible, corporeal quality along with its 'spiritual' dimension. This coming-into-being entails 'a full stretching to the point where the person can stretch no more' (p. 51). Here, the narrator marks one's becoming as a process of alteration that is built on a certain plasticity of experience. It is a stretching out beyond our limits, both figuratively and literally, occasioning a different form of being. Hers is a unique bodily existence where the 'blood is thankful' and where 'pain is exacerbated life' (p. 51), and yet this existence pushes into unknowable spaces and becomes 'something more magical and more graceful' (p. 56) than what we can even contemplate or physically inhabit.

Lispector attends keenly to what it is we can neither articulate through words nor capture through understanding. In the novel, existing, living and becoming are treated synonymously with residing at a threshold. And it is in this space of the threshold where each of us is born as a unique being—and not just once as in our first birth, but where each of us is transformed again and again. The narrator pleads: 'Don't you see it [my existing] is like a child being born?' (p. 51). Becoming is a birth that is experienced in a field of sensibility through which one 'feels the tumult of newness' (p. 20). A newness that evokes fear and apprehension like a soon-to-be-born infant. She writes: 'But now I want plasma, I want to feed directly from the placenta. I'm a little frightened, still afraid to give myself over since the next instant is the unknown' (p. 3). In figuratively being born, we enter into the next instant again and again, living (but never *re*living) the newness that is ours in each moment of the present. What is striking about Lispector's language is the mixture of the visceral concreteness of the body with the ephemeral, anticipatory state of the 'next instant'. This 'next instant' is always imminent and open to surprise ('Something is always about to happen' (p. 43)) and at the same time it is always predictable in its very unpredictability: 'And the only thing that awaits me is precisely the unexpected' (p. 44). Connecting the 'unexpected' here to birth stands somewhat in contrast to dominant preoccupations of western philosophy that instead identify death 'as the only thing that awaits us all'. In proposing natality as a model of unique becoming as opposed to mortality as our common final act, Lispector renders the nature of our existing as recurrent, and not something that takes its form against the background of a future finality.[7]

Like our first birth, our subsequent ones are not easy. Because they are accompanied by a deep uncertainty of the future, by the mystery of the 'next instant', living in the present can also be painful. The narrator expresses her quiet disappointment: 'Oh, living is so uncomfortable. Everything presses in: the body demands, the spirit never ceases, living is like being weary but being unable to sleep—living is upsetting' (p. 78). That is, to live in the present means that life becomes a 'delicately real' (p. 56) experience, where the veils through which we usually sense the world are cast off, even if only momentarily. The stories we use to plot the world and ourselves are the shifting sands upon which our uniqueness becomes precariously, if inevitably, attached but through which we cannot experience life fully.

Towards the end of the book, the narrator recounts a moment where this fullness of living appears. It is a moment of sensation of coming into being, a sensation of 'silence and light terror' (p. 71):

> Because today, July 25, at five in the morning, I fell into a state of grace. It was a sudden sensation, but extremely soft. Luminosity smiled in the air: precisely that. It was the world sighing. I don't know how to explain it, in the same way that you don't know how to describe the dawn to a blind man. It's unsayable, what happened to me in a sense form . . . (p. 71).

The aesthetic character of this state of grace, its 'sense form', remains unamenable to language. The narrator acknowledges that in its unsayability, the sensations remain just that, sensations, residing between spirit and body. It is as if they have an aura of untouchability and unapproachability hanging about them. She continues:

> In that state, beyond the tranquil happiness that irradiates from people and things, there's a clarity that I call lightness only because in grace everything is so light. . . . The body is transformed into a gift. And one feels it's a gift because one is experiencing, directly from the source, the suddenly unquestionable gift of miraculously and materially existing. . . . [Unlike the grace of the saints] it's simply the grace of a common person who suddenly transforms it into something real because it's common and human and recognizable. . . . Discoveries, in this sense, are unsayable and uncommunicable. And unthinkable.

That's why, when the state of grace came over me, I remained seated, quiet, silent. It's like an annunciation. Not preceded by angels, however. But it's as if the angel of life came to announce the world to me (pp. 72–73).

Lispector puts into relief the exquisiteness of living—an exquisiteness that is fleeting; for like all states no matter how graceful or magical, the moment of their appearance must pass. Coming into being is a one-off affair, flooded, however, with sensibility that can only be talked about as memory and reflection, and never to be relived at the same moment again. What is so striking about the passage here is the juxtaposition of Lispector's imagery of angels, miracles and gifts with the sheer banality of transformation: it can and does happen to anyone. Such moments of becoming, living, existing, are not just for sages, saints, or venerables. As the narrator claims, 'I wasn't meditating at all, there was no religiousness in me. I had just finished my coffee and I was simply living, sitting there with a cigarette burning down in the ashtray' (p. 73).

What Lispector's novel portrays is the ordinariness of the extraordinary event of becoming, and the extraordinary transformation that emerges amidst the ordinariness of our lives. She relays in poetic detail the time and space of transformation that takes hold of us again and again, redolent with anxieties and fears, as well as with the glory and sheer delight to be had in the moment. Although she writes of the instantaneousness of becoming, without plan or intentionality, hers is not the regular language of epiphany; in coupling it to birth it becomes an epiphany located in the small and subtle gestures of everyday life. Her work is a powerful, imaginative display of the liminal aspects of transformation. Educationally speaking, the metaphor of birth gives us an alternative imaginary of the kind of changes we seek to inspire in students, even if such changes are not within our control. That is, we 'conceive' educational demands for students' transformation and introduce students to new information and experiences; there is implicit in this that the student will in turn emerge as not someone merely different than before, but also renewed in her becoming.[8] Pedagogically speaking, the aesthetic sensations that accompany this becoming signal the concrete, contextual nature of existing, for it is in our acute awareness of the instant, and the people and things that are part of this instant, through which a 'state of grace' is experienced. Thus, it is in relation to our material surroundings that we transcend the limits of ourselves. And this, I think, has something important to say to education, given the concrete realities of classroom life: the relationships to other bodies, other sensibilities, other ideas. What therefore remains to be explored more thoroughly here is precisely this relational, contextual aspect of becoming, and the ways in which metaphors of this liminal space of relationality might provide a more fulsome picture of the existential, transformative character of education.

THE LIMINAL QUALITY OF RELATIONSHIPS

Perhaps no other philosopher has devoted herself to mobilising metaphors of liminality more than Luce Irigaray. Her feminist project is one of transforming patriarchal symbolic practices through recourse to emphasising the relational, embodied qualities of human becoming which acts, she claims, to counterpose the primarily masculine imagery of depictions of ontology. As Caroline Wilson's chapter in this book outlines, such a project echoes what Luisa Muraro refers to as the maternal symbolic; it is a way of instituting new modes of relationality through the mobilisation of an alternative language. In line with this, Irigaray has focused on developing metaphors that speak to the time and space in between self and other, in between identity and difference. Hers is a philosophy of relationality through which she attempts to rethink human becoming as always already located in this experience of the threshold, and like both Lispector and Muraro, frequently writes of birth, newness and natality as well as integrating aspects of female corporeality into her language. In this sense, her work speaks directly to the pedagogical idea of transformation at the same time as it is firmly anchored in relationships.

One of Irigaray's most compelling metaphors is what she refers to as the 'placental economy', or placental exchange, which provides her with a way of drawing attention to the threshold where human existence itself is rooted in an encounter with the unknowable other. 'One of the distinctive features of the female body is its toleration of the other's growth within itself without incurring illness or death for either one of the living organisms' (1993b, p. 45). In a conversation with Hélène Rouch, an embryologist, Irigaray claims that this economy operates according to a different logic than that usually accorded it by patriarchal discourse. I quote from Rouch:

Firstly, I'll just remind us what the placenta is: it's a tissue, formed by the embryo, which, while being closely imbricated with the uterine mucosa remains separate from it. This has to be reiterated, because there's the commonly held view that the placenta is a mixed formation, half-maternal, half-fetal.

However, although the placenta is a formation of the embryo, it behaves like an organ that is practically independent of it. It plays a mediating role on two levels. On the one hand, it's the mediating space between mother and fetus, which means that there's never a fusion of maternal and embryonic tissues. On the other hand, it constitutes a system regulating exchanges between the two organisms . . . (1993b, pp. 38–39).

Women are not in an undifferentiated state with the child *in utero*. They are *not one*. Despite current popular discourse around motherhood which often positions women as being in a state of fusion with their foetuses, or regulates mothers' bodies under the assumption that everything they do has an *im*mediate impact upon the unborn child, Rouch and Irigaray postulate a very different conception, highlighting the placenta's *mediating* role between self and other. This complex system of mediation is best captured again by Rouch:

The embryo is half-foreign to the maternal organism. Indeed, half of its antigens are paternal in origin. Because of this the mother should activate her defense mechanisms to reject this other to her self. . . [Yet] the placenta isn't some sort of automatic protection system. . . . On the contrary, there has to be a recognition of the other, of the non-self, by the mother, and therefore an initial reaction from her, in order for placental factors to be produced. The difference between the 'self' and other is, so to speak, continuously negotiated (1993b, pp. 40–41).

Here we see that the placenta is other to the mother, as is the foetus. In order for placental development to occur, this otherness that is the embryo must be 'recognised'. Life itself is dependent upon the *recognition of an other*. It is not dependent upon incorporating the other to make it one; rather, life is dependent upon a self-other relationship where each remains separate, yet interrelated (the placental exchange). The placenta is between mother and child, acting not as a barrier, but as a substance which mediates their exchange. It is not a 'border', but a membrane, a porous threshold which regulates mother-embryo interaction and yet keeps their otherness intact. As Rachel Jones (2011) writes, 'It thus allows differences to remain palpable between two beings who are nonetheless not straightforwardly separable' (p. 161).

Irigaray's next move is to see this 'economy' as a metaphor for reimagining existence as itself a relation to otherness. Thus, Irigaray moves from the raw materiality of the placenta as a biological substance, to its signification as a metaphor for the transcendent qualities of existence—transcendent in that human becoming is not simply about a biological interchange, but about an interaction with something other that exists beyond one's own corporeal limits. It approaches, for Irigaray, an ethical engagement with 'mystery', even if it is also incarnate. 'The placental economy is therefore an organized economy, one not in a state of fusion, which respects the one and the other. Unfortunately, our cultures . . . neglect or fail to recognize the almost ethical character of the fetal relation' (1993b, p. 41).

This ethical aspect of liminality is central to Irigaray's project, as it consists in respecting the otherness of the other. In order to highlight this relation, she elsewhere draws on the metaphors of touch and caress[9] as another way of approaching what she refers to as the 'sensible transcendental' (1993a, p. 32): a sensible experience of the other which calls into being the 'unforeseeable nature of contact with otherness, beyond its own limits' (1993a, p. 211). That is, our becoming is in a sensible, material relation with an other which simultaneously enables us to exceed ourselves, to engage with the mystery of the unknowability of the other. Echoing the 'placental economy' here as one of exchange, the metaphors of touch and caress are mediating thresholds of becoming. I quote Irigaray at length:

No nourishment can compensate for the grace or work of touching. Touching makes it possible to wait, to gather strength, so that the other will return to caress and reshape, from within and from without, a flesh that is given back to itself in the gesture of love. The most subtly necessary guardian of my life is the other's flesh. . . . As he caresses me, he bids me neither to disappear nor to forget but rather to remember the place where, for me, the most intimate life is held in reserve. Searching for what has not yet come into being for himself, he invites me to become what I have not yet become. To realize a birth that is still in the future (1993a, p.187).

This birth that is 'not yet' is rooted here in the tactile, sensory dimensions of contact. Touch is a searching for what has not yet come into being at the same time as it 'invites' the other, through its grace, into this shared space for which there are no words, but only sensations. Such contact, consistent with Irigaray's emphasis on the sensible transcendental, opens up toward an unknowable future. The *moment* of contact—the *instant* as Lispector would say—is what enables each of us to exceed to ourselves and to become someone who has not yet been defined. Thus touch is not only about material limits, but always gestures to an opening of spirit through which a new birth is possible.

Irigaray's attempts to call into being the inbetweenness of relationality through metaphors such as the placenta and the caress, offer us two windows of insight into the qualities of relationships relevant for human becoming: 1) a respect for the otherness of the other; and 2) a respect for the other's becoming, that is, a respect for other's future—a becoming that is 'not yet'. In the first instance, in terms of education, respect for otherness forms the bedrock for bringing an ethical sensibility to our relationships. When read through the placental economy, the teacher-student relationship becomes one of mediation and exchange. Although each bears a different role, they nonetheless are linked through the porosity of the classroom and the practices they engage in within it (such as the texts they read, or the art they create, or the material spaces they inhabit). Such porosity is not about becoming fused or unified, but only works from a respect for the other's becoming. Resonating with Conroy's liminal education and teacher disposition here, the placental economy allows us to revision teacher-student relationships as having existential value for both parties, whereby each meet in an encounter that actually moves beyond the limits of their educational roles. In the second instance, the respect for the other's future becoming would seem to be particularly suited to education, since future-oriented discourses constantly frame our reasons for teaching certain subject matter and for valuing certain kinds of academic performance over others. But the difference here is that it is only through the present moment that the future can have meaning. For example, in Irigaray's metaphor of touch, it is in one's contact with an other in the here and now through which the future opens up. This means that it should not be left solely to policy makers and curriculum developers to decide what kind of adults we want children to be in the future (or what kind of professionals we want adult students to become), but to find ways in our teaching to allow the future to be open-ended. This requires an engagement in the present moment—in all its subtlety—that resists its co-optation in an already defined future. Mobilising touch as a metaphor of pedagogical relationships means signalling that education is very much about the sensibilities incurred in the everyday contact teachers and students have with one another and how those sensibilities can then open up the question of becoming to a personal future that remains outside the dictates of politicians and other stakeholders in education—a becoming that is, as Irigaray says, 'not yet'. Thus what Irigaray's metaphors offer is a way of grounding the relational quality of transformation, making our interactions within educational settings bearers of ethical and ontological implications.

LIMINAL PEDAGOGICAL RELATIONSHIPS AND EDUCATION

If we shift from metaphors of growth or stages or outcomes, to ones involving the liminality of living, existing, and becoming—between body and spirit—then the teacher-student relationship correspondingly shifts. The specifically pedagogical, transformative relationship is therefore not about control or predicting the future, about learning a particular piece of subject matter, or about measuring outcomes, although these are all significant aspects of our educational work. It is, rather, about making room within educational discourses for the kind of existential, liminal aspects of the teacher-student relationship which already go on, even if we fail to name or address them. This does not mean that I think everything in education has to do with human becoming, or that we simply need to mobilise the term 'sensible transcendental' or 'placenta' or 'birth' and all will fall into proper focus. It is, rather, that in order to have some nuance in our educational practices, we need to begin to appreciate the subtle, unnameable dimensions of our life that do indeed have a profound impact on the kinds of teaching and learning that go on in our classrooms. This is why metaphor is so important, for the task is not to define, circumscribe, or predict these aspects of relationality, but to bring them into our sphere of attention so that they then can take their place within our conceptual work on education and our practical work with students. Acknowledging the inbetween spaces through which we become who we are in this moment, beyond the rigid intentionalities that often frame the work of teaching, opens up the possibility for approaching policy, assessment, and curriculum not only as guidelines, documents, or discourses, but fundamentally as *practices* that are always being played out materially, between bodies in the present, and unpredictably, against a future that is always unknown. So it is not that the future-oriented questions of what we teach and why we teach it are not central to the task of education; it is not that teachers (particularly in elementary and secondary education) can ignore the role they play in socialisation or that teachers can simply refuse to make academic judgements; it is that there is more than this to the work we do—if, that is, we believe that education indeed can have some transformative potential. It seems to me that if we are going to resist the increasingly market economy terms that are used to define our work, we need alternative vocabularies that can help us to manoeuvre around them better and to become more aware of the times that small moments of grace, those instants of living transformation, actually make a difference to who we as students and teachers become in the process.

This means using a language in our theorising and in our ways of reflecting upon practice that neither erases these relational dimensions, nor simply celebrates them, but that is mindful of how they offer texture and depth to our everyday engagement with curriculum, evaluation, and interpersonal encounters. This is not a conceptual language that attempts to capture fully the aesthetic dimensions of becoming, but a language that admits of its own limits in that it can never stand in for the experience itself. This is not to claim that experience is unmediated, but simply that it is its own 'thing' in the instant it happens, not given to replication or encapsulation. Thus, thinking about our encounters with students through metaphors of liminality gives us a way of approaching these encounters without entirely co-opting them under the hubris of understanding. As Wilson in Chapter 2 emphasises, language helps to name what has previously been left unnamed; at the same time, however, such naming does not suture over the experience of embodied existence. Touch, natality, newness and exchange are not definitions of what experience *is*, rather they offer us a method and approach for appreciating that these experiences shape profoundly the conditions of our educational settings. When we think of the common vulnerability teachers experience standing up in front of a class, the anxieties that grip students about to read aloud in front of their peers, the fear of failure, of which O'Donnell in this volume writes, that prevents students from speaking—all this cannot be 'converted' into language. Theorising and reflecting differently, through metaphor, through the liminal imagination, means *approximating* the aesthetic experience of existing and becoming, without assuming that our language can act as a substitute for the experience itself. At the beginning of this chapter, I wrote of the goosebumps on my skin and the teacher's breath on my cheek, and I 'name' an experience; but that experience still stands outside of understanding. What this chapter has had as its central focus is in fact how the limits of our understanding do not determine the limits of what happens to each of us in the moment of living, in the moment of becoming. Taking seriously the liminal experiences of our pedagogical relationships, with all their subtlety, ineffability *and* materiality, can help us reimagine the transformative potentialities of the educational landscape. In other words, not understanding our pedagogical experiences might just be the very life-affirming and risky stuff out of which education can be made.[10]

NOTES

1. Castoriadis (1997) refers to pedagogy, stemming from the Greek *paideia*, as a process through which the newborn becomes a human being (pp. 129–130).
2. As will be seen in the discussion below, drawing on Lispector, spirit involves not only an intangibility, but a sense of being unbounded.
3. Deleuze rejects the idea of metaphor, claiming that it has been inherently tied to identity and analogy. Yet, his own use of rhizomes, lines of flight, and indeed the definition of the philosophical concept itself seems to intimate nonetheless a mode of thought that metaphor has often served to depict. I am using the term 'metaphor' instead of 'concept' in order to allude to the traces of literary (and indeed aesthetic) meaning that inhere in our philosophical renderings of educational practice.
4. See Masschelein's (2010) discussion of the importance the present and paying attention have in the context of an educational experiment.
5. Although not addressing directly the question of liminality, see also Maxine Greene's (1978, 2004) work on the relation between becoming and the arts.
6. The Portuguese title is *Agua Viva*, or literally, living water.
7. Natality, as it appears in Lispector's novel, is not the same as Hannah Arendt's (1959) reading of the term. The former is built on the experiential, corporeal aspects of becoming, while the latter is concerned with narrative and speech.
8. This metaphor of birth here functions differently than the Socratic mid-wife model of teaching, since for the latter, the idea is about 'delivering' from the m/other something that is already there, whereas for the former emphasis is not on the delivery as such, but on the moment of entering the world.
9. Her discussion of touch and the caress are part of an interpretative critique of Emmanuel Levinas's (1969) use of the terms in his *Totality and Infinity*.
10. I would like to acknowledge the feedback I received from the anonymous reviewers and from my fellow contributors to this volume.

REFERENCES

Arendt, H. (1959) *The Human Condition* (New York, Anchor Books).
Castoriadis, C. (1997) *World in Fragments: Writings on Politics, Society, Psychoanalysis, and the Imagination*, D. A. Curtis, trans. (Stanford, CA, Stanford University Press).
Conroy, J. C. (2004) *Betwixt and Between: The Liminal Imagination, Education and Democracy* (New York, Peter Lang).
Deleuze, G. and F. Guattari. (1994) *What Is Philosophy?* G. Burchell and H. Tomlinson, trans. (London, Verso).
Dewey, J. (1969) [1938] *Experience and Education* (New York, Collier Books).
Greene, M. (1978) *Landscapes of Learning* (New York, Teachers College Press).
Greene, M. (2004) *Releasing the Imagination: Essays on Education, the Arts, and Social Change* (New York, National Association of Independent Schools).
Irigaray, L. (1993a) *An Ethics of Sexual Difference*, C. Burke and G. C. Gill, trans. (Ithaca, NY, Cornell University Press).
Irigaray, L. (1993b) *Je, Tu, Nous: Toward a Culture of Difference*, A. Martin, trans. (New York, Routledge).
Jones, R. (2011) *Irigaray: Toward a Sexuate Philosophy* (London, Polity).
Levinas, E. (1969) *Totality and Infinity: An Essay on Exteriority*, A. Lingis, trans. (Pittsburgh, PA, Duquesne University Press).
Lispector, C. (1989) [1974] *The Stream of Life*, E. Lowe and E. Fitz, trans. (Minneapolis, MN, University of Minnesota Press).

72   *S. Todd*

Lusted, D. (1986) Why Pedagogy? *Screen*, 27.5, pp. 2–14.
Masschelein, J (2010) E-ducating the Gaze: The Idea of a Poor Pedagogy, *Ethics and Education*, 5.1, pp. 43–53.
Todd, S. (2003) *Learning from the Other: Levinas, Psychoanalysis and Ethical Possibilities in Education* (Albany, NY, State University of New York Press).

5
'You Have to Give of Yourself': Care and Love in Pedagogical Relations

MARIT HONERØD HOVEID AND ARNHILD FINNE

INTRODUCTION

In order to reach a better understanding of relationships in pedagogical practices we believe our language about relationships needs to be broadened and deepened. To do this, we draw on French feminist philosopher Luce Irigaray's notion of 'two', and what a relational space between 'two' entails for developing an alternative form of mutual understanding and what educators actually do in their practices. We first conceive of this relational space as one which always involves a liminal space of in-between where human interaction occurs. We then address human interaction in terms of what forms our will and makes us do what we do in relational contexts. Here, we draw upon American philosopher Harry G. Frankfurt who writes about 'care' and how what we care about represents a volitional drive. According to Frankfurt, what we 'care about' organises, in some ways, what we do, how we act and how we behave (Frankfurt, 1988). Furthermore, we explore his notion of love in relation to his notion of care and in so doing elaborate more fully what is at stake in our pedagogical interactions. Finally, we offer some thoughts about why a more complex theory of actions is needed in order to broaden and deepen our language of pedagogical relations and what this means for reimagining pedagogical relationships.

What provoked our inquiry into care and love in pedagogical relations was a series of interviews conducted with four female school leaders from the area around Trondheim, Norway. We learned something about how actions in a practice can be framed after interviewing them about their experiences of being principals and of having responsibility for their school. When the interviews were interpreted, what the school leaders said and especially the way they said it caught our

Re-Imagining Relationships in Education: Ethics, Politics and Practices, First Edition. Edited by Morwenna Griffiths, Marit Honerød Hoveid, Sharon Todd and Christine Winter. Chapters © 2015 The Authors. Editorial organization © 2015 Philosophy of Education Society of Great Britain. Published 2015 by John Wiley & Sons Ltd.

attention. What became evident in the description of personal practice and statements made by some of the leaders was the way they depicted their work in terms of relationality, which particularly lent itself to an exploration of the role care and love play in pedagogical relationships. When a person talks and acts (as a school leader) she not only transmits a content (a *what*), but also a *way* of leading, and furthermore she expresses something about what she cares about (Frankfurt, 1988) as a person and a school leader. What we care about is closely linked to our will and thus what forms the way we act. This chapter does not take up a qualitative analysis of this material, but rather uses a couple of statements as a springboard for elaborating some of the theoretical aspects that we believe are necessary in order to reach a better understanding[1] of human actions and relations in pedagogical practice.

We understood an expression used by one of the principals, 'you have to give of yourself', to have a significant meaning. It said something about what this school leader believed to be a guiding principle for herself in the relations she has with staff and students in her school. But it also conveyed something deeply personal about what she was guided by in her leadership. A day in school can be very unpredictable for a school leader. Many things can happen and most of them are unscheduled. Some of these events will challenge her normal way of acting and the kinds of judgement her leadership enables or limits her to make. Similarly, another school leader talked about keeping an 'open door' to her office, which signalled an acceptance of being 'disturbed' and an open invitation to be engaged in whatever happened throughout the day.[2]

We have interpreted what these leaders said as a sort of attentiveness that they showed towards an open and dynamic space of relations and what it required of them.[3] Living and leading in a changing and dynamic web of relations challenges and drains you as a person— especially if you have committed yourself to be engaged fully as a leader. But at the same time this space seems to be where new energy and engagement for what leaders do can be found; it is also through the relationships in this dynamic web that the possibility of new life is generated. In other words, 'giving of yourself' does not entail a loss of oneself, but that by 'giving' one might receive something back that will shape who one becomes as a leader. Similarly, by keeping an 'open door' a leader might signal that she is ready to become engaged whenever someone needs her and thus be open herself to change.

In this chapter we have taken these two expressions, 'to give of yourself' and to keep an 'open door', as a point of departure for our theoretical exploration of relationships in education. What we aim to address has to do with living in/with relations as a dynamic and always changing pattern that will require something of and do something with the persons living in/with it. This reflexive side to relationships is not something defined by planned and strategic actions, but it does require a teacher's or leader's presence in a different way than is currently taught in most courses on management and leadership.

We discuss this aspect of presence and interaction and what they entail in light of these statements and with reference to the idea of a relational space 'in-between' (Hoveid, 2012). We then explore what forms human (inter)action in this relational space through the notions of care and love.

THE NOTION OF 'TWO' AND A RELATIONAL SPACE OF 'IN-BETWEEN'

The notion of 'two' runs as an underlying theme in Luce Irigaray's writings and is made explicit in the titles of the books: *To Be Two* (2001) and *Democracy Begins Between Two* (2000). Her primary concern is the urgent need for our society, and education we would add, to grant full recognition of both the genders which makes society (and education) function. The being 'two' in Irigaray's texts is a somewhat provocative stance towards the tendency to reduce being into oneness, or sameness. Sharon Todd writes with reference to Irigaray:

> The relationship of coexistence is about representing what lies *between* the two in a way that disregards neither their radical separateness nor their singularity as individual subjects (2009, p. 127, italics in original).

According to Irigaray, this notion of 'two' is a constant reminder that, at least in our Western ways of thinking, we tend to reduce our understandings of the world and of the other into sameness. This means that on an individual level we tend to subordinate what others say or do into our own way of understanding. However, for Irigaray: 'As soon as I recognise the otherness of the other as irreducible to me or to my own, the world itself becomes irreducible to a single world: there are at least two worlds' (Irigaray, 2008, p. x). Her point is that if traditional Western ways of thinking and acting tend to reduce the understanding of the other back to one, and thus to sameness,[4] we shut down the possibility of otherness, of that which is 'not same'. Irigaray's argument is that these reductions to sameness, to one—as developed over many generations—seem to have a very strong hold over the way we perceive ourselves and the world as humans.[5]

In Irigaray's own writings, she challenges this idea of sameness through writing strategies invoking different metaphors and through developing texts where other images of who women and men can become and what lies between us emerge. As Rachel Jones argues: 'The question, for Irigaray, is whether we think being in terms of any kind of oneness, unified essence or identity, or whether we allow that being—and thus, human being—is two. . . . [T]he "being" of "*being-two*" is found *in-between*' (Jones, 2011, p. 22 Italics in original). As we understand it, 'two' is important in order to uphold the possibility of creating a space between. 'Two' constitutes a difference that refuses to be collapsed into one and the same. In a passage from *To Be Two* (2001), Irigaray expresses that in order to recognise the other I cannot subject him to my laws (also meaning universal law); that is, unless he remains a mystery to me, my way of recognising him will only result in my domination of him:

[M]arry ethicality and truth in my relationship with the other: I think of the other as the mystery which he is for me, as a truth, certainly, but always as one which is unknown to and inappropriable by me, unable to be dominated or universalized; change the relation between love and truth: respecting the mystery of the other through love implies that this respect for a truth which will never be mine modifies my, our relationship with the truth. Instead of being light opposed to darkness, or knowledge opposed to ignorance, truth is light which does not give up mystery, light which illuminates without revealing; never total, never authoritarian or dogmatic, but light always shared between two subjects irreducible to one another (Irigaray, 2001, p. 110).

For Irigaray, respecting the mystery of the other is what could alter our interpretations of the world between us as humans and thus also what humans perceive to be true. For our purposes here, we are not so much concerned with Irigaray's discussion about truth but rather with her way of perceiving relationships as irreducible to one another. It is this notion of 'two' that, to our minds, opens up to other understandings of relationships *between* people expressed in lived experience. The passage from Irigaray speaks about the possibility of altering the way we are accustomed to ordering the world between us. Accepting her notion of 'two' challenges inter-subjective relations based on a hierarchical ordering whereby the other is always subsumed to the one in power.[6]

From a position above others and where people are subsumed under the control of *one* there is no reason for listening or inquiring into who this other might be, how she *thinks* and *speaks*, differently.[7] The practice which becomes paramount for the notion of 'two' is that it requires an ability to listen, to listen to that which has not yet emerged, to listen to that which you do not already know. Irigaray stresses what listening can do if we try to establish a relationship that can encompass 'two':

> *I am listening to you* is not to expect or hear some information from you, nor is it the pure expression of sentiment (a rather naïve aim of psychoanalysis sometimes). *I am listening to you* is to listen to your words as something unique, irreducible, especially to my own, as something new, as yet unknown. It is to understand and hear them as the manifestation of an intention, of human and spiritual development (Irigaray, 1996, p. 116, italics in original).

The Irigarayan notion of 'two' is difficult to grasp. If 'you' are someone and 'your' words something, 'I' cannot possibly know—how can 'I' then recognise 'you'? Irigaray states that to hear 'your' words as a manifestation of an intention, of human and spiritual development, is crucial for this understanding of the other and thus of 'two'. This is then necessary for a space in-between to appear.

In our reading the conception of 'two' is not confined to a dyadic reading, it has to do with a 'being-two' which can be found 'in-between'. As Jones writes '. . . Irigaray's style lies in her disruption of conceptual oppositions such as form/matter, self/other . . . while resisting capture by a logic that insists on dividing everything up into "one" (side) or the "other" ' (Jones, 2011, p. 18) . For us, as we said in the introduction, this conceptualisation of a relational space is a necessary aspect of reimagining relationships and it gives another possibility for interpretation of pedagogical practices.

The practice of keeping an 'open door' policy, as one school leader mentioned, can be read as a sign: it was possible for anyone working in that school to come in and present themselves and whatever problems or happy events they wanted to share. If this 'open door' were merely an opening into a room where others who entered would be compelled to conduct themselves and think in just one way, the leader's way (in other words, to become dominated), then there would have been no real 'open door' at all. An 'open door' entails creating a space where the other is listened to, where someone hears the manifestation (as Irigaray writes) of an intention, a beginning; this space is both an acknowledgement and a description of this idea of 'two' that is found in-between the self and the other.

When you make plans and lead groups of people (for instance as a school leader) in an organization you are, on the one hand, dependent on developing and upholding structures that are recognisable to all within the institution and that people can turn to when they have doubts about what to do and how to act. Working within these structures and implementing regulations are necessary activities for most leaders. On the other hand, it is the everyday life of a leader, the way she acts and approaches others, how she acts and reacts, that will determine what kind of leader she becomes. What she has tried to put in place in order to govern the organisation and those who work within it represents a background for her practice. It is the responses to actions that she gives and receives from those she works together with that will determine what kind of relationship her leadership expresses.

It seems that this space of relationships in pedagogical practice, this space 'in-between', has not yet been articulated fully in research or in courses devoted to leadership. In some way we could say that we live it, but we do not know how to address it or talk about it (Hoveid, 2009). Perhaps if we started by listening for the other, we could discern another way of perceiving relationships, thus changing the relation between ethicality[8] and truth, as Irigaray suggests.

In order to reimagine relationships in pedagogical practices we believe this notion of 'two' opens a(nother) point of departure for understanding those relationships. Beginning in a notion of 'two' allows us to attend to practice where the other is listened to and acknowledged and it allows us to pay attention to those practices that tend to be overlooked in leadership in education. In order to reach better understandings of relationships, we wish to turn now to address the ways in which the leaders expressed themselves. That is, not only did they through their descriptions of 'giving yourself' and keeping an 'open door' say something substantive about relationships, but the ways in which they talked (form rather than content) conveyed something about what they felt and were moved by in their actions. As we interpret it here, they told us that they *cared*. Thus in order to complement the idea of relational space as 'two', we turn now to explore a notion of care and how it guides human action.

'CARING ABOUT' IN HUMAN (INTER)ACTION

When a leader or teacher is engaged in an pedagogical practice she will inevitably be governed by objectives that she has to account for and by moral or normative standards for what it is she is doing. To put it a little differently and crudely: accountability and what one (believes one) knows, on the one hand, and morality or how one acts towards others, on the other hand, seem to be two key issues when one discusses pedagogical practice. Drawing on the work of Harry G. Frankfurt, we now explore what is meant by the notion that people act in accordance with 'what they care about', with what is important to them and what they love. Frankfurt's philosophy is concerned with what compels humans to act, and to ask what kind of 'drives' can be identified for what we do as humans; that is, what is it that moves people in their choices and in their actions? In response, Frankfurt develops a notion of care as something which frames our actions. His notion of *care*, however, is not primarily about caring *for* the other, but rather deals with *caring about* or having concern for something, as we explore below.

Before we engage further with human action that is guided by 'care' and 'love' we first need to elaborate in what way Frankfurt's idea, that our actions are guided by 'what we care about', relates to the more common ways of categorising human action. In the opening part of his essay 'The Importance of What We Care About', Frankfurt (1988) states that philosophers have primarily addressed two large sets of questions. The first set constitutes the domain of epistemology, the second, ethics or morality. What is interesting for our purposes here is that Frankfurt moves beyond an understanding of human interaction understood exclusively either in terms of what we know or can know to be true (epistemology) or upon decisions of what is right and wrong (morality). Between what we can know and what is right and wrong there is a field, especially when we inquire into pedagogical practices, of what it is we *do* and how this can be framed—a field of which these two dominating areas of philosophy cannot give sufficient accounts. Frankfurt argues instead that there is a third branch of inquiry: '. . . concerned with a cluster of questions which pertain to another thematic and fundamental preoccupation of human existence—namely, *what to care about*' (1988, p. 80, italics in original).

In everyday life we are not always articulate about what we do, but even so there are some things that move us to act in certain ways—this is so even when it comes down to habitual actions in everyday life (Stern, 2004). On this view, motives or intentions are important in order to understand human action. Frankfurt writes in the introduction to the book *Necessity, Volition and Love*: 'The significance of volitional necessity in our lives is by no means confined, of course, to its role in cognition. It is manifestly pertinent as well to our attitudes, to our choices and to our actions' (Frankfurt, 1999, p. x). This brings us to the heart of Frankfurt's argument: if what we do is not totally based on chance, habits or us being totally subject to social structures, then human action is intentional. Thus, what we do, or why we act, is in some ways also guided by our own initiatives, meaning that there are motivational forces that make us do some things instead of others. This does not, of course, mean that we can have control over everything we do or that we can make a rational account of why we did what we did: it means that we have the capacity to take the initiative and to create a sort of coherence in our lives. The fact that we have a capacity to initiate action does not, however, necessarily mean that we always use it.

Frankfurt writes, 'Human beings are extremely complicated; they tend to be ambivalent and inconsistent in many respects, and they are resourceful. This makes them elusive' (1999, p. 161). This indicates that human (inter)action can always be made subject to different interpretations. As such, it is this field of human actions (and behaviour) we believe is important to explore further and to develop a more nuanced language about in order to be able to reimagine human relationships as a space in-between.

In pedagogical practices, relationships between people direct us towards interpretations of the actions of the people involved. We have previously stated that we see the 'being two' in the 'in-between' as a characteristic of a relational space that upholds difference. What Frankfurt's work on action offers is a way of understanding what frames our actions in this space. We are primarily concerned with actions we have described as leadership—but as we will see, Frankfurt's notion of care and his idea that humans act according to what they *care about* will entail a much wider understanding of human (inter)action.

Frankfurt writes of care within his larger concerns about the possibility of autonomy and of a human will that could be anchored in something other than Kant's pure will. As he frames it: 'The pure will has no individuality whatsoever. It is identical in everyone, and its volitions are everywhere exactly the same. In other words, the pure will is thoroughly *impersonal*. The commands that it issues are issued by no one in particular' (1999, p. 132, italics in original). Through an analytical argument Frankfurt shows how unlikely it is that what each one of us considers important (to oneself) is the same for all of us. He adds: 'It seems even less likely that the one thing about which each one of us cares most is the moral law' (ibid.). He structures his argument around the notion of love as a special aspect of care, in a similar way as Kant structures his argument on autonomy and pure will, but without losing the connection to individual particularity. It is worth quoting Frankfurt at length in order to exemplify his difference from Kant.

According to Kant, a person's volitions are related to his will . . . only insofar as he is following the austerely impersonal dictates of the moral law. In fact, however, the same relation between volition and will holds when a person is acting out of love. Love is, of course, paradigmatically personal. Nevertheless, the unconditional commands of love are not, as Kant suggests, adventitious elements of a person's will. They are essentially integral to it, for what a person loves is a defining element of his volitional nature. . . . Thus, the personal grip of love satisfies the conditions for autonomy that Kant believes can be satisfied only by the impersonal constraints of the moral law (1999, p. 132).

Frankfurt states that Kant's notion of a person's ability to act autonomously can only derive from the essential character of his will, and this will must be under the command of a 'universal' law. The argument by Frankfurt is that when a person acts out of care, and especially when guided by love, then a person is put under the same kind of obligation—but this time in a deeply personal and thus singular way. What we contend is that when humans act there are certain motivational forces at play and that understanding this intentionality (i.e. what motivates, the volitional necessity, that make people act as they do, whether they are conscious of it or not) is crucial also to understanding interaction between people. 'The fact that someone cares about a certain thing is constituted by a complex set of cognitive, affective, and volitional dispositions and states' (1988, p. 85), Frankfurt writes. Sometimes you are able to express directly what you care about—and we believe one of the school leaders did that when she said, 'you have to give of yourself '[when you are a leader]. However, as Frankfurt states: 'It certainly cannot be assumed that what a person cares about is generally under his immediate voluntary control' (1988, p. 85). This means that human interaction is also informed by this complexity of intentionality and unknowability. Thus, as Frankfurt suggests, neither morality nor knowledge can provide a sufficient answer to how a person should live or why she act as she does. Instead, it is by exploring what we *care about* and the love this entails that we can better understand the complexity of human relationships in general and pedagogical relationships in particular.

CARE AND THE LOVE IN-BETWEEN

As one gets older one sometimes wonders about what one has done in life and why things happened in the way they did. Sometimes luck or misfortune seems to be the only plausible answer. Chance events certainly shape a lot in our lives, but human beings are not entirely powerless or agentless: when a person acts there are also volitional 'forces' at play. To say that a person *cares about* something is not the same as saying that she likes something or merely that it is important to her and it also differs from saying that she wants it, prefers it or judges it to be valuable (Frankfurt, 1999, pp. 158–163). According to Frankfurt, caring is a fundamental, constitutive feature of our lives, caring is less about *what* we care about, but *that* we care. Frankfurt writes:

> Creatures like ourselves are not limited to desires that move them to act. In addition, they have the reflexive capacity to form desires regarding their own desires—that is regarding both what they want to want, and what they want not to want (Frankfurt, 2004, p. 18).

Thus, caring is also reflexive, meaning that when we care we identify ourselves with what we care about. Exercising the capacity to care provides us with continuity and coherence in our volitional lives, because humans pursue what they *care about*. 'Suppose we cared about nothing. In that case, we would be creatures with no active interest in establishing or sustaining any thematic continuity in our volitional lives' (1999, p. 162). This means that through care one's actions are given a direction and as humans we are defined by what we care about.[9]

Furthermore, as acting human beings there is undoubtedly a lot we do because we feel or believe we know what to do. This may even be expressed through an obligation or as a duty to do things a certain way. In whatever way these obligations and duties are imposed on us we have learned that it is our responsibility to act according to what we know. If we have queries about what a person has done in a concrete pedagogical practice, about why she acted as she did, this is often raised by the question: How could she do this? In this line of questioning there is implicitly already a judgement, usually implying that what she did is morally improper. The point to be drawn from Frankfurt is that if our understanding of human action only has these alternatives, epistemology and morality, then there is a lot in human interactions and relationships that we do not hear or see, and consequently do not and cannot understand.

In a pedagogical practice many actions are gauged against the register of what we can know or the register of moral obligation, and thus the field of education is often referred to as a normative discipline. However, when we act as humans there is also a volitional necessity at work, and acquiring a more elaborate vocabulary about how this volitional necessity informs what we do in pedagogical practices is important in order to gain a better understanding of leadership and relationships in education. As part of developing such vocabulary, we turn to Frankfurt's elaboration of care in the form of love. Here he not only identifies love as a mode of caring, as we have seen above, but also demonstrates its power in human will and in our actions and relationships to others.

Arguing that love is connected to our will does not imply that we have voluntary control over what we love. One of Frankfurt's arguments is that love engages the one loving. This engagement is created through the love for the other and it means that it is not my willingness to love but rather by my willingness to be engaged by love, which is the forming structure. Thus, his argument runs counter to the idea that love is under a person's voluntary control:

> . . . love is essentially a somewhat non-voluntary and complex volitional structure that bears both upon how a person is disposed to act and upon how he [*sic*] is disposed to manage the motivations and interests by which he is moved (1999, p. 165).

This forming structure that love has is interesting. Love shapes us in a way that is different from other motivational drives, because, in loving 'there are no necessary truths or a priori principles by which it can be established what we are to love;' (Frankfurt, 2004, p. 130).

Frankfurt distinguishes between active and passive love. Passive love has to do with the will being acted upon (heteronomous) and active love has to do with the will determining itself in relation to another (autonomous). A passive love means that the will is acted upon and Frankfurt connects this with a sort of self-interest connecting the one loving to her object of love. In passive love a person is thus more preoccupied with her own good and what she can benefit (from love) than what she can do that would benefit her object of love or whom she loves. 'But love does not need to be based upon self-interest' (1999, p. 133). Instead, there is also a love of a different kind, an active love. The one loving is then motivated by an interest in the loving itself. This means that it is not driven by a self-interest, which would turn it into passive love. Active love may imply that the one loving will be rewarded and will experience the value this love has for her. So 'although active love as such is valuable to the lover only for the sake of the benefits it provides to his beloved, it is also true that it is valuable to him for its own sake' (1999, p. 134, fn). In this way love configures our will and we can thus distinguish between love driven by self-interest and love guided by the act of loving itself.

Love happens and love shapes our purposes and priorities and in this respect love is both personal and unconditional. An example of this unconditional love is a parent's love for her/his children. Most parents love their children, not because they must love them or because they seek to gain something from them and derive benefits from their love. Most parents simply love their children because they love them—unconditionally. This (active) love is not guided by duty or moral obligation, but we invest ourselves in it and it implies a selflessness. Acting out of love is configuring my actions according to my love, rather than me configuring what or who I love.

On this account, love means that I have to listen to/for you. If 'I' keep on speaking, and if I keep on imposing *my* words, *my* ways of understanding the world, then there is very little space left for love. This is why 'listening' is crucial, for 'I' cannot speak and at the same time hear what the other is saying—her words, her presence. This is often a difficult task for educators who are more accustomed to being the master of words and of what should be said—and thus not speaking is something frightening for many teachers and school leaders.

We believe this raises interesting interpretative possibilities as to what makes people act as they do in pedagogical practices. In studies of leadership and in organisational theory there is usually a concern about how leaders needs to be more strategic, more rational and more goal oriented. However, in their leadership roles, teachers and principals might also be motivated by love. The object of love could be many different 'things': it could be the love of learning, or for the children to give them possibilities to flourish through education, or for the school and those who work in it. As we have argued this is the kind of love that entails a selflessness, but at the same time it is the kind of love which is engendered by care at a deeply personal level. As an educator, a person will invest herself in this kind of love because this is what creates the motivations, the reasons for why she keeps on being engaged as a leader or a teacher.[10]

While Frankfurt argues that love is unconditional and selfless, Irigaray takes this one step further by insisting, in one of her essays that the reception of the other is sought and received in an almost absolute silence (1996, p. 115). For as she argues 'I am listening to you prepares the way for the not-yet-coded, for silence, for a space for existence, initiative, free intentionality and support for your becoming' (ibid., p. 116). In love there is openness and when it happens, one can both approach it and be approached by it. There is a creation of a space as we are formed by love, rather than us forming it as a rational act. What Frankfurt's notion of love helps us to understand is that love is part of a complex volitional structure. As we have already stated, love is not formed by my will, but by my willingness to be engaged by love. If I love, then I seek that which I love. In their approach to love, where the 'two' different philosophers, Irigaray and Frankfurt, woman and man, somehow touch, give breath to each other (in Irigaray's words), is the notion of love as something unappropriable. Irigaray's expression, 'i love *to* you',[11] could then with Frankfurt's notion of love maybe also be expressed as 'i *will* love *to* you'.

Human (inter)action can always be made subject to new interpretations, and this is one of the reasons why Frankfurt describes it as elusive (1999). So why bother to interpret at all? Whenever we think we have understood what people do, and why they do it we always have to take into account that there is something we did not see or hear, something we did not understand. Re-imagining relationships in education, for us, has to do with how one's understanding is framed, how it can be expanded and why one tends *not* to listen for or see that which has not yet come into existence. This way of listening would entail listening for the initiative, for intentionality. If a person's actions are motivated by (active) love she will try to listen for this intentionality, for the other whom she loves. She will give the other space and not appropriate her beloved. Instead she will act in ways she thinks will benefit her beloved. If love creates a space for the initiative, free intentionality and possibilities for listening to the other, then our argument is that relationships in education cannot be fully understood if they are interpreted exclusively in terms of what we know (epistemology) or in terms of how to behave (morality). If love creates, then we have to approach the web of human relations in all its messiness, including its generative, fecund and sometimes destructive sides. Our picture of this web is not one that is spun as by a spider, intricate and systematic, always leading back to a single centre, but rather as one created by kittens who have gone haywire with a ball of yarn, with at least two ends somewhere in a knotted mess. Participating in this web of relations means knowing that it will form you, but not how; in other words it means knowing that if you 'give of yourself' you will regain yourself, but differently. Thus, when one school leader said: You have to 'give of yourself', we interpreted this as a statement expressing something very personal and that she cared deeply. The two statements that set off this inquiry into care and love in pedagogical relations, 'you have to give of yourself' and the need to keep an 'open door' has taught us that what these school leaders expressed does not have to do with duty, obligation or virtue; it has to do with that complex space of interaction motivated by something deeply personal and allows for a reception of the other that both Frankfurt and Irigaray call love.

INTERPRETING RELATIONS IN PEDAGOGICAL PRACTICES REQUIRES A MORE COMPLEX THEORY OF ACTIONS

If we want to explore the field of relationships between humans in terms of both care and love in pedagogical practices, we believe this has to be done through both theoretical/philosophical explorations and more concrete studies in order to expand our notions of human interaction. Our take on this is that we need these studies in order to develop a language and understanding that can encompass broader meanings in the field of education and leadership today.

This chapter began with two statements from two school leaders—'you have to give of yourself' and keeping 'an open door'. These led us to investigate some aspects of human relationships in education that are rarely touched upon in pedagogical literature. Through the notion of 'two' as a recurrent theme in Irigaray's philosophy there is a possible way to acknowledge the 'in-between', that is, the space of rationality. Reimagining this human space of relationships in terms of 'two' is a rejection of appropriation, of dominations, of sameness. We think such a space, where there is enough room for differences to flourish, is necessary to safeguard in pedagogical practices, and not least in leadership in education. For this space 'in-between' to appear we agree with Irigaray that it is necessary to listen for the intentionality of the other. In pedagogical practices it is more customary that the intentionality of the one in charge of the learning activities is imposed on to the other(s). This belongs, so to speak, to the 'nature' of teaching and leadership as pedagogical activities. But if a space for the other is given, then a space in-between can appear, and differences can emerge. Thus, we think that if a head teacher keeps an 'open door' this could be an invitational space, a sign of caring about the people with whom one works, a sign of creating a space where 'being-two' is possible. Love as a motivational drive on the part of educators cannot completely safeguard this space, but we believe it represents a possible beginning. Without such concern it is even unlikely that a space for the other can be created in education, we would argue. So by keeping 'an open door' to this 'being-two' we believe the wider goal of what education is about can be achieved.

It is important to explore these relationships in pedagogical practices and the possibilities for flourishing that they have. Leadership in education is under much strain and leaders in education today are like managers in manufacturing industries, being asked to deliver an outcome. The outcomes of education are hard, if not at times impossible to measure, and even harder to predict. Since we believe good education is also about a wider flourishing, beyond measurement, we think it is necessary to identify and speak about practices that defy the measurable.[12]

In order to inquire about these possibilities we find that it is necessary to develop another language about what constitutes actions in this space between people. Both Irigaray and Frankfurt address care and love as an aspect of human flourishing. Our claim is that we have to address these aspects of human (inter)action in order to understand better what we already do and what we can do better in pedagogical practices. In educating for the future we need to remember this. In an age where measurement for accountability purposes is forced upon school leaders internationally it is easy to forget and thus it is difficult to listen for that which simply cannot be measured.

NOTES

1. This expression is inspired by a reading of Paul Ricoeur (1994) on hermeneutics. Like him we hold that there is no such thing as a full or final understanding, but what we can aim for in our encounters in social practices is a better understanding.
2. And of course it could signal and mean a lot of other things.
3. For a nuanced elaboration of relationality between body and spirit, see Sharon Todd (Chapter 4).
4. The idea of sameness of one is also a critique of the idea of a universalised one, as in the Kantian versions of pure reason. For Irigaray it is a matter of securing an embodied and worldly transcendence and not transcendence into oneness as in a 'marriage between mind and God where all ties to the world of sensation has been severed' (Irigaray, 1993, p. 15).
5. And perhaps this is especially noticeable in the practice and politics of education today when so many aspects are reduced into something measurable (Biesta, 2010).
6. For a more elaborate discussion of female authority see Caroline Wilson (Chapter 2), or Jones who addresses: 'Re-reading Diotima: Resources for a Relational Pedagogy' (Chapter 1).
7. We acknowledge that this might seem a bit categorical.
8. We make a distinction between moral and ethics (in line with Paul Ricoeur), as we believe Irigaray also does. The moral domain refers to that which is defined by the normative and ethics is about seeking a good life with and for others.
9. This means our identity is shaped by what we care about. This line of Frankfurt's theory is not addressed in this chapter.
10. In our Scandinavian context teaching is also framed in terms of leadership, i.e. classroom leadership (and not classroom management).
11. The translation of Irigaray's text uses lower case for i (not I).

12. For an elaborate discussion of current developments in school policy and curriculum, see Christine Winter (Chapter 7).

REFERENCES

Biesta, G. (2010) *Good Education in an Age of Measurement. Ethics, Politics, Democracy* (Boulder, CO, Paradigm Publishers).

Frankfurt, H. G. (1988) [1982] The Importance of What We Care About, in his: *The Importance of What We Care About* (Cambridge, Cambridge University Press), pp. 80–94.

Frankfurt, H. G. (1999) *Necessity, Volition and Love* (Cambridge, Cambridge University Press).

Frankfurt, H. G. (2004) *The Reasons for Love* (Princeton, NJ, Princeton University Press)

Hoveid, M. H. (2009) Læreres utdanning: et arbeid med personlig språkbruk: pedagogisk filosofiske medieringer om mulighetene for utvikling av praktisk fornuft gjennom arbeid med språkbruk. [Teachers Education. A Work with Personal Language Use: Pedagogical and Philosophical Mediations about the Possibilities of Developing Practical Wisdom through Work with Language-Use]. Trondheim, NTNU, PhD Thesis.

Hoveid, M. H. (2012) A Space for 'Who'—a Culture of 'Two': Speculations Related to an 'In-Between Knowledge', *Ethics and Education*, 7.3, pp. 251–260.

Irigaray, L. (1993) *An Ethics of Sexual Difference*, C. Burke and G. C. Gill, trans. (Ithaca, NY, Cornell University Press).

Irigaray, L. (1996) *I Love to You. Sketch of a Possible Felicity within History*, A. Martin, trans. (London, Routledge).

Irigaray, L. (2000) *Democracy Begins Between Two*, K. Anderson, trans. (London, The Athlone Press.)

Irigaray, L. (2001) *To Be Two*, M.M. Rhodes and M. F.Cocito-Monoc, trans. (London, The Athlone Press).

Irigaray, L. (2008) *Sharing the World* (London and New York, Continuum).

Jones, R. (2011) *Irigaray* (Cambridge, Polity Press).

Ricoeur, P. (1994) *Oneself as Another* (Chicago, IL, University of Chicago Press).

Stern, D. N. (2004) *The Present Moment in Psychotherapy and Everyday Life* (New York, W.W. Norton & Company).

Todd, S. (2009) *Toward an Imperfect Education. Facing Humanity, Rethinking Cosmopolitanism* (Boulder, CO, Paradigm Publishers).

6
Another Relationship to Failure: Reflections on Beckett and Education

AISLINN O'DONNELL

DO I ASK TOO MUCH?

Our ideas depend on dialogue with others, but it can be easy to forget their origins in those relationships that orient our intellectual lives. The chapters by Caroline Wilson, Sharon Todd and Rachel Jones in this book serve as a reminder of the importance of acknowledging our relational origins and our debt to others, helping us become more attuned to the ways in which the genesis of ideas is often bound up with the lives of others, our interlocutors. This chapter was born in failure, the failure to have an idea, or more precisely the failure to generate an idea of which I could be named the sole progenitor. It began with conversations in a prison on Samuel Beckett and pedagogy, conversations that emerged from our classes in philosophy. This chapter is dedicated to the man, the student in my class, whose interest in Beckett and whose illuminating readings of his writings invited me to reimagine failure.

Given the manner in which many, though not all, of his characters display antipathy toward children, and, unlike Luisa Muraro (see Caroline Wilson, Chapter 2), seem to be convinced that it would have been better to never have been born (but since one has been, one must persist), whilst evincing a committed incapacity to be in any ordinary sense 'productive citizens', the writings of Samuel Beckett might seem a peculiar choice when reflecting upon philosophy of education. Yet, if one wishes to look at the world through a different lens, through those occupying its underside or its outside, then Beckett helps one do so without condescension or pity. His writings prompt consideration of some of the ways in which humans are situated on a graduated scale of recognisable humanity, teaching us how to develop another relationship to failure. His views on success, prestige and failure are traced through the denizens and anti-heroes of his prose and plays. His

Re-Imagining Relationships in Education: Ethics, Politics and Practices, First Edition. Edited by Morwenna Griffiths, Marit Honerød Hoveid, Sharon Todd and Christine Winter. Chapters © 2015 The Authors. Editorial organization © 2015 Philosophy of Education Society of Great Britain. Published 2015 by John Wiley & Sons Ltd.

characters tend not to have much understanding of what is even meant by a 'normal', flourishing human life. Says one his most infamous characters, Molloy, of manners, 'On this subject I had only negative and empirical notions, which means that I was in the dark, most of the time, and all the more completely as a lifetime of observations had left me doubting the possibility of systematic decorum, even within a limited area' (Beckett, 1979, p. 25). Slapstick and bawdy humour puncture the erudite witticisms of the so-called intellectuals and philosophers he portrays. In later writings, Beckett's images of the human become ever more subtractive, bare, intensive and generic, more like the wind or light, eliminating those all-too-human attributes that serve not only to identify and classify, but also to distinguish us from one another: each one becomes utterly singular, in a way that resonates with some of the descriptions offered by Rebecca Adami and Sharon Todd in this book. Characters, even those made manifest through ebbs of intensity and bare descriptions of movement and breath, are often absorbed with preoccupations, rituals and programmes that seem foreign to those of ordinary humans. At moments they experience delight in the world and even ecstasy; much of the time they simply go on, living lives that elude familiar forms of narrative or temporal structure. Yet a closer look at their practices, observations and questions pushes us to question the purported logic of our own regimes of living, and to pay more attention to our unruly minds. Beckett's works are difficult and their themes might seem foreign to the concerns of those of us who work in education, but they are instructive because of their contemplations upon the human condition and their reflections upon ethics.

It is seldom that one finds such characters being either judgemental or displaying too much concern about what others think of them. It is not difficult to find something liberating in this indifference, not to others *per se*, but to what others make of us. Such indifference does not foreclose gestures of kindness or solidarity with others. Often Beckett's characters make clear our profound dependence on others, as well the difficulty of getting along: couples like Vladimir and Estragon, in *Waiting for Godot* (Beckett, 2006), or Mercier and Camier, in the novel of the same name (Beckett, 1994b), do not need to understand each other, or even have anything in common, to stick with one other. The apparent disregard for what is supposed to constitute a 'successful' human life can give consolation to those who feel cowed by the pressures of success, allowing a space for the rather basic question of 'why' to be asked—Why do I desire this? Why do I seek recognition from them? Why is my career so important? Why do I need to know this? When in *Worstward Ho*, Beckett writes, 'Ever tried. Ever failed. No matter. Try again. Fail again. Fail better' (1983, p. 7), this serves to comfort. The kindly 'No matter' does not allude to prospective success or achievement but rather seems to encourage: 'Don't worry', 'Keep going', 'Keep trying', 'On'. It is unsurprising that artists have been drawn to this phrase, and indeed toward the end of this chapter I will examine some of these practices.[1]

There are two interwoven strands in this chapter. One questions the emphasis on competition and achievement in contemporary education and its implications for our relationship to failure. The second, strongly influenced by Beckett, explores ways of reimagining our relationship to failure in such a way that allows us to reflect on what matters in life.[2] We may come to wonder whether we ask too much of humanity and of education when faced with images of mastery, autonomy, competition, potential, competence, flourishing and perfection that continue to inform philosophical principles that underpin educational practice. Christine Winter, Rebecca Adami, and Caroline Wilson, in particular, underline the corrosive effects of such aspirations. It may be wiser, as Sharon Todd suggests in *Toward an Imperfect Education: Facing Humanity, Rethinking Cosmopolitanism* that we temper our expectations of what education might achieve, and likewise to blunt and diminish those ambitions that tend to be most bolstered by a culture of competitiveness and standards that is, *de facto*, cultivated in many educational systems. Education cannot serve as the solution to society's ills and failures. Throughout his writings, one of Beckett's targets is education. The educational endeavour is often provocatively described as an exercise of relative futility, which offers, nonetheless, a form of distraction and an occasionally pleasant, occasionally taxing, way of passing time. In *The Unnameable*, the voice, Worm, seems confused by this practice, failing to grasp what the purpose of such an activity might be, although it seems nonetheless to have left its mark, for good or ill.

What puzzles me is the thought of being indebted for this information to persons with whom I can never have been in contact. Can it be innate knowledge? Like that of good and evil. This seems improbable to me. But what they were most determined for me to swallow was my fellow creatures. In this they were without mercy. I remember little or nothing of these lectures. I cannot have understood a great deal. But I seem to have retained certain descriptions, in spite of myself. They gave me courses on love, on intelligence, most precious, most precious. They also taught me to count, and even to reason. Some of this rubbish has come in handy on occasions, I don't deny it, on occasions which would never have arisen if they left me in peace (Beckett, 1979, p. 273).

Although some might read such words as nonsense or even cynical, they have the effect of deflating grandiose claims of the impact of education in order to return us to reflection upon what matters in life. This comes to pass without self-indulgence, self-hatred, pessimism or delusion, allowing us to be rather more circumspect about what we educators do. It reminds us that little of the knowledge transmitted to students, even with vigour, passion and enthusiasm, is digested or assimilated, but that ideas seep through nonetheless, and playing with them can be rather enjoyable. So much of what Beckett writes under-lines the bleakness and futility of human existence. The expectation that we could ever escape this suffering serves only to compound it. Still, what I find most moving in his characters is they persist in spite of this, and as they do they find small comforts, decency and cama-raderie. Perhaps this is as much as we can hope for.

AN ANTI-HEROIC CURRICULUM

Rather than seeking to eliminate failure, it is more interesting to think about how the concept of failure could be reimagined if, as Beckett suggests, failure is not accompanied by disappointment but became simply what we *do*, rather than being something we *are*. It might afford a greater capacity to discern which kinds of failure are prefer-able and why we seem incapable of acknowledging the futility of many of the ways in which lives are spent, or expended. Failure is inevitable in practices that remain open to the world, through which the 'unknown' is allowed breathing space rather than resisted in an endless quest to master, confine and navigate the terrain of the known. For Beckett, failure is just part of what it is to be human and what matters is that one persists without seeking sanctuary in the hope of future salvation, transcendent or worldly. If we are closed to the possibility of failure, then we are closed to life's openness and unpre-dictability: we make of ourselves impermeable gods. Looking at failure in this light is not simply a matter of making the rather obvious statement that even when we set goals for ourselves (goals which can often be, in Beckett's view, rather unreflective and pointless), these are often frustrated or interrupted. More importantly, it asks us to question the ethics of those who refuse to countenance failure, seeking control and/or justifying success in their chosen sphere at any cost. In this respect, Beckett asks us who we become if we refuse to allow failure into our lives. However, he is not suggesting that we should seek out failure or despair; we should take comfort where we can and find solace in such happiness that comes into our lives. Krapp, in *Krapp's Last Tape*, only retrospectively understands the significance of his moment of happiness, but he does not live in regret:

> Past midnight. Never knew such silence. The earth might be uninhabited.
>
> *Pause.*
>
> Here I end this reel. Box—*(pause)*—three, spool—*(pause)*—five. (*Pause.*) Perhaps my best years are gone. When there was a chance of happiness. But I wouldn't want them back. Not with the fire in me now. No, I wouldn't want them back (Beckett, 1994a, p. 22).

Ruth Cigman (2001, and in Chapter 9) has argued that the question is not whether one should seek happiness but rather *how* we should do so. *How* we go about living also matters for Beckett. Although he would not have such confidence in the possibility of happiness, his writings bring us to ask ourselves not only *why* we have certain aims, but also *how* we attain such aims. Those who find their desires and objectives are seldom frustrated are viewed with some suspicion, as they tend, in his view, to be indifferent to the effects of their actions on the lives of others and the earth: capitalism is consummately tyrannical in its indifference to the lives of others. Such people readily find ways of explaining away their cruelty or indifference. This is not to suggest that we might have a perfect state of affairs were people to become more enlightened, but the world might become a little less brutal were we to face reality and face humanity.

In his book *Simone Weil and the Intellect of Grace*, Henry Finch comments on the continuation of a Roman legacy in education systems populated, broadly speaking, by heroes; even the undertrodden in the stories of the curriculum overcome in their own way, and those who do not are to be pitied or given charity. Sharon Todd observes that:

> [t]he idea that education can ameliorate certain global conditions under the sign of humanity is a worrying proposition, not least because it fails to recognize that the very injustices and antagonisms which are the targets of such education are created and sustained precisely through our human talent for producing them (2010, p. 9).

We tend to promote a broadly positive and hopeful idea of humanity in education. Beckett's writings prompt consideration of some of the ways in which reimagined curricula might introduce a more gentle and minimal set of principles, evocative of a politics of decency rather than one of flourishing. Whilst there is an understandable desire to see the next generation as the one capable of resolving the horrors of the world, perhaps it might be more helpful to children and students were there to be more honest descriptions about the state of the world and the prospects for most human lives. Curricular stories could describe anti-heroes like Beckett's characters, who are tramps, refugees, clowns, psychiatric patients and denizens—those usually made invisible or set to the margins of systems—in a way that avoids presenting people as objects of pity in need of welfare or moral transformation or, perhaps worse, as exotic outsiders, since such approaches tend to consolidate the role of agency with the 'privileged'. Unfortunately, benevolent gestures can unwittingly serve to reinforce hierarchical relationships, creating a feeling of self-satisfaction on the part of the benefactor whilst making of the beneficiary an object of pity.

How one responds to the one who has nothing, reveals who one is. How one responds to having nothing also reveals something of oneself. But unlike fairy stories, there is no moment of redemption or transformation at the end of the stories. In the *Trilogy*, Molloy rejects gestures of pity and charity with vehemence.

> Let me tell you this, when social workers offer you, free, gratis and for nothing, something to hinder you from swooning, which with them is an obsession, it is useless to recoil, they will pursue you to the ends of the earth, the vomitory in their hands. The Salvation Army is no better. Against the charitable gesture there is no defence that I know of. You sink your head, you put out your hands all trembling and twined together and you say, Thank you, thank you lady, thank you kind lady (Beckett, 1979, p. 38).

Unfortunately, it is easy to be blind to one's motivations and to the secret pleasures that arise through pity and charity rather than compassion. Gestures of benevolence can reinforce the ways in which another is seen (and sees himself or herself as lesser, depending on how much power one holds in a given situation).

Of the desire for prestige and the power that accompanies such gestures, Finch writes that, '. . . prestige like everything illusory, is based on imagination. It is the imagination that gives people the fascinating power to seem more than human, enabling them to treat with contempt the nobodies beneath them who accept this treatment with pleasure' (1999, p. 65). The most reliable ways of securing prestige are fear, cruelty and terror, which can take more or less evident form. In cultures that see themselves as meritocratic, failure to conform or attain the 'goods' of 'recognition', 'agency' or 'material well-being' (to put a more acceptable gloss on prestige, power, or money) can mean that one is seen or sees oneself as individually blameworthy. However, there remain those, like Beckett, who simply refuse to accept that these constitute the goods of a human life. He does not see 'lessness' as a matter for moral condemnation or solicitude, and he does not presume that those who have power are to be envied.

THE IDOLS OF PRESTIGE, PROGRESS AND PERFECTION

The confusion is not my invention. We cannot listen to a conversation for five minutes without being acutely aware of the confusion. It is all around us and our only chance now is to let it in. The only chance of renovation is to open our eyes and see the mess. It is not a mess you can make sense of (Beckett quoted in Driver, 1961, p. 22).

Beckett's writings offer an honest, if devastating, commitment to the surgical excision of any remnants of delusions, illusions, utopias, salvific narratives or ideals that might give false comfort to a human life. He strives to articulate an ethical position that, rather than taking refuge in speculation about how the world ought to be, helps human beings to respond courageously to how things are—'how it is', as he writes. This is described well by John Calder who says, 'The presence of evil cannot be denied. The most casual look around reveals it everywhere, it is always in a dominating position and the most that can be done by those endowed with moral instincts is to combat it, under duress, with every possible sacrifice and personal inconvenience' (2001, p. 41). He argues that the message of Beckett's work is 'in saying to as much of humanity as will listen, that if it learns to forgo personal ambition and think in terms of cooperation, compassion and companionship, it will be happier' (2001, p. 138). Whether or not Calder is correct in his analysis, it serves as an interesting provocation to those of us working and participating in systems of education. It moves one to ask what effect the principle of competition has on the experience of education, to what extent the control mechanisms of an administered society affect relationships to failure, and, whether what Sarah Ahmed (2010) describes in *The Promise of Happiness* as the normalising injunction to be happy forecloses or brackets the affective complexity which is constitutive of a human life. Some will suggest that concern with what others think of us can serve to motivate ethical action, yet one could counter that the mere existence of another human being demands a response of kindness, decency, civility and care, whatever that person may think of us. Indeed, a supererogatory ethic would not require recognition for such gestures.

We are thus invited to think of failure as an inevitable dimension of being human in the world to which our response is simply to persist. This clear-sighted realism seeks to see things as they are, rather than always hoping for a better world and imagining better human beings. Any betterment that arises is singular and often temporary, involving small efforts to alleviate suffering where it is witnessed, rather than the construction of *grand projects* of social engineering. Beckett's writings challenge and draw to light the corrosive effect of some of the fundamental aims and assumptions shaping educational practice and policy, in particular, as I have indicated, the principle of competition and the quest for prestige, in respect of which liberalism and libertarianism maintain an agnostic position. Instead of flourishing or even autonomy, a more measured, more gentle and renunciative approach to education and to life is suggested. This is does not mean a life of unabated despair: life involves many moments, some of absurdity and curiosity, others provoked by experiences of the joys of memory, the open skies and muddy landscapes. A so-called 'successful' life can be impoverished and insensible. For some it will seem heretical to rail against the idols of progress, perfection and production that have come to mark social relations in contemporary liberal democratic capitalist societies: a brief glance at many course descriptions, curricular principles, mission statements, and 'philosophies' of educational institutions reveal that perfectionist, progressive and aspirational discourses continue to define implicitly and explicitly the way in which humanity is understood in education, whilst the emphasis on competence and measurable outcomes underscore that what matters is success measured against standards. Given the *de facto* use of bell curves in many courses, it is peculiar that little attention is given to the impossibility of universal success. This is not to say that all should not pass examinations, but rather that we should be more truthful about the prospects of failure and more circumspect about their function—many of my first year students write in their philosophy essays of how they now dread thinking because of the way in which the need for success in examinations over-determined and distorted their experiences of learning. Some forms of assessment are valuable whilst others undermine the relationship to education. I also see this in prison where many of the men with whom I work failed to meet the required national standards in schools, and thus felt themselves to be failures. Children see through all of this quite quickly once they enter school. To question such aspirations can appear both obtuse and wrong-headed. Surely we ought to encourage the growth, autonomy, achievement and flourishing of children and young people in education? However, competition rooted in comparison contributes to a way of relating to failure that understands it in terms of one's being and one's failure to match up to others.

FEELING LIKE A FAILURE

The relationship to failure raises a range of questions in respect of both students' self-conceptualisation and their relation to their peers, to those in authority and to societal norms. If the dominant way of understanding failure in education is to judge success in relation to a standard or norm, then failure is a relative term contingent upon what that standard or norm prescribes. Failure understood in relation to success itself presupposes that there be a standard to serve as a benchmark, be it conventional, statistical and/or artificial. One compares oneself with others in that process. The principle of competition determines how and whether one matches up that standard and to one's peers. However, it is not inevitable that failure be understood from within an economy of comparison or competition. One might think from the perspective of failure and incompetence, emphasising not outcome but process. Certain ways of failing can be helpful and useful (although, of course, others are not, such as moral or ethical failure). Failure can be uncoupled from judgement and expectation, and the relationship between failure and experimentation in contemporary art practice, as we will see below, helps us to better understand how. This raises the question of whether practices and institutions of education need to be reimagined in order to bracket conventional understandings of success, so that failure might come to be understood not as *being* a failure and as a deficit of being—a relatively new concept according to Scott Sandage (2010)—but in terms of the activity of failing. This is not to make failure the *telos* of one's actions, which would return it to the framework of success, but rather invites us to think about failure and incompetence in terms of experimentation and the 'trying things out' that is immanent to any practice. This might serve as a counter-balance to those discourses that emphasise success or happiness. Might a counter-narrative to that of autonomy, agency, productivity and flourishing make a difference to students' self-understanding, relationships with others and relationship with failure? John Calder suggests that,

> [a] service that Beckett has done for many is to take away their fear of inadequacy. The pressure of education, of parents, and of society itself to be successful, an achiever, a person of means and power, is always great. The purpose of such ambition can only be itself. . . . The very effort of achieving something in the world tends to inhibit the ability to ask why and any desire to find a meaning or purpose to the effort, other than self-aggrandisement (2001, p. 138).

Calder perhaps over-states matters in speaking of self-aggrandisement, but it allows us to reflect upon the goods of a human life, and the values that ought underpin it, however he is right in pointing to students' fear of inadequacy. One form of resistance commonly exercised by students is silence, but what causes this? When I asked my students, who continued to remain resolutely silent in tutorials on critical thinking, why students don't participate, they spoke of a familiar litany of reasons: fear, lack of confidence, fear of looking stupid, fear of getting it wrong, fear of failure. However, a propensity to focus on the psychological dimensions of fear tends to occlude a broader political, social, economic or cultural analysis of the desire for success, mastery and competence and the correlative fear of failure in the lived experience of everyday life. One of the problems facing my students is that they had come to understand failure solely in ontological terms, construed through the language of identity as a noun, as something one is, rather than as a verb, as something one does. This is not to suggest, as behavioural psychology sometimes does, that one's actions and one's being are separate—there are times at which our failures, be it through action or inaction, strikes painfully at the heart of who we feel we are. However, students in classrooms will rarely have done something to merit such self-approbation and shame, yet still they view failure in terms of their identities. If failure is construed in ontological terms, and if enquiry into the conditions for and consequences of this relationship to failure is lacking, this can lead to quasi-behavioural reactions to perceived failure or the possibility of failure: the slightest hint of *being* lacking in some way can bring students to experience affective responses that are part of the same family of social affects that includes shame, embarrassment and humiliation. This is instructive. Although not an affect itself, these affects that are associated with the experience of the *fear* of failure, rather than necessarily failure itself, are social affects; that is, they are precipitated by the (anticipated) judgement of the other or the failure to meet a perceived standard.

This is a delicate area. There are areas in life in which we might be said to be lacking in our relation to others through indifference, insensitivity, cruelty or ambition. There are times when we rightfully feel ashamed because we have fallen short of our values. Shame reveals to us that our lives are bound up with those of others; however, shame becomes pernicious when the anticipated response of others operates in such a way as to preclude us from living honestly and in accordance with our values. A comparative culture that sees the path to human flourishing as one premised upon an ideology of competition is the culture of contemporary capitalism. However, despite the emphasis on success for all, it is the failure to be successful in the terms dictated by society that is the dominant tenor of life in contemporary capitalist, liberal society. Bare refusals to participate in such an economy could help to interrupt the dominant logic of contemporary capital premised on such a principle of competition. This is why, says Calder, 'His [Beckett's] many written statements on the folly of ambition and the irrelevance of failure to anything real are among his most potent and comforting, because they help to remove a major anxiety. There is neither fault nor shame in failure' (2001, p. 9), adding, '[h]is self-identification is always with the victim' (2001, p. 106). Calder's keen observation that failure is irrelevant to anything real in Beckett is an important one, yet, of course, Beckett is acutely aware that often we fail to live a life that is ethical, and this is not a form of failure that is irrelevant.

FEAR OF FAILURE

Yes, I once took an interest in astronomy. I don't deny it. Then it was geology that killed a few years for me. The next pain in the balls was anthropology and the other disciplines, such as psychiatry, that are connected with it, disconnected and then connected again, according to their latest discoveries. What I liked in anthropology was its inexhaustible faculty of negation, its relentless definition of man, as though he were no better than God, In terms of what he is not. But my ideas on this subject were always horribly confused for my knowledge of men was scant and the meaning of being beyond me (Beckett, 1979, p. 38).

Beckett's wry descriptions of education, through the voices of his characters, offer a rather more circumspect and modest vision of education and its achievements. Yet, Molloy, Worm and Moran's reflections are not traversed by fear, but only by mild confusion and occasional over-identification with those purported aims. They seem a far cry from John Holt's descriptions of children in his classic text *How Children Fail*. Holt's descriptions of the experiences of children in schools are resonant with the experiences of my students in teacher education, both as students and as student-teachers. Failure in schools, as elsewhere, is understood in relation to the perceived judgement of others. For many, schooldays constitute a period of unrelenting failure to match the expectations of the teacher, the standards of the national curriculum, and the knowledge of one's peers. Oddly, a fear of failure affects even those deemed most competent and apparently successful within the educational system. Thus, the other becomes, not one on whom I may depend or who may depend on me, or someone in relation with whom I may come to constitute myself, but simply a generic marker indicating my relative success or failure.

I suggest that it is not failure *per se* that precipitates a feeling of humiliation, shame or fear, but anticipated judgement: not being able to do something should not necessarily elicit the fear, shame, deference, ambition and paralysis that have come to be associated with the prospect of failure. In a set of diary entries, Holt considers the relationship to failure held by the children in his classes. Schools cultivate, in his view, *producers*, rather than *thinkers*. Producers look for the right answer, certainty and approval and become concerned if they do not receive affirmation or if they get the wrong answer. Holt wonders about the responses of children to the prospect of failure. 'Kids often resist understanding, make no effort to understand, but they don't often grasp an idea and then throw it away. . . . Can a child have a vested interest in failure?' (Holt, 1964, p. 19). Rather than face the prospect of getting a wrong answer, they disengage: 'The child must be right. She cannot bear to be wrong, or even to imagine that she might be wrong. When she is wrong, as she often is, the only thing to do is to forget it as quickly as possible' (1964, p. 27); or they panic: 'She closes her eyes and makes a dash for it, like someone running past a graveyard on a dark night. No looking back afterwards, either' (1964, p. 24).

Holt writes of one child, 'She also knows the teacher's strategy of asking questions of students who seem confused or not paying attention. She therefore feels safe waving her hand in the air, as if she were bursting to tell the answer' (1964, p. 27). Holt calls one strategy 'guess and look', that is, try to figure out from bodily and vocal cues the answer the teacher wants. Teachers themselves can become so obsessed with *their* right answer that they fail to hear the response of the child, intelligent as it may be. Describing the tenor of classroom life, he says,

> Their attention depended on what was going on in class. Any raising of the emotional temperature made them prick up their ears. If an argument was going on, or someone was in trouble, or someone was being laughed at for a foolish answer, they took notice. Or if you were explaining something so simple that all the rest knew it, they would wave their arms and give agonized, half-suppressed cries of O-o-o-o-o-oh!' [. . .] But most of the time, when explaining, questioning or discussing was going on, the majority of children paid little attention or none at all (1964, p. 35).

(Even though fifty years have passed since Holt's book was published, many people currently working in teacher education who are accustomed to supervision in primary schools will be as familiar as he was with those half-suppressed cries in certain schools.) The complicated relationship between teaching and the children's experience of, relationship to, and attempts to avoid failure is traced through these descriptions. A further difficulty compounds matters—the teacher's self-image, hopes and desires. Holt writes, 'The conscientious teacher thinks of himself as taking his students (at least part way) on a journey to some glorious destination, well worth the pains of the trip' (1964, p. 36), however this was not how children understood school and learning. They felt that they were in school because they had to be. They had no real idea of where they were going, or why, but they knew that they had to complete the tasks set before them if they wished to avoid trouble.

Holt portrays the lived experience of children in visceral terms claiming that many children are scared most of the time in schools, even those schools that are kindest and gentlest, saying to witness the behaviour of some children is akin to an animal fleeing danger. He asks us to pay attention to the expressions on children's faces, the way that they turn to observe one another, and their bodily comportment when he remarks, 'Now it begins to look as if the expectation and fear of failure, if strong enough, may lead children to act and think in a special way' (1964, p. 39). Part of the difficulty lies in the constant expectation of success, a culture that values right answers rather than process, and behavioural management strategies that do not acknowledge the child's natural curiosity and desire to learn but that are premised on the idea that children need to be coerced into learning. Holt feels that we put children under intolerable and constant pressure to meet predetermined standards and to match the abilities of their peers. In response to this he proposes a thought experiment for teachers. 'But suppose every teacher in the school were told he had to do ten pages of addition problems, within a given time limit and with no mistakes, or lose his job' (1964, p. 52).

Another dimension to the problem is the broader cultural relationship to failure that conceives it in the ontological terms outlined above, whereby failure is seen as revelatory of the inadequacy of the self. Holt acknowledges this whilst wondering why this is the case, 'Of course, we adults tend to see all small, specific failures, of our own or of children, as proof of general failure, incompetence, worthlessness. Is it a cultural matter? Are there no people in the world for whom it is not a disgrace to do something badly?' (1964, p. 59). Even strategies of praise and affirmation can unintentionally serve to exacerbate feelings of worthlessness, in particular when encouragement to meet the 'self-concept' attributed to one has been confounded. Rather than being an instance of *failing*, it constitutes a failure of *being*. It is perhaps for this reason that 'The strategies of most of these kids have been consistently self-centred, self-protective, aimed above all else at avoiding trouble, embarrassment, punishment, disapproval or loss of status' (1964, p. 59); this is similar to the list of the reasons offered to me when I asked my students why they did not speak in tutorials. As Holt recognises this is debilitating in many ways, including for thinking: there is a difference between the figure of the 'idiot', like Molloy, who refuses to know what 'everyone knows', and the scattered, panicked response to the invitation to thinking and living outlined in the above quotations. A further danger is that children come to develop a particular relation to authority that conceives of it in terms of control, coming to desire the approval of the Master or the Other, who may present himself or herself, as Britzman (2006) argues, as a being without vulnerability, averse to risk, wholly adequate, godlike, wholly rational, without prejudice, and without fear. This image of autonomy without dependency is a powerful one in education, as Rachel Jones, in Chapter 1, underlines. This is compounded by the confusion that teachers make between good character and good behaviour—good character may require contesting authority and going against the grain, and such gestures by children often meet with hostility and punishment by teachers.

The consequence of this is put starkly by Holt, 'We destroy this capacity above all by making them afraid, afraid of not doing what people want, of not pleasing, of making mistakes, of failing, of being *wrong*. Thus we make them afraid to gamble, afraid to experiment, afraid to try the difficult and the unknown. Even when we do not create children's fears, when they come to us with fears ready-made and built-in, we use these fears as handles to manipulate them and get them to do what we want' (1964, p. 165). This, I suggest, leads to the translation of failure of doing into failure of being. Why is it seen as a failure of one's *being* to be unable to *do* something?

I'LL GO ON

Certain of Molloy's pious statements resonate rather uncomfortably with Holt's observations. He says,

> I have only to be told what good behaviour is and I am well behaved within the limits of my physical possibilities. And so I have never ceased to improve, from this point of view, for I used to be intelligent and quick. As far as good will is concerned, I had it to overflowing, the exasperated good will of the over-anxious . . . And if I have always behaved like a pig, the fault lies not with me but with my superiors, who correct me only on points of detail instead of showing me the essence of the system, after the manner of the great English schools, and the guiding principles of good manner, and how to proceed, without going wrong, from the former to the latter, and how to trace back to its ultimate source a given comportment (Beckett, 1979, p. 25).

Molloy does his best to respond to cues but he doesn't really understand the point of it all. Indeed, Beckett's characters never quite fit, nor do they know what to do, but, unlike most of the children described by Holt, they are not weighed down by a sense of inadequacy born of comparison with others: being adequate or inadequate is scarcely an issue for them.

Let us briefly imagine what education might be like if our relationship to failure were to be reimagined. What if educational institutions were spaces in which we tried things out? What if they were an exercise in 'infancy', perpetual beginning, exposure and searching curiosity, as Rachel Jones, in Chapter 1, describes. This does not imply a lack of persistence, diligence, attention, or that we would never complete anything (completion and success are not equivalent terms) but it means we might be liberated from the forms of judgement that paralyse agency, and it might permit poetic ruptures with cynicism and even a heightened awareness of the subtleties of the 'everyday'. A cue could be taken from contemporary artists like Francis Alÿs. Alÿs engages in acts that are often impossible, futile or useless, such as seeing how long he can wander with a 9mm pistol in his hand through Mexico City before being arrested, or spending nine hours pushing an ice block through city streets until it melts, or deploying a group of five hundred volunteers to use shovels to move a sand dune four inches. These exercises allow for a poetic disruption of the everyday, and can also serve to reveal the reality of many of our working activities. Ignoring the imperative of efficiency, Alÿs scrawls axioms such as 'Maximum effort Minimum result' in his notebooks. Mark Godfrey referring to his ice-block pushing, writes, 'Here for the first time, the artist dramatized the aphorism that "sometimes doing something leads to nothing", expending maximum energy with minimum results. The action reflected on the everyday pursuits of all those working in the streets around him, and more generally on the vanity of the modernising efforts of successive Latin-American governments' (Godfrey and Biesenbach, 2010, p. 18). The axiom of 'maximum effort minimum result' does not so much prescribe as describe in a way that also forces Western culture, with its emphasis on productivity and efficiency, to ask, what, with all our efforts, are we really doing? Do we have anything to show for it all? Alÿs's works have the same kind of effect as Beckett's characters—the uselessness of their actions can serve as a hiatus provoking a distance from the immediate situation in which it seems obvious what must do and who one must be. We are forced us to ask ourselves why we assume our own actions have greater value than those of Murphy or Molloy.

The fear of failure experienced by my students and those described by Holt presupposed the possibility of being adequate and even successful. A wilful blindness to the fact that not everyone can be 'winners', 'heroes', 'achievers' or even 'all they can be' persists, and there is insufficient questioning at a policy level about which aspirations ought to be valued, or whether they are even desirable. To what extent is an honest contemplation of the human condition permitted in schools or colleges? A relationship to failure is shaped through systems of assessment that rely on benchmarks and standards, by standardised testing such as PISA, and by cultures in schools and universities that reward success and differentiate students through high stakes testing. This is not to suggest that an alternative would be the kind of 'entrepreneurial' culture increasingly promoted by businesses seeking to intervene in educational life, as this also sets its sights on success and ignores the inevitable hierarchy that emerges. Is there another way of imagining the human condition that might allow for a more subdued, nuanced and kinder philosophy of education? This is particularly important when educating future teachers whose own fears and standards may forbid the kinds of open experimentation and play with children that can invite critical enquiry, curiosity and exploration, as well varying material engagements through practice in different disciplines. We could learn from the ways that young children explore the world and bring some of that attentiveness, interest and absorption into our own relationships with the everyday.

A preliminary sketch of a Beckettian philosophy of education might include the following: we are inadequate, but we muddle through; the world is a mess, but we should face our situation with courage; education will not change much, but for all that, it is often an enjoyable distraction; we should be decent to other human beings, forgoing personal ambition and the desire for prestige; there is no ultimate *telos* to a human life, but still we persist, on; and we should try things out, experiment, without undue concern about success or failure. Perhaps then experiences of education might be more tolerable. Perhaps. Rather than experiencing oneself as a failure, one fails, fails again, fails better, fails worse.

NOTES

1. I think here of Bruce Naumann, Fischli and Weiss, Francis Alÿs, Thomas Hirschhorn or Fluxus who try and tried to undermine a desire for control, mastery or autonomy, welcoming more gentleness, humour, weakness or experimentation in both their work and in the relationship cultivated with those encountering, or participating in, the work.

2. Whilst I acknowledge that there is an extensive literature on failure and education, one contribution that Beckett makes is to help us to understand failure as part of the human condition. This is, in part, why he and others of his generation are so critical of the administered society that seeks to eliminate risk. This is a different point to the one made by writers like Melanie Philips who challenges the idea that no one should fail. Similar criticism have been made in special needs education. The normative position that no one should fail, fails to acknowledge the reality that we do fail, and in many different ways. Children understand condescension. Conversely, there is a good deal of literature that focuses on the effort to eliminate failure because of its effects on self-esteem. However, perhaps, the real problem is learning how to fail. This is not to advocate an acquiescent position that accepts under-resourced classrooms, poor treatment of children, and so forth. This would constitute a kind of moral or ethical failure which Beckett deplores, but it is to explore a way of looking at failure that has perhaps not been sufficiently explored in the literature.

REFERENCES

Ahmed, S. (2010) *The Promise of Happiness* (Durham, NC, Duke University Press).

Beckett, S. (1979) *The Beckett Trilogy: Molly, Malone Dies, The Unnamable* (London, Picador).

Beckett, S. (1983) *Worstward Ho* (London, Calder).

Beckett, S. (1994a) *Krapp's Last Tape and Other Dramatic Works* (New York, Grove Press).

106   A. O'Donnell

Beckett, S. (1994b) *Mercier and Camier* (New York, Grove Press).
Beckett, S. (2006) *Waiting for Godot* (London, Faber & Faber).
Britzman, D. (2006) *Novel Education: Psychoanalytical Studies of Learning and Not Learning* (New York, Peter Lang).
Calder, J. (2001) *The Philosophy of Samuel Beckett* (London, Calder).
Cigman, R. (2001) Self-Esteem and the Confidence to Fail, *Journal of Philosophy of Education*, 35.4, pp. 561–76.
Driver, T. (1961) Beckett by the Madeleine, *Columbia University Forum*, IV, Summer.
Finch, H. (1999) *Simone Weil and the Intellect of Grace* (New York, Continuum).
Godfrey, M. and K. Biesenbach (2010) *Francis Alÿs: A Story of Deception* (London, Tate).
Holt, J. (1964) *How Children Fail* (Harmondsworth, Penguin).
Sandage, S. (2010) The Invention of Failure: Interview with Sina Najati [2002], in: L. Le Feuvre (ed.) *Failure* (London, Whitechapel).
Todd, S. (2010) *Towards an Imperfect Education: Facing Humanity, Rethinking Cosmopolitanism* (Boulder, CO, Paradigm).

7
Curriculum Knowledge, Justice, Relations: The Schools White Paper (2010) in England

CHRISTINE WINTER

A major problem besetting education today is what is referred to as the attainment gap, that is, the inequalities in schools in terms of educational outcome between learners with different backgrounds and capabilities.[1] The attainment gap is important because benefits accruing from an education are substantial and where such a gap exists, it leads to large disparities in the quality of life many young people can expect to experience in the future. The attainment gap relates to the concept of 'educational equity'. Although both educational equity and equal educational opportunity fall under the overarching concept of educational equality, 'equity' is not synonymous with 'equal opportunity'. Equity means 'all social groups achieving a similar profile of success with the same proportion doing well or poorly at school' (Collins and Yates, 2011, p. 111). It involves treating students fairly although differently, based on differences of need. It means that equitable educational outcomes or results are achieved regardless of the social, economic, cultural and personal characteristics of the learner. In contrast, 'equal educational opportunity' refers to the idea that every learner should have equal access to an equally good education, requiring, on most accounts, the same allocation of educational resources. In the latter case, given their different social backgrounds, learners' needs differ and some learners will achieve more success than others in a standardised education system (Brighouse and Swift, 2008). Of course, the above is a simplistic rendering of a highly complex and contested field, as the work of Calvert (2013), Espinoza (2007), Nash (2004), Schouten (2012), Jencks (1988), and Bronfenbrenner, (1973), as well as contributions to this book (Adami, Jones, Shuffelton and Wilson) attest.

Sociologists of education have made important contributions to the 'attainment gap' debate by examining the role student characteristics

Re-Imagining Relationships in Education: Ethics, Politics and Practices, First Edition. Edited by Morwenna Griffiths, Marit Honerød Hoveid, Sharon Todd and Christine Winter. Chapters © 2015 The Authors. Editorial organization © 2015 Philosophy of Education Society of Great Britain. Published 2015 by John Wiley & Sons Ltd.

and background play in influencing educational attainment from both a qualitative research perspective (See, for example, Gillborn and Kirton, 2000; Gillborn and Mirza, 2000; Sveinsson, 2009; and Reay, 2006, 2012) and from statistical analyses (for example, Demack, Drew and Grimsley, 2000; Raffe *et al.*, 2006; Cassen and Kingdon, 2007; Hirsch, 2007; Strand, 2008; and National Equality Panel, 2010). Despite these researchers' collective recommendations to change educational resourcing mechanisms, curriculum, pedagogy, assessment and teacher education policies and practices, the political will to reform policy in line with such recommendations remains faint and the attainment gap persists. This does not mean that policy makers eschew equal opportunity/equity data and arguments in their reform and promotion of education policy. Attainment gap statistics are used by governments in line with the 'policy by numbers' discourse (Rizvi and Lingard, 2010; Lingard, 2011), as a lever to drive technicist and performative governance policies of target-setting, monitoring of inputs and outputs, inspection and close surveillance of teachers under the banner of educational equity (Clarke, in press). Discourses of attainment (and more specifically under-attainment) become the means of pathologising learners by locating 'the problem' within the group of students who are suffering as opposed to locating it within the education system that produces under-attainment (Gillies, 2008).

The notion of a 'gap' between attainment levels of groups of learners points towards questions about relations between the 'high-attainers' and the 'low-attainers'. For example: what is the nature of the 'gap'? why does it exist? what are the differences between the groups of learners? are educational opportunities equal, equitable? Taking the theme of 'relations' as alluding to 'connections', 'attachments', 'affiliations', 'associations' between things in education—the 'things' may be people, such as in the relations between teacher and student, the relations between the self and the other. Alternatively, the 'things' may be concepts, such as language and its relation with meaning; social class in relation to examination results; the relations between philosophy and education, and the relations of central concern here, those between curriculum and justice. This chapter is replete with these kinds of 'relations'. However, in working with the ideas of French philosophers Emmanuel Levinas and Jacques Derrida (as I do below), I am conscious of how language operates in its creation of associations like causation and binary oppositions; language has a tendency to totalise and close down other ways of thinking than those which are expressed. The idea of 'relations' being 'between' things pushes one into a 'this' and 'that' (and maybe 'and the other') thinking space. This is a space where some 'thing' is related to some 'thing' else, and whilst boundaries direct thinking towards the 'things' and their 'relations', they simultaneously restrict the opening of new thinking spaces where the instability, undecidability and irruption of language which these philosophers acknowledge, can unfold to make room for the other. Thus, in the chapter, I adopt a 'light-touch' approach to relations, one that Derrida describes as a 'relation without relation' (1997, p. 14). He uses this phrase to portray his critique of Heidegger's privileging of gathering (*Versammlung*). Derrida argues that the condition of my relation to the other is dissociation, not gathering, because the former opens up a space for the incoming of the radically singular other (ibid., p. 14).

CURRICULUM KNOWLEDGE IN ENGLAND: A BRIEF BACKGROUND

One particular direction of thought in the debate about educational equality has recently focused on curriculum knowledge, as researchers discuss which configurations of knowledge might provide a just education for all students (Whitty, 2010; Collins and Yates, 2011; Yates, 2013; and Young, 2013). The 'new' sociology of education movement in England in the late 1960s and early 1970s at the London Institute of Education, spearheaded by Michael Young (1971) promoted the 'voice discourse' stance, whereby working class underattainment in school was claimed to be due more to the nature of the curriculum on offer in school than to the 'deficit' cultures of learners' homes and communities (Whitty, 2010). The solution to the inequity problem according to this argument involves constructing curricula on the basis of different kinds of knowledge content for different groups of students. In other words, it is about constructing curricula with differentiated knowledge bases. An example developed in school Humanities in 1960s England was Lawrence Stenhouse's Humanities Curriculum Project (HCP). Stenhouse described HCP curriculum knowledge as 'a vernacular equivalent of the classics' (1980, p. 248), written for youngsters considered to be 'of average and less than average ability (Schools Council/Nuffield Foundation, 1970, p. 6) who had been neglected through a traditional academic curriculum'.[2] Such differentiation of curriculum knowledge for different groups of students is problematic in the sense that some configurations of knowledge are valued more highly by society than others.

This leaves a second option. A common configuration of curriculum knowledge is assumed to be appropriate, indeed, an entitlement for, all students, whatever their backgrounds and deemed capacities.

In England and Wales in 1988, The National Curriculum, with its common knowledge base that all students in state schools were legally required to study was introduced to replace a diverse range of school curricula. But a common core curriculum leads to the problem of the decision about what and whose knowledge should be taught and why. Given differences in resources and in student characteristics, curriculum knowledge will be read in different ways according to students' class, culture and social relations (Apple, 1996, p. 33). As we have seen, over the last 40 years in England, various debates have taken place amongst education professionals, politicians and the media about the problematic relationship between curriculum knowledge and equity, leading to several stances, to name a few: the 'new' sociologists of education in the 1970s; the cultural restorationists of the 1980s; the supporters of critical pedagogy and postcolonial theory; the neoliberals of the turn of the century; and most recently the 'core knowledge' brokers of the 2010 Schools White Paper in England.

THINKING CURRICULUM KNOWLEDGE ALONGSIDE LEVINAS AND DERRIDA

Reforms are currently underway in the English education system to change both the kind of curriculum knowledge students learn in school and the curriculum framework through which the teaching, learning and assessment of that knowledge takes place. In the pre-election words of Michael Gove, the Secretary of State for Education, the reforms will 'make opportunity more equal in our society' (2009). Five folds of the reform are relevant to the discussion here. The first concerns performativity. Here, the focus is on raising standards in student test and examination scores and on raising the quality of the examination system (DfE, 2010, paras. 12, 4.4–4.6), in both cases in order to match the best performing education systems overseas. Second, the policy plans to give teachers increased autonomy (ibid., paras. 12, 4.4). At the same time the third fold involves extending school accountability for student performance through measures which include greater financial transparency, use of data to compare school performance, reformed performance tables and reformed Ofsted inspections (ibid., para. 17–20). The fourth policy fold focuses on raising standards for 'children from poorer families', those described as 'deprived' (ibid., para. 20, bullet 4) and/or 'vulnerable' (ibid., para. 16, bullet 7). In response to criticisms that the National Curriculum is overcrowded, the Government proposes the fifth fold: a focus on 'essential knowledge and understanding' (ibid., para. 4.1) in the form of academic subjects (ibid., para. 12), with 'clear expectations for what children must know and be able to do at each stage' (ibid., para. 10). In spite of the acknowledgement of 'other' learners, this renewed governance of education is taking place through a policy replete with totalising discourses of authoritarianism and regulation which, I argue later, leave little obvious space for those students who 'fail' by not fitting the dominant 'rules of engagement' (see also the work of Aislinn O'Donnell, Chapter 6).

Two philosophers who help probe and trouble the discourses of curriculum policy reform in England are Emmanuel Levinas and Jacques Derrida. Both are interested in going beyond ontology or 'what is' and 'what is thought to be', into the pre-originary realms of being, where an openness to the other in effect structures subjectivity itself. For Derrida, these concerns are tied to the operations of language. He shows that whatever form language takes it serves to deny accurate representation of the object it describes and instead is characterised by deferral, dissemination, undecidability (Derrida, 1982). Deconstruction allows the cracking open of pre-suppositions surrounding the assumption that words have stable and self-sufficient meanings. Reading deconstructively makes way for the chain of traces that reveal the incoming of the other, that allow for those who do not fit the discourse to enter, and in so doing, directs us to a 'justice to come' (Derrida, 1992, p. 27). In Derrida's famous words: 'Deconstruction is justice' (ibid., p. 15). The responsibility of deconstruction is to disrupt those taken-for-granted meanings of curriculum discourses by opening them up and releasing them from their metaphysical assumptions to see what or who may have been overlooked, marginalised and omitted in the process of curriculum-making. The idea is that through this transgressive act, affirmative and more ethically just ways of knowing, making, and doing curriculum might be instituted.

The concept of justice, however, runs into some trouble, since any attempt to define justice needs to accept that it cannot be defined. In other words, if justice is always to come, it cannot rest upon a self-present meaning from which everything can be determined: 'One cannot speak directly about justice, thematise or objectivise justice, say "this is just" and even less "I am just" without immediately betraying justice' (ibid., p.10). Any declaration of justice implies a calculability, a conceptualisation, a theorisation, a pinning down of meaning that assumes a pure and self-sufficient presence, whereas justice is 'infinite, incalculable, rebellious to rule and foreign to symmetry, heterogenous and heterotropic' (ibid., p. 22). This does not mean that justice should be abandoned. Indeed, even though justice remains 'an experience of the impossible' (ibid., p. 15), there is no greater responsibility than the pursuit of justice. The possibility of justice, 'a justice to come' (ibid., p. 27), should always be kept open through a deconstructive relation to language. Derrida looks to the *aporia*, the impossible crossing or passage (1993, p. 8), for the unexpected arrival of the other, for the release from totalising ways of thinking. He stresses the unlimited responsibility involved in deconstruction, a thought echoed by John Caputo when he writes about the *aporia*:

> Only then is there a genuine 'responsibility' which means the need to respond to a situation that has not been programmed in advance, to invent new gestures, to affirm an unstable identity that differs from itself. That impossibility is the only possible invention, the invention of the other . . . (Caputo, 1997, p. 120).

In describing Derrida's understanding of justice as infinite, incalculable, and heterogenic, Caputo suggests a comparison with Levinasian ethics (1997, p. 136). Levinas offers an opportunity to engage with a call for goodness that, in the spaces of deconstruction, reaches beyond any doctrinal or totalising rules, principles or criteria governing human behaviour. In this sense, Levinas takes a step further than Derrida does by bringing to the surface his view that justice arises through the realisation of one's responsibility to the Other: 'Levinas wants to overturn the primacy of ontology, and he wants to do this by showing that fundamental to our being, indeed prior to our *being* is our responsibility to the Other' (Standish, 2008, p. 59). The responsibility for the other does not operate within an economy of return, conditioned by reciprocity or 'give and take' (Levinas, 1996, p. 44). It is unconditional. It is an infinite obligation to respond to suffering. The ethical relation to the other sees the subject responding to and taking responsibility for the needs of the other without reward or payback. In explaining the relation between the subject and the other as one-to-one, face-to-face, Levinas seeks to move beyond the constraints of totalising discourses in which we are all trapped to witness ethics in the encounter between the subject and the bare and unadorned human face of the other, uncontaminated by cultural dispositions (Levinas, 1996, p. 53). The ethical encounter is prior to ontology, to language, to subjectivity.

Learners develop their subjectivities, their becoming who they are as subjective individuals and as members of communities and society, through relations with the language and ontology of school curriculum knowledge. Curriculum knowledge is about language and meaning; it offers an opportunity to examine how the ethical relation might become a possibility as a horizon of thought; how it might open up the ethical relation to the other. Like Derrida, Levinas understands that justice cannot be discussed in terms of pre-determined definitions or principles which serve to totalise thinking. He proposes two directions of thought: autonomy and heteronomy.

The primacy of ontology marks the first direction of thought that Levinas calls 'autonomy'. Autonomy recognises humans to be free when they think rationally and act according to their own will. Levinas questions autonomy on the grounds that it excludes the relationship to the Other that he claims comes before Western rationality (Chalier, 1995, p. 6). He argues that this version of autonomy reduces the Other to the condition of the self, the personal, the individual, to 'man's [*sic*] ego' (Levinas, 1998, p. 48). Autonomy as self-determination, personal freedom and morality, and as a long established aim of Western education systems, takes on a form Levinas rejects. Autonomy fails on two counts: because we cannot live together freely without agreeing to limit our freedom and because Western autonomy involves humans as rational subjects seeking to understand the world as it is already known, thereby denying the possibility of alterity (Strhan, 2012, p. 80).

Levinas' second and contrasting direction of thought he calls heteronomy. This involves a movement that goes beyond autonomy as self-sufficiency and freedom to choose. Catherine Chalier describes heteronomy as the place 'where morality is rooted . . . morality is not associated with my reasonable will or reasonable freedom, but in my aptitude to welcome the neighbour in such a way that his [*sic*] life will be more important to me than my own' (1995, p. 7). Morality arises in a person when she becomes aware of her freedom in the eyes of the other who is not free, who is suffering, who is vulnerable. By welcoming the neighbour or stranger as more important than herself, she demonstrates a morality beyond freedom. Heteronomy involves the casting off of self-sufficiency, and opening the self to responsibility to the Other, to the debt to the Other. 'Rather than a subject who chooses, autonomously, to accept responsibility for others, I am responsible for and to the other person before I am capable of choice, and only become a subject in heteronomy' (Strhan, 2012, p. 82). The ethical responsibility for the other comes before everything. Levinas proposes that it is only when I have responded to the call of the other by accepting responsibility for the other that I can accept and use my sense of freedom. Encouraging students and teachers to recognise their autonomy in schools involves an awareness that we can only become autonomous after we recognise that we live in a community and society in which we depend on one another (Strhan, 2012, p. 91). In a similar vein, Chapter 3, Amy Shuffelton argues the need to recognise our interdependency before our autonomy, in the context of raising children.

Levinas and Derrida provide both troubling and yet promising thoughts for a consideration of curriculum knowledge and structure in the contemporary educational climate of international competition, regulatory structures and measurement of effectiveness. Derrida's challenge to the assumed security of meaning surrounding the language of standards discourses can be drawn upon in relation to proposed regimes of performance management for accountability purposes. Likewise, his suggestion of undecidability threatens the notion of undisputable truth as resident in the 'essential knowledge' of school subjects as well as punctures belief in totalising concepts that enframe and pin down that knowledge in neat and tidy schemes. Levinas' rejection of autonomy and his commitment to the ethical encounter with the other makes us think again about the dangers of curriculum as pre-defined knowledge, imposed by external interests, and prepared for speedy consumption according to a menu of 'what works', irrespective of the background and cultural disposition of the learner.

To see how the ideas discussed above 'rub alongside' an example of curriculum policy, I turn next to the document *The Importance of Teaching: The Schools White Paper* (DfE, 2010), published six months after the current Conservative/ Liberal Democrat Coalition Government came into power in Britain. Disapproval, on the part of the Government, of both the multiplying of awards[3] in a wide range of academic and vocational subjects and of the supposed ease with which students could gain high grades in these awards led the Government to introduce into the English education system a new curriculum structure through the 2010 White Paper. The language of the policy is dominated by discourses of international competition, autonomy, standards and traditional conceptions of school subject knowledge.

THE IMPORTANCE OF TEACHING: THE SCHOOLS WHITE PAPER (DfE, 2010)

The authors of the White Paper argue that the policy aims to raise the standard of the English education system in relation to its international competitors. It states in the Foreword: 'What really matters is how we're doing compared with our international competitors. That is what will define our economic growth and our country's future.

The truth is, at the moment we are standing still whilst others race past'.[4] This is accompanied by the promise of 'a tighter, more rigorous, model of the knowledge which every child should expect to master [*sic*] in core subjects at every key stage' (DfE, 2010, para. 11). The 'equality argument' underpinning the White Paper is that an externally prescribed common core curriculum will provide an entitlement for all to achieve social mobility, the Government's view of one of the main purposes of the education system, particularly for 'disadvantaged' youngsters: 'Our schools should be engines of social mobility, helping children to overcome the accidents of birth and background' and 'the soft bigotry of low expectations' (DfE, 2010, Foreword).[5] How such a social mobility-for-all movement can succeed within a competitive education system based on the selection of 'winners' through a prescribed and regulated curriculum and assessment regime poses fresh questions about the theme of justice in the Schools White Paper.

The new model of knowledge formulated in The Schools White Paper for the General Certificate in Secondary Education examinations (GCSE[6]) is located within a challenging curriculum framework in which grade boundaries are raised, end-of-module examinations are replaced with end-of-course examinations and opportunities to re-sit examinations through the course of the programme of study are removed. These measures are introduced to counter 'qualification inflation'. Two recent additions have been made to the policy reform. The first is the shift from lettered to numerical grades. Instead of eight grades, A*–G, where A* is the highest, the new system of grading institutes ten grades, where 9 is the highest, 1 is the lowest and U is unclassified.[7] The change aims to provide more differentiation between students achieving the higher and middle grades, and 'improve the spread of grades', according to the Qualifications Authority, Ofqual (2013, p. 6). Extending the number of categories in the selection process involves a supposedly more 'precise' filtering mechanism for differentiating between those who 'succeed' and those who 'fail' in the high stakes assessment system. The second new policy involves the abolition of coursework and controlled assessment[8]—both being school-based assessment methods. The new GCSEs will be 'fully linear', and externally marked end-of-course examinations will become 'the default method of assessment' (Ofqual, 2013). Restricting assessment methods to written, 'terminal', summative examinations, limits the range of practical and intellectual capabilities students are able to demonstrate.

Another arm of Coalition policy introduced via the White Paper is a high-stakes policy mechanism, the English Baccalaureate (E-Bacc).

Although neither an award nor a qualification, it contributes, in the form of a performance indicator, to the rank position of schools in the examination league table. In order to 'qualify'/'count' for an E-Bacc, a student must gain five or more GCSE passes at top grades A*–C in a restricted number of traditional subjects, namely, English language, mathematics, science, a foreign language and either history or geography (computer studies was added to the list later). The E-Bacc imposes a status hierarchy on the school curriculum by privileging six subjects, excluding Art, Design and Technology, Drama, Food Science, Music, Religious Education and Sports Studies which offer approaches to knowledge that are different from that of the traditional academic subjects comprising the E-Bacc.[9] Given its key role as a performance indicator, early research findings (Hobbs, 2013) indicate that, in response to the E-Bacc policy, schools are adapting their curriculum frameworks by influencing students' and parents' choice of GCSE subjects on the basis of perceived intellectual 'ability' to score a high grade in order to boost the school's attainment league table position. Students who are predicted to achieve below a C grade in a subject, yet enjoy learning the subject, will be dissuaded from studying it, because of the future impact on the schools' aggregated E-Bacc scores, and hence on school performance. The opposite is also true in that students who may wish to study a non-E-Bacc subject but who are considered capable of gaining a grade C or higher in an E-Bacc subject will be 'encouraged' to 'opt for' the latter instead of studying the subjects they might enjoy and excel at. Under the E-Bacc, performance in league tables, unsurprisingly, becomes the basis for subject choice in schools.

With respect to relations between the curriculum and learners, the reforms herald an extension of levels of state control over student experience of curriculum and introduce an increasingly fine-grained stratification and grading of students on the basis of externally pre-scribed and administered assessment criteria. Measuring educational experience is re-cast through a narrow focus on academic attainment within a system determined to differentiate, select and reward some students over others (Gillies, 2008). Opportunities for students to achieve high grades, especially amongst those with limited access to cultural and material resources, will decrease. The new relation between the curriculum and teachers serves to de-professionalise the latter by taking away teachers' rights to plan and teach coursework and to evaluate, critically, their students' responses to their teaching. Tight specification and, it is argued, improved objectivity of rules and criteria in the curriculum framework will challenge the ability of teachers to recognise and take responsibility for the needs of the culturally, economically and linguistically heterogeneous populations of students in their classrooms.

The final curriculum reform to be considered here is that of curriculum knowledge. The move away from a skills or competency-based curriculum was driven by the Coalition Government's call for the reinstatement of 'real knowledge'. 'Real knowledge' in the Government's eyes consists of traditional neo-conservative knowledge which is re-packaged and re-branded as the knowledge of the liberal education movement. Gove takes the descriptors of liberal education knowledge and applies them repeatedly to traditional neo-conservative knowledge, saying, for example that core knowledge is 'one of the central hallmarks of a civilised society' and 'a chance to be introduced to the best that has been thought and written' (Gove, 2009, p. 3). In Gove's words, it encapsulates 'a shared appreciation of cultural reference points, a common stock of knowledge on which we can all draw, and trade' (ibid., p. 4). It 'must embody their [students'] cultural and scientific inheritance, the best that our past and present generations have to pass on to the next' (DfE, 2010, para. 4.7).

The 'real knowledge' promoted by the 2010 White Paper bears more affinities to the 'core knowledge', of the neoconservative educational foundation[10] in the USA led by E. D. Hirsch than to the knowledge of liberal education espoused by Richard Peters and Paul Hirst of the London School of the 1960s and 70s. Hirsch's 'core knowledge sequence', comprises 'What every American needs to know' in the form of a 'coherent, cumulative, and content specific grade-by-grade curriculum' (Hirsch, *et al.*, 2002). The White Paper (DfE, 2010) states that 'All children should acquire' (para. 4.1) or 'be expected to master' [*sic*] (para. 4.6) core knowledge, and that teachers should know 'how to convey knowledge effectively and how to unlock understanding' (para. 4.8). In the White Paper core knowledge is predetermined knowledge, stable and unproblematic, something to be 'retained' and 'applied' by students. It is claimed to be important for accountability, as it represents 'a body of knowledge against which achievement can be measured' (para. 4.2). The new curriculum will 'act as a new benchmark for all schools'. Parents will be able to use this 'slim, clear and authoritative' curriculum 'to see what their child might be expected to know at every stage in their school career' (para. 4.12). Parents will be able 'to hold all schools to account for how effectively their child has grasped the essentials of, for example, English language and literature, core mathematical processes and science' (DfE, 2010, para. 4.12).

It would be foolish to argue that an education system should not be 'rigorous' or accountable. But an examination of the underpinning totalising principles and concepts on which the curriculum knowledge of such a system is built provides clues about the (im)possibility of that system opening a space for justice, for the ethical relation to the other. Intensification of high stakes assessment regimes, teachers making subject choices for students and prescribed cultural restorationist knowledge close down opportunities for the arrival of the other and for the expression of ethical responsibility necessary to address the attainment gap. Totalisation of knowledge, according to a predetermined scheme for the transmission of particular cultural values is at work through the 'core knowledge' concept, but totalisation of the teaching and learning processes in the form of transmission of knowledge within the banking system (Freire, 1972) is evident too, as the teacher is assumed to 'pass on' and 'convey' core knowledge which the learner 'acquires', 'masters' [sic] and 'applies'. Driven by the 'race to the top' in the global market, the 2010 White Paper policy reform is dominated by increased curriculum prescription, regulation and technicisation which not only make ethical questions about the sensitivity to students' subjectivities, to the demand of the student as the other, redundant, but obstructs the teacher from fulfilling her or his ethical responsibility to the student, instituting and reinforcing, to my mind, a cycle of violence[11] and injustice.

    In the next section, I turn towards a re-invention or re-imagination of curriculum as/through relations. This turn is made in response to Walter Humes' and Tom Bryce's (2003) claim that post structuralists 'fail to move beyond deconstruction' in order to offer practical solutions to serious education policy problems. Humes and Bryce describe this failure as 'a kind of intellectual dereliction' (p. 186). In an attempt to avoid this accusation, or show that it is a wrong assumption in the first place, because it is based on a misunderstanding of the potential inventiveness and ethical commitment of certain forms of poststructuralism, I argue that Derridean and Levinasian thinking can inform the official curriculum by disrupting its taken-for-granted totalising concepts and by making an unconditional demand for the responsibility to the other. How this might be worked towards is explained below.

REIMAGINING CURRICULUM (AS/THROUGH RELATION)

To 'apply' Derrida's and Levinas' thinking to curriculum in the form of a neat and clear programme of instruction for teachers or policymakers would be to subscribe to the very totalising and instrumental tendencies to which they object. But, as Strhan (2012) argues, the thinking of these two philosophers does disturb—profoundly—

existing curriculum orthodoxies and makes us think about the impossible: how things might be different if we attend more to the potentialities and imperatives for justice in curriculum knowledge configuration and structure. The works of Sharon Todd and Paul Standish are helpful in indicating two directions this might take. The former is interested in the role of curriculum within pedagogical relations (Todd, 2001, 2009) and the latter in the role of curriculum knowledge as ways in which the relation to the other might be realised (Standish, 2004, 2008). Like other authors in this book (Greenhalgh-Spencer, Todd and Hoveid and Finne), Todd and Standish argue for the cultivation of practices and knowledge that are open, plural and diverse at the same time as valuing the unique and singular.

Todd reminds us that we cannot consider curriculum knowledge and its framework outside the pedagogical relationship: 'Curriculum . . . is neither just a cultural or political instrument divorced from the concrete practices of teaching, nor a solipsistic rendering of personal or autobiographical knowledge' (Todd, 2001, p. 446). Arguing that curriculum plays a role in pedagogical relations between the subject and the 'other', she reminds us that within this is an ethical relation bearing the unlimited responsibility of the 'I' to respond to the needs of the other in such a way **that secures her right to be other**. This is an obligation that cannot be ignored. Within relations, 'curriculum lends substance to the process of "learning to become": it is the symbolic raw material that students use, discard or rewrite in making meaning for themselves. Curriculum is, thus, fundamental to the symbolic elaboration necessary to ego-making' (Todd, 2001, p. 446). In a curriculum framework made up of a pre-determined, fixed configuration of knowledge, imperatives of grade comparisons in a culture of competition and the stratification of students into 'high', 'middle' and 'low' attainment categories, relations between the teacher and the learner will be reduced to those that are less than ethical on Levinas' understanding. The knowledge component of the curriculum, 'delivered' by the teacher under pressures of accountability, may be oppressive and inappropriate to the other who is the student, because it shows no respect for her otherness, her alterity. Students respond to curriculum in unpredictable ways, but when knowledge is prescribed, closed down and imposed on students, it effects a violence in denying their otherness. The Schools White Paper does our students an injustice by assuming it can institute meaning in advance through curriculum objectives, assessment criteria and regimes and impose a fixed and totalised curriculum knowledge within pedagogical relations.

The second direction of thought is interested in how curriculum knowledge might *constitute* the relation to the other. Standish argues that curriculum is a matter of language, and the relation to the other occurs through language. Through language the curriculum becomes one way the relation to the other can be realised. Totalising forms of curriculum knowledge, such as core knowledge, assume and emphasise the goal of students acquiring comprehensive knowledge and gaining 'mastery' over that knowledge. Instead, Standish suggests that an ethical relation with the language of the curriculum (knowledge) allows the teacher and student to develop deconstructive attitudes towards knowledge and to go beyond curriculum specifications and objectives. Cracking open the totalising effects of language reveals other knowledge, other ways of knowing that cannot be predicted, and that fascinate, puzzle and excite the learner (Standish, 2008, p. 64). The teacher is not an operator who teaches disciplinary and technical 'tricks' to drill students to gain high scores in examinations, but is instead a sensitive and engaged guide towards knowledge that is intrinsically rich and bears potential to extend student thinking along unexpected and inventive paths. Given the momentary nature of our ethical engagement in teaching and learning, the teacher attends to the students' needs, exercising an ethical care that exceeds the demands of the technical aspects of the curriculum. The teacher understands, too, that the knowledge bound up in disciplinary subjects is not a closed shop—an 'other' knowledge demands a sensitivity to different points of view, opportunities to move beyond the boundaries of the subject, to attend to intuition, creative imagination and 'lateral as well as linear thinking' (Strhan, 2012, p. 136). The teacher acknowledges that school subjects should never take for granted their existence, but should forever self-interrogate, adopt a questioning role towards their own other of knowledge, 'pursue little sideroads, or venture into unmarked areas—open knowledge up, find a way to read "otherwise" ' (Caputo, 1997, p. 76). This does not lead to a rejection of the knowledge of the classic disciplines, but disrupts their taken-for granted authority and allows an investigation about what they omit, how, why and what alternative knowledge might be.

However, there is never enough time or resources for teachers to attend to the needs of their students. And, of course, teachers have serious responsibilities to their students, parents and communities. They are employed by the state, so it is difficult for them to protest against those totalising curriculum policies and practices with which they are compelled to comply in schools. According to Strhan, they are not de-politicised or re-politicised in their role, 'but are rather always and already political and ethical subjects' (2012, p. 181) because they make political and ethical decisions about how they respond to the *aporia* of concrete situations of injustice in their daily

interactions with students and colleagues. Awareness amongst teachers of their political and ethical responsibilities and discussion of the
dilemmas they face, with students and colleagues in schools, in
subject association fora, the media, HEIs and wider society, give rise
to spaces in which these issues can surface, gain prominence and
encourage the generation of inventive responses to the needs of the
other. Thinking about curriculum as/through relations, alongside
Derrida and Levinas, provides a disturbing and liberating dimension
to this awareness and discussion. It goes beyond curriculum, beyond
teaching and learning as acts of coercion and compliance, to the
promotion of a non-violent means of realisation of being in the world.
It jettisons the idea of language as representation in order to open up
language to fresh ways of understanding the world. It offers partici-
pation by students, teachers and community in emergent networks of
responsible relations to explore curriculum knowledge through human
interactions and communications which are recognised as always and
already steeped in ethics and politics.

The Schools White Paper promotes the idea that a tightly controlled
curriculum structure and pre-determined official knowledge for the
school curriculum serve as an entitlement leading to increased educational equality for all students. I argue a different case. First, that a
tightly regulated and controlled curriculum structure which seeks to
increase distinctions between successful and unsuccessful students
and schools on the basis of comparison, differentiation and individu-
alisation, leading to increased labelling, will decrease educational
equality and influence student subjectivities in ways that are socially
and educationally divisive and unjust. Second, the imposition of core
knowledge is unjust in the sense that it does not respect the life-worlds
and perspectives of the other since it is externally imposed, culturally
fixed and tightly defined, obstructing access to and engagement with
that knowledge for certain social groups. Third, the external prescription and definition of curriculum knowledge as unproblematical and
fixed exerts a sclerotic effect on meaning, denying access to rich,
exciting and ethically just ways of thinking for all students.

Curriculum as/through relations draws attention to the links
between language, discourse, subjectivity and curriculum, and how
taken-for-granted discourses of performativity, autonomy, accountability and core knowledge can settle, rest and remain undisturbed in
the individual, national and international psyche until they are tracked
down and we are compelled to think otherwise. Thinking otherwise,
beyond the self, provides an interruption from outside the discourse,
from heteronomy, where an opportunity to see curriculum as other
opens up—curriculum as inventive, bold, strange, demanding and

enriching. Opening up our eyes to a curriculum otherwise, engaging with and attending to curriculum through the ethical relation to the other seems to offer a possibility for an ethically just future.

NOTES

1. A student from a 'more socio-economically advantaged' background 'outperforms' a student from an 'average background' by the equivalent of a year's education in reading (OECD, 2010, p. 14). In English maintained schools in 2003 a 32% difference existed between students from 'professional' and 'other/not classified' backgrounds gaining 5+ GCSE grades A*-C (DfE, 2006, p. 42).
2. Other examples of differentiated curriculum knowledge bases existed in England during the 1990s and early 2000, when, despite the existence of a National Curriculum, New Labour allowed schools to choose to teach either the discrete subjects of Geography, History and Religious Education, or a competency/skill-based curriculum like Opening Minds (Bayliss/RSA, 1999).
3. Awards are the qualifications students obtain by taking external examinations organised by institutions referred to as 'awarding bodies'. These institutions were called 'examination boards' in England in the past.
4. The Expert Panel Report (DfE, 2011) highlights the countries which are 'racing ahead' as China, Hong Kong SAR, Singapore, South Korea and Taiwan: 'the assumption here is that deep engagement with subject matter, including through memorisation where appropriate, leads to deeper understanding' (sec. 8.6).
5. Academies, free schools and independent schools are not required, legally, to follow the National Curriculum. They are charged, instead, with providing a broad and balanced curriculum.
6. GCSE is a 2-year programme of study usually taken by students aged 14–16. Examinations are now only available at the end of the 2-year programme.
7. It will be impossible to compare the new grades with the current A*–G grades.
8. Controlled assessments 'take place under supervised conditions and are either set by awarding organisations and marked by teachers, or set by teachers and marked by awarding organisations' (Ofqual, 2010). Course work does not require supervised conditions.
9. Change to the E-Bacc policy was introduced in October, 2013, when the number of subjects qualifying for the E-Bacc was raised from 5 to 8.
10. E. D. Hirsch's Core Knowledge Foundation is a traditional conservative education movement, not one founded on the liberal education tradition.
11. 'Violence'. The word derives from the work of Paulo Freire, where he writes oppression that negates humanity entailing violence which is not necessarily of a physical kind (Freire, 1972).

REFERENCES

Apple, M. W. (1996) *Cultural Politics and Education* (Maidenhead, Open University Press).
Bayliss, V. / RSA (1999) *Education for the 21st Century*. Online at: http://www.thersa.org/__data/assets/pdf_file/0005/2885/opening-minds-education-for-the-21st-century.pdf
Brighouse, H. and Swift, A. (2008) Putting Educational Equality in its Place, *Educational Finance and Policy*, 3.4, pp. 444–466.

Bronfenbrenner, M. (1973) Equality and Equity, *Annals of the American Academy of Political and Social Science*, 409, pp. 9–23.

Calvert, J. (2013) Educational Equality: Luck Egalitarian, Pluralist and Complex. Paper presented at the PESGB annual conference, New College Oxford, 22–24 March.

Caputo, J. (1997) (ed.) *Deconstruction in a Nutshell* (New York, Fordham University Press).

Cassen, R. and Kingdon, G. (2007) *Tackling Low Educational Achievement* (York, Joseph Rowntree Foundation).

Chalier, C. (1995) The Philosophy of Emmanuel Levinas and the Hebraic Tradition, in: A. T. Peperzak (ed.) *Ethics as First Philosophy* (London: Routledge).

Clarke, M. (in press) The Sublime Objects of Education Policy: Quality, Equity and Ideology, *Discourse: Studies in the Cultural Politics of Education*. Available online at: http://www.tandfonline.com/loi/cdis20

Collins, C. and Yates, L. (2011) Confronting Equity, Retention and Student Diversity, in: L. Yates, C. Collins and K. O'Connor (eds) *Australia's Curriculum Dilemmas: State Cultures and the Big Issues* (Melbourne, Melbourne University Press).

Demack, S., Drew, D. and Grimsley, M. (2000) Minding the Gap: Ethnic, Gender and Social Class Differences in Attainment at 16, 1988–1995, *Race, Ethnicity and Education*, 3.2, pp. 117–143.

Department for Education [DfE] (2006) *Statistics of Education: Trends in Attainment Gaps 2005* (Norwich, HMSO).

Department for Education [DfE] (2010) *The Importance of Teaching: The Schools White Paper* (London, The Stationery Office Ltd.).

Department for Education [DfE] (2011) *The Framework for the National Curriculum: A Report by the Expert Panel for the National Curriculum Review* (London, DfE.). Online at: https://www.gov.uk/government/uploads/system/uploads/attachment_data/file/175439/NCR-Expert_Panel_Report.pdf

Derrida, J. (1982) Différance, A. Bass, trans., in his: *Margins of Philosophy* (Chicago, IL, Chicago University Press), pp. 1–27.

Derrida, J. (1992) Force of Law: The 'Mystical Foundation of Authority', in: D. Cornell, M. Rosenfeld and D. G. Carlson (eds.) *Deconstruction and the Possibility of Justice* (London, Routledge).

Derrida, J. (1993) *Aporias*, T. Dutoit, trans. (Stanford, CA, Stanford University Press).

Derrida, J. (1997) The Villa Nova Roundtable: A Conversation with Jacques Derrida, in: J. Caputo (ed.) *Deconstruction in a Nutshell* (New York, Fordham University Press).

Espinoza, O. (2007) Solving the Equity-Equality Conceptual Dilemma: A New Module for Analysis of the Educational Process, *Educational Research*, 49.4, pp. 343–363.

Freire, P. (1972) *Pedagogy of the Oppressed* (Harmondsworth, Penguin).

Gillborn, D. and Kirton, A. (2000) White Heat: Racism, Underachievement and White Working Class Boys, *Journal of Inclusive Education*, 4.4, pp. 271–288.

Gillborn, D. and Mirza, H. S. (2000) *Educational Inequality: Mapping Race, Class and Gender* (London, OFSTED). [Office for Standards in Education.]

Gillies, D. (2008) Educational Potential, Underachievement and Cultural Pluralism, *Education in the North*, 16, pp. 23–32.

Gove, M. (2009) A Comprehensive Programme For State Education. Speech to the Centre for Policy Studies, 6 November. Online at: http://www.thersa.org/__data/assets/pdf_file/0009/213021/Gove-speech-to-RSA.pdf Accessed 3 September 2013.

Hirsch, D. (2007) *Chicken and Egg: Child Poverty and Educational Inequalities* (London, Child Poverty Action Group).

Hirsch, E. D., Kett, J. F. and Trefil, J. (2002) *The New Dictionary of Cultural Literacy: What Every American Needs to Know* (New York, Houghton Mifflin).

Hobbs, K. (2013) The Constitution and Implementation of the English Baccalaureate: Implications for Educational Equality. Student presentation to EdD programme, University of Sheffield School of Education, 19 October.

Humes, W. and Bryce, T. (2003) Post-structuralism and Policy Research in Education, *Journal of Education Policy*, 18.2, pp. 175–187.

Jencks, C. (1988) Whom Must We Treat Equally for Educational Opportunity to be Equal?, *Ethics*, 98.3, pp. 518–533.

Levinas, E. (1996) Meaning and Sense, in: A. T Peperzak, S. Critchley and R. Bernasconi (eds) *Emmanuel Levinas: Basic Philosophical Writings* (Bloomington, IN: Indiana University Press), pp. 33–64.

Levinas, E. (1998) Philosophy and the Idea of Infinity, A. Lingis, trans, in his: Collected Philosophical Papers. (Pittsburgh, PA, Duquesne University Press).

Lingard, R. (2011) Policy as Numbers: Accounting for Educational Research, *Australian Educational Researcher*, 38, pp. 355–382.

Nash, R. (2004) Equality of Educational Opportunity: In Defence of a Traditional Concept, *Educational Philosophy and Theory*, 36.4, pp. 361–377.

National Equality Panel (2010) *An Anatomy of Economic Inequality in the UK* (London, Centre for the Analysis of Social Exclusion, London School of Economics and Political Science).

OECD (2010) *PISA 2009 Results: Overcoming Social Background* (Paris, OECD).

Ofqual (2010) GCSE Controlled Assessments. Online at: http://webarchive.nationalarchives .gov.uk/+/http://www.ofqual.gov.uk/qualifications-assessments/89-articles/21-gcse-controlled-assessments. Accessed 28 January 2014.

Ofqual (2013) *Reforms to GCSEs in England from 2015*. November (Coventry, Office of Qualifications and Examinations Regulations).

Raffe, D., Croxford, L., Iannelli, C., Shapira, M. and Howieson, C. (2006) *Social Class Inequalities in Education in England and Scotland* (Edinburgh, Centre for Educational Sociology, University of Edinburgh).

Reay, D. (2006) The Zombie Stalking English Schools: Social Class and Educational Inequality, *British Journal of Educational Studies*, 54.3, pp. 288–307.

Reay, D. (2012) What Would A Socially Just Education System Look Like?: Saving the Minnows From the Pike, *Journal of Education Policy*, 27.5, pp. 587–599.

Rizvi, F. and Lingard, R. (2010) *Globalizing Education Policy* (London, Routledge).

Schools Council/Nuffield Foundation (1970) *The Humanities Project: An Introduction* (London, Heinemann).

Schouten, G. (2012) Fair Educational Opportunity and the Distribution of Natural Ability: Toward to Prioritarian Principle of Educational Justice, *Journal of Philosophy of Education*, 46.3, pp. 472–491.

Standish, P. (2004) Europe, Continental Philosophy and the Philosophy of Education, *Comparative Education*, 40.4, pp. 485–501.

Standish, P. (2008) Levinas and the Language of the Curriculum, in: D. Egea-Kuenhe (ed.) *Levinas and Education: At the Intersection of Faith And Reason* (London, Routledge), pp. 56–66.

Stenhouse, L. (1980) Reflections, in: L. Stenhouse (ed.) *Curriculum Research and Development in Action* (London, Heinemann).

Strand, S. (2008) *Minority Ethnic Pupils in the Longitudinal Study of Young People in England*. Extension Report on Performance in Public Examinations at age 16 (Warwick, University of Warwick).

Strhan, A. (2012) *Levinas, Subjectivity and Education: Towards an Ethics of Radical Responsibility* (London, Wiley Blackwell).

Sveinsson, K. P. (2009) *Who Cares About the Working Class?* Runnymede Perspectives (London, Runnymede Trust).

Todd, S. (2001) 'Bringing More Than I Contain': Ethics, Curriculum and the Pedagogical Demand For Altered Egos, *Journal of Curriculum Studies*, 33.4, pp. 431–450.

Todd, S. (2009) *Toward an Imperfect Education: Facing Humanity, Rethinking Cosmopolitanism* (Boulder, CO, Paradigm).

Whitty, G. (2010) Revisiting School Knowledge: Some Sociological Perspectives on New School Curricula, *European Journal of Education*, 45.1, pp. 28–45.

Yates, L. (2013) Revisiting Curriculum, the Numbers Game and the Inequality Problem, *Journal of Curriculum Studies*, 45.1, pp. 39–51.

Young, M. D. F. (1971) *Knowledge and Control: New Directions for the Sociology of Education* (London, Collier-Macmillan).

Young, M. D. F. (2013) Overcoming the Crisis in Curriculum Theory: A Knowledge-Based Approach, *Journal of Curriculum Studies*, 45.2, pp. 101–118.

8
Re-Thinking Relations in Human Rights Education: The Politics of Narratives

REBECCA ADAMI

INTRODUCTION: TENSIONS IN HUMAN RIGHTS EDUCATION

The demography in Europe is changing and many classrooms are becoming increasingly heterogeneous as to learners' cultural, ethnic, religious, ideological and gendered backgrounds. At the same time, as Panigrahi observes, '. . . schools are sometimes affected by deep-seated national stereotypes of others, overly nationalistic sentiments and views of history, and contemporary ethnic, religious and political tensions' (2007, p. 134). This poses a tension, particularly given the plans to introduce Human Rights Education (HRE) as part of national curricula when there is lack of critical analysis of the possible effects of such plans (see Peters, 2013).

Learners with particular beliefs may feel estranged by the portraying of some values, cultures and religious faiths as threats to the 'universalisation' of human rights in HRE, especially when so called 'defenders' of human rights are set up as a pre-defined category of a homogenous 'us' restricted to certain kinds of national, ethnic, cultural, religious or socio-economic belongings. Examples of this estrangement of groups of people include the debate on so-called 'Asian values', addressed and problematized by Anthony Langlois (2001) and the presumed clash between so-called 'Islamic values' and human rights, critically analysed by Michael Ignatieff (2003) and Elizabeth Bucar and Barbra Barnett (2005).

Additionally, when human rights' violations are repeatedly placed in non-Western societies, their urgency seems restricted to certain parts of the world, hence limiting the discourse that claims universality of such rights. Ignatieff (2003) calls into question human rights when used as 'a political trump card' against a collective notion of

Re-Imagining Relationships in Education: Ethics, Politics and Practices, First Edition. Edited by Morwenna Griffiths, Marit Honerød Hoveid, Sharon Todd and Christine Winter. Chapters © 2015 The Authors. Editorial organization © 2015 Philosophy of Education Society of Great Britain. Published 2015 by John Wiley & Sons Ltd.

'otherness'. Brooke Ackerly (2008) explores the universality of human rights in her book, *Universal Human Rights in a World of Difference*:

> There has been significant debate about the question of human rights and Confucianism and of human rights and Islam. There are disagreements within those traditions themselves about whether rights can be understood within the tradition, if some transformation of the tradition is necessary to recognize them, and if so, how to transform the tradition in order to accommodate human rights (2008, p. 109).

Ackerly raises here the ongoing negotiations in different traditions that are under constant transformation, read through notions of justice, equality and human rights. The moral clashes between human rights and religious value systems risk being simplified for several reasons: first, because culture, religion or human rights do not exist independently of human beings and human relations; and second, speaking of human rights as 'a framework' or 'a secular religion' underestimates the billions of human beings in the world who act and speak of human rights in a multitude of ways. As a Christian, for example, one might acknowledge the multitude of interpretations and traditions that exist *within* Christianity by virtue of relations one has with unique individuals who, no matter how different in their outlook on the world, confess themselves to the same faith. This relational complexity and access to counter-narratives[1] within cultures, religions and traditions challenge any educator in the field of human rights.

There seems to be a general understanding that human rights are born in Western culture. For this reason, critical discussions by Western scholars on the compatibility between human rights and traditions within Christianity and Catholicism have been marginal. Jack Donnelly (2003), amongst others, claims that human rights are inherently Western, but that they do not necessarily violate the values of non-Western societies and traditions. The dominant narrative of the origin of human rights is reified through the work of Jack Donnelly (2003), Ronald Dworkin (1977) and Patrick Hayden (2001). The urgency of human rights loses its potential for political imaginary if presented as a *fait accompli* and conflated with a certain (Western) outlook on the world. How do we face dominant narratives in relation to human rights without estranging persons who might feel uncomfortable in being labelled as 'the other' in relation to a seemingly 'universal' subject?

In order to explore narrativity as political action in human rights education and the relevance of uniqueness and plurality in this endeavour, the chapter first makes a shift from particularity as a collective identity of the other (for example, as found in narrative literature of 'Afro-American studies' or 'women's studies', as proposed by Martha Nussbaum (1998)) towards the need for plurality in any conception of rights in cosmopolitan thinking, as argued by Sharon Todd (2010). The aim is to gain a notion of human rights learning that moves away from identity politics, from *what* we are, and instead engages with unique relations in plural classrooms, where *who* one is is addressed through the notion of life narratives (see Adriana Cavarero, 2000).

The chapter then turns to Hannah Arendt and her positing of the dangers of not taking responsibility as educators to introduce students to a world which they are to transform, while at the same time keeping an openness towards students' unique narratives. In emphasising that the notion of human rights is based upon a plurality of narratives I draw on the notion of counter-narratives proposed by Michael Peters and Colin Lankshear (1996).

A RELATIONAL APPROACH IN HUMAN RIGHTS EDUCATION

There are many ways to think about relations in education.[2] In my chapter, I place narrativity and the sharing of narratives at the centre of relations in HRE. Indeed, I view such relationality as being achieved through narrativity, in an ontological view of narrativity that Adriana Cavarero has developed further and which she draws from the work of Hannah Arendt.

That narrativity can be seen as political action is implied in Arendt's understanding of political life and subjectivity; life is lived in community with others who are different, and our human condition is this plurality.[3] We cannot decide who we are and then, by will, disclose ourselves in relation to others. Rather the narratives through which we get a glimpse of ourselves are fleeting and dynamic, and are relational creations. Our narrative birth is through the political act of narration where others 'receive and interpret the acts of each new arrival by addressing, implicitly, to him the question: "*who* are you?" ' (Kristeva, 2001, p. 58). Accordingly, narrating human rights in relation to life stories is not concerned with 'learning *about* the other' (see Nussbaum, 1998); neither is it concerned with 'learning *from* the other' (see Todd, 2003) but rather 'learning *in* relations' through narratives.

The narrative approach to HRE presented in this chapter provides a move away from questions of *what* we are, as posed in relation to non-discrimination in HRE, to focus more on questions of *who* we are and how human rights can be articulated through our lived experience. By contrast, a major field in HRE[4] focuses on overcoming exclusion in human relations, as raised through the question 'what are you?' in order to be able to respond: 'you are equal in rights and dignity, even though you might be a woman, gay, transsexual, a child, from a minority, etc.' A majority of HRE scholars[5] has, due to the non-discriminatory 'nature' of the subject of human rights, treated HRE as politically neutral and/or intrinsically good, and thus paid little, or no, attention to the harmful asymmetry of its pedagogical relations and the potentially dis-empowering effects embedded in the discourse. I argue that relations in HRE may actually increase feelings of exclusion and marginalisation in the making of otherness (even though the intentions are to reach inclusion and feelings of dignity). Narrating human rights as experiences of violence can lead to increased suffering of learners in recalling injustice that may lay bare the discrepancy between the fixed and 'neutral' wording of HR texts and the social reality of injustice and inequality.

In my critique against a view of HRE as politically neutral I use Arendt's notion of narration as political action due to the relational view of politics she presents (2005). According to Arendt, an action, or narration, cannot be seen in isolation or be judged through the intentions of the initiator, since actions receive their political significance in how they are received by others. Human rights educators cannot, therefore, hide behind 'good intentions'. This is further exemplified in the dominant historical narrative of human rights that is being reified in HRE, when human rights scholars connect the notion of human rights to the Enlightenment and to Western culture. HRE then risks becoming problematic if it is to *enlighten* people in other parts of the world. The danger in treating human rights as a secular religion has been criticised by Miia Halme (2008), who observes the colonial and imperialistic tendency of so-called 'human rights experts' in the Scandinavian Network of Human Rights Experts (SCANET) as being generally white and Western, whereas learners are targeted as coming from Southern parts of the world. Equally important here is the work of Marie-Bénédict Dembour (2006), who offers a Marxist, feminist and cultural-relativistic reading of the Universal Declaration of Human Rights (UDHR) in raising awareness of the danger in an uncritical 'belief in human rights' (2006, p. 20). For this re-thinking of relations in learning human rights, the chapter argues that HRE needs to address both competing historical narratives on the drafting of the Universal Declaration on Human Rights (UDHR) as well as unique life narratives of learners.

THE UNIVERSAL DECLARATION OF HUMAN RIGHTS FROM 1948: BASED ON DIFFERENT HISTORICAL NARRATIVES

To educate about human rights is to educate about selected parts of its history, which calls into question which competing narratives from the past are to be selected. The drafting process of the Universal Declaration of Human Rights (UDHR) in 1946–48 involved people with different religious and cultural backgrounds and may tell us something about the challenge and complexity of human rights learning today. The post-war period was a time when faith in human reason and development had been shattered through the acknowledgement of the horrors of the Holocaust. During the process of finding hope and asserting a human dignity that had been devastated through human cruelty, the delegates to the United Nations Human Rights Commission (who had been appointed the task of writing a first draft of the UDHR that would later be negotiated and amended through different UN bodies) asked UNESCO to set up a Committee to discuss whether there was any universal legitimacy of human rights in different philosophical and ideological strands of thought (cf. Adami, 2012).

The UNESCO Committee on the Philosophical Foundation for the Rights of Man [*sic*] collected written contributions from different parts of the world that would be discussed and later published in a report to the UN Commission on Human Rights, called *Human Rights: Comments and Interpretations*. In this report, which is available through the UNESCO archives in Paris, we find texts on the historical origins of the notion of human rights in Islam, Hinduism, Confucianism, Communism and many more. Mahatma Gandhi was one of the contributors. What is noteworthy is that the list of human rights in the UNESCO report was almost identical to the list of rights that the UN Drafting Committee presented to the UN Commission on Human Rights, which served as the first draft of the thirty articles in the UDHR (cf. Adami, 2012).

The problem that seemed initially to lie in the foreground, both in formulating human rights in 1948 and in human rights education today, is the supposed polarity between 'universal' and 'particular' values. Yet, after the extensive political sessions and philosophical discussions in 1946–48 between individuals from different parts of the world, the polemic shifted and was identified instead as existing between different particular value systems themselves, and not between universal practical principles of human rights and diverse cultural, religious, or ideological traditions (cf. Adami and Schumann, 2013).

If the aim of human rights learning is not about the reaching of consensus on a universal, philosophical and ideological foundation, then how are learners and educators supposed to keep an openness to conflicting and sometimes antagonistic narratives on human rights? In order to explore the possibility of students creating something new in HRE, I turn to the concept of 'counternarratives', developed by Peters and Lankshear (1996) to illustrate the possibilities for critique and for the creation of narratives that challenge dominant narratives of human rights in education. Counternarratives enable learners to relate experiences in their lives to cultural narratives that are not static, but under constant negotiation and change, hence increasing the space for negotiation and for creating something new in HRE. In this sense, counternarratives serve to turn human rights into something more than abstract words, into something that is actually urgent and meaningful for a unique 'who' in particular contexts, to use Arendtian terminology.

HUMAN RIGHTS LEARNING IN A WIDER UNIVERSAL CONTEXT

Previous research in educational philosophy on cosmopolitanism has widely discussed the relationship and presumed dichotomy between universality and particularity in relation to human rights and learning (see Hansen, 2008; Rizvi, 2008; Todd, 2007, 2010). When human rights are seen as a Western project based on a set of particular narratives, such as in connection to secularism, liberalism and western humanism, as has been problematised further by Donnelly (2003), Hayden (2001), and Tesón (1985), then other ways of reading human rights risk being silenced in HRE. This relation between locality and universality, and the conflict between dominant and marginalised interpretations of human rights, has been discussed specifically in earlier research on cosmopolitanism and education. I will briefly mention two strands of thought that reflect these concerns: *liberal cosmopolitanism*, represented in the work of Martha Nussbaum[6] (1998) and *critical cosmopolitanism*, a critical-ethical position within cosmopolitanism, represented in the work of Sharon Todd (2010).

Nussbaum (1998) advocates a liberal education where learners are expected to 'understand the world and the other' through what Nussbaum calls 'narrative imagination' (1998). This imagination aimed at empathy is described by Nussbaum as 'the ability to think what it might be like to be in the shoes of a person different from oneself' and upon this make acts of judgement (1998). The liberal education that Nussbaum is proposing for cosmopolitan awareness consists of studies of 'non-western cultures', of 'women's studies' and of 'Afro-American studies' (1998). The need to learn about the unknown and different other is seen as a way to overcome fear and lack of compassion towards people of 'other' religions, cultures and gender. Although I feel sympathetic with the view for raising the need for literature studies in humanities in order to develop 'narrative imaginary', I depart from Nussbaum's urge to learn about a collective other as a way of achieving a sense of global citizenship through emotions such as empathy. Such emphasis on the importance of cultural and gendered collective traits of identity risks reifying generalised and exotifying characteristics of people, and loses the focus on the unique and concrete other, whom, I argue, one cannot grasp through the reading of literature, or through narrative imagination, but only through the intimate space of sharing unique life narratives, urgent for *you* and *me* here and now.

Nussbaum's appeal to narrative in the form of literature is due to her belief that 'narratives are more able to impart the truths of moral philosophy than are the texts of the moralists', according to Mark Dooley (Dooley, 2007, p. 175).[7] Whereas Nussbaum wants to explicate certain moral 'truths' through the use of literature in education, Arendt's (2005, 2006) notion that it is through a multitude of world-views that we come to a certain freedom is in my view more helpful for the challenges facing HRE. For Arendt, freedom is about seeing the world in all its complexity, which is made possible by the plural conditions of the public sphere. This is not to be interpreted as a relativistic approach that claims to abandon universality altogether; rather it means that in order to reclaim the universality of human rights, the political condition of plurality and, ultimately, uniqueness need to be addressed as relational conditions of that universality. Hence narratives are relational through speaking, writing and listening, and provide unique aspects of a whole that one single person cannot grasp through reason based on autonomy. This view of narrative as relational expands Nussbaum's appeal to literature for narrative imaginary, which seems to reside in the individual's sovereign capacity to feel compassion for 'others'.

Critical cosmopolitanism, the second strand of thought to be considered here, has raised critique on similar lines as I have here—a critique that works against the defining of individuals as social categories, and stresses the complexity and plurality of a unique other. Todd (2010) draws a distinction between the terms 'cultural diversity' and 'plurality', where the latter 'requires acknowledging a unique *who* that emerges in the context of a narrative relation that not only cannot be reduced to social categorizations, but that itself is political' (Todd, 2011, p. 104). Todd seeks a 'more robust conception of plurality' where plurality is not just representing cultural belongings but is based on uniqueness (2011, p. 102). Todd's reframing of universalism is an important shift in cosmopolitan thought that raises critique against the exclusion of persons in appeals to rights that do not take into account both plurality and uniqueness.

Human rights have been criticised as proclaiming universalism at the expense of taking into account particularism and cultural diversity. One can, for instance, see Fazal Rizvi's (2008) exploration of cosmopolitan learning as being locally anchored as a response to a liberal view of human rights that can be found in Martha Nussbaum's (1998) defence of liberal education. Rizvi stresses that learning takes place in particular settings, which are relational rather than influenced by abstract values. He discusses a cultural awareness which implies the understanding of culture as essentially dynamic rather than static (2008, p. 23), as opposed to Nussbaum's view of learning 'about' the other, as belonging to a static, and 'graspable' value-laden culture.

Although Rizvi's critique in defence of particularity is valuable and important in shedding light on a generally taken for granted conflation of liberalism and human rights, it lacks a reimagining of pedagogical relations that actually welcome a plurality in classrooms. Here I find it useful to think instead of particularity as narratives in different spheres that influence the study of human rights. It is not as easy as 'reading the human rights through particular contexts' since, as Rizvi states, these are not fixed reference points, but under constant internal contestation.

The difference found in people's uniqueness allows learners to read human rights through conflicting and sometimes antagonistic cultural narratives. Beneath the seemingly relativistic argument is the narrative foundation of making human rights come alive through the life experiences people narrate in educational relations. These narrations connect the unique and unrepeatable story of someone with the universally shared notion of 'equality as justice' as asserted in the creation of human rights. This narrative turn in human rights learning, I suggest, has significant political as well as educational implications.

RELATIONS THROUGH NARRATION: REIFYING OF RENEWING THE WORLD?

And education, too, is where we decide whether we love our children enough not to expel them from our world and leave them to their own devices, nor to strike from their hands their chance of undertaking something new, something unforeseen by us, but to prepare them in advance for the task of renewing a common world (Arendt, [1954] 2006, p. 193).

In her essay 'The Crisis of Education' (in Arendt, 2006), Hannah Arendt raises her concern for the role of politics in education, where she is critical of the ways in which adults leave it to the next generation to assume responsibility for the world. According to Arendt, politics, as an arena between equals, differs from education as an authoritative institution of unequal power relations between educators and learners. Education, in Arendt's view, is the creation of a separate world for children, where they take no part in the world of their parents and where young people are left to the authority of grown ups, who in a sense become representatives for the world, and who have the responsibility to introduce the young into our common world. Arendt's concern is whether we love our children, and the world, enough to enable children to take responsibility for renewing it in the future. The task is two-fold, as I see it: to introduce the new generation into the world, and at the same time 'not to strike from their hands their chance of undertaking something new' (2006, p. 193).

Arendt is concerned with education as a public institution governed by a political nation state. She sees the vulnerability of children in education when they are exposed to the public eye, in their process of becoming (2006). Arendt warns us that an education built on political utopias, such as the realization of human rights for all, risks being presented as something which already exists (2006, p. 173). However, human rights as a political imaginary has not yet been fully defined, and it is precisely this indefinability, in my view, where the possibility for renewal of the world lies. The danger in rendering the potential of renewal in terms of an already existing political imaginary of human rights lies in the reification of human rights as being connected to a certain strand of political or ideological thought, such as when human rights are reinforced by education as being an exclusively Western, liberal project.

> Instead of joining with one's equals in assuming the effort of persuasion and running the risk of failure, there is dictatorial intervention, based upon the absolute superiority of the adult, and the attempt to produce the new as a *fait accompli*, that is, as though the new already existed (2006, p. 173).

Like Arendt, I am sceptical of our ability as educators to assume responsibility for the world, and given the focus of this chapter, for human rights in the world, if educators do not engage with the political imaginary that can arise in narrating human rights through the uniqueness of each and everyone's lived experience. This potential for political imaginary is lost at the moment that we, as educators, narrate human rights as something fixed, based on a single philosophy or ideology, and renders them into a project compatible with only certain life views and incompatible with the unforeseen element of renewal in people's uniqueness. A human rights education, as an open space where learners' unique experiences of rights are welcomed, is a relational space where human rights come alive and take on different forms and colours. If students are to assume responsibility for the world as grown-ups, in the sphere of political community, it will be through the arrival of unique beings who claim space through an equal recognition of difference.

When Nussbaum stresses the need to learn 'about the other', to include literature studies on women, minorities and other religions, the problem is not, following Arendt, that the literature is generally homogeneous and that the inclusion of other types of marginalised stories and narratives fill the educational setting with stereotypical representations. The problem addressed is rather *how* narratives are told, listened to and shared in education. We must ask ourselves if we, as educators, in our good intentions, reify relations of a plural 'us' and 'others' in pedagogical relations, or if we allow for students to bring in the new and unexpected that come with the open question of 'who are you?'

In HRE, then, there may be present dominant narratives on human rights as based on Western philosophy (whatever 'Western' may be represented as in that specific context) or we may have included non-Western philosophies and narratives on human rights. Nevertheless, the importance of the pedagogical relation, between 'you' and 'me' is based on the openness, trust and attentiveness we as educators can create together with our students, so that each and every student, in her uniqueness, may bring something new, and feel trusting enough to question and create new counternarratives that work against those which are represented in the classroom.

COUNTERNARRATIVES IN A WORLD OF PLURALISM

Man [. . .] exists—or is realized—in politics only in the equal rights that those who are most different guarantee for each other (Arendt, 2006, p. 94).

If equality is not a reality, but a political project, as Arendt intimates above, then how can human rights learning re-claim its political significance in thinking a future which is not yet? A crucial question that arises from the idea that pedagogical relations are themselves unequal while appealing to an equality in a world characterised by plurality, is whether one can hold cosmopolitical assumptions about certain universal claims of equality between people and at the same time respect the differences found in people's uniqueness. This question finds its pragmatic relevance and urgency for anyone interested in speaking of the universality of human rights while at the same time keeping an openness to the uniqueness in people's lived experiences. There is a constant dynamic here where the particular feeds into lived experiences, as a way of understanding *who* we are in relation to *how* we are perceived by others in terms of both dominant narratives and counternarratives of what it means to be a woman, gay, straight, immigrant.

According to Peters and Lankshear (1996), 'to understand contemporary times is a matter of recognising the diverse and subtle ways in which our everyday lives are impacted and interrupted by cultural and political struggles between "official" narratives and the counternarratives that emerge in contestation to them' (1996, p. 1). In 'Postmodern Counternarratives' Peters and Lankshear develop a concept for exploring the politics of education within the everyday struggles for human identities and loyalties (ibid.). They distinguish between two spheres of counternarratives: the first as directed to the past and its historical dominant narratives and the second consist in the counternarratives of cultural and political contestation in the present. My aim with using the concept of counternarratives is to extend its meaning so as to understand counternarratives as the stories that distinguish 'you' from 'me', not only 'they' from 'us'.

The first sphere of counternarratives, according to Peters and Lankshear, 'observes the existence of counternarratives which function generically as a critique of the modernist partiality for 'grand', 'master' and 'meta' narratives' (1996, p. 2). They can be seen as a critique 'of the philosophies of history accompanying the grand claims concerning Man, Truth, Justice' (ibid.) that are seen as 'representing the West, and 'America' as the last projection of European ideals' (ibid.). Following this note, the grand stories on the origin of human rights have served to legitimate the myth of enlightened Western ideals, whereas in fact there are many counternarratives within Western history of thought and outside, of what is bluntly meshed together as 'Western'. This myth of a 'Western' origin of human rights has been criticised by other scholars (see Donnelly, 2003; Ignatieff, 2003; Morsink, 1999).

The second, related dimension of 'counternarratives' that Peters and Lankshear explore is those stories 'that counter the "official" and "hegemonic" narratives of everyday life' (1996, p. 3), which uphold a sense of a common set of national, cultural and religious traditions and values in people's lives. It is these legitimising stories that disrupt and impact on people's sense of self, influencing in different ways their processes of becoming. These counternarratives in our daily lives are what Peters and Lankshear refer to as the stories of 'those individuals and groups whose knowledge and histories have been marginalized, excluded, subjugated or forgotten in the telling of official narratives' (ibid.).

Since I am interested in how people relate to cultural narratives when sharing their lived experiences on human rights, I find it useful to think in terms of these counternarratives that create opportunities for contestation and negotiations of hegemonic and dominant narratives on human rights in classrooms. I aim at moving beyond this binary that both Nussbaum (2006), and Peters and Lankshear (1996) are preoccupied with in education, namely to achieve a balance between narratives as local and cosmopolitan. Although sympathetic with the notion that particular narratives influence how we understand ourselves, I assert nonetheless that the notion of counternarratives can also be used to introduce into education that new element which, as Arendt argues is found in every newborn person through their uniqueness and difference.

Counternarratives in this sense are not told through collective voices, or people speaking in groups. There is always an author, a sender of a message, and that person is a singular 'you' who claims to represent a plural 'us'. This act of speaking and writing narratives about identities becomes political action when received by another, who is a singular 'you'. It is important to stress, here, that there is a responsibility to pay attention to *how* we listen to different stories of otherness that claim to be the collective voices of groups and 'cultures'. Even though these 'cultural narratives' might play a significant role in shaping a sense of self, as Marianne Horsdal (2012) argues, they nevertheless cannot grasp or replace the uniqueness and unrepeatable tale of every person, and should be seen as narratives that try to represent a social myth of sameness. So, instead of continuing to 'strike a balance' between cosmopolitanism and particularism in relation to human rights education, I focus next on how cosmopolitanism can be interpreted as local spaces of diversity that can open up in classrooms, where both plurality and uniqueness can be voiced in pedagogical relations and on the political imaginary that so arises.

NARRATIVITY AS POLITICAL IMAGINARY IN PEDAGOGICAL RELATIONS

Being seen and being heard by others derive their significance from the fact that everybody sees and hears from a different position (Arendt, 1958, p. 57).

Arendt argues that it is precisely through the multitude of perspectives (in this sense of human rights) that a sense of consistency appears, 'a sameness in its utter diversity' (ibid.). A plurality of narratives on human rights frees individuals from their limited perspective on the world, on what human rights can mean in the world. When different and agonistic narratives on human rights meet in spaces of plurality, the meaning of human rights becomes more 'true' in an Arendtian sense, happenings in the world are revealed to us as more complex when seen from a variety of perspectives (2005, p. 95).

The notion of politics as relational and as a space created in words and action between human beings, as developed by Arendt, is crucial for highlighting the political potential in human rights education, a potential that is ontologically dependent on plurality and narrativity. Freedom of speech means nothing if there is not someone who can listen, interpret and respond, thereby making the initiating act political. Political action occurs in-between human beings, in a political relationality where one is dependent on the singular, unique other who is different in order to create politics together.

Arendt argues that the aim of politics—its promise—is freedom. Freedom, which should not be conflated with isolation, can only be experienced and achieved together with others in the spontaneity of political action. Politics lies outside of the individual, and only comes about in her community with others. Freedom could, in this sense, be read as being based upon a plurality of different narratives on human rights that enriches and frees learners to draw from a multitude of interpretations of human rights. The political potential of renewing the world hence lies in how human rights are reified or negotiated in educational relations. Since narratives are constrained by nationalism, sexism and racism, counternarratives serve to increase the relational space for speaking and acting in classrooms.

Although Arendt writes that education should be kept separate from politics as a free space for children to develop in creativity and play, rather than a space through which to form their political capabilities, she does not suggest that actions in educational settings automatically become politically significant for the future in the way they are intended. In the words of Arendt: '. . . even the children one wishes to educate to be citizens of a utopian tomorrow are actually denied their own future role in the body politic, for, from the standpoint of the new ones, whatever new the adult world may propose is necessarily older than they themselves' (2006, p. 174). What is dangerous, remarks Arendt, is when adults, as authorities in education, do not reflect on, take responsibility for, or take seriously, the political dimension of their words and actions in relation to unique individuals.

Learning human rights through lived experience puts learners and educators at risk due to the vulnerability accompanying the relational sharing of narratives. Ultimately I make the claim that the act of sharing human rights experiences, in spaces marked by plurality, is best described as 'narrativity as political imaginary', since these educational relations have the potential to renew the world; to re-negotiate *who* is seen as an equal in political spaces. To expose one's experiences as contained in one's life story puts the learner at risk, a risk of exposing their vulnerability in relation to others. As Arendt so eloquently argues, the acts of speaking or writing in public are political acts that demand courage. *How* human rights will be interpreted in the future is limited only to the plurality of different narratives shared in a political space that is under constant re-negotiation.

I want to reemphasise two points here: first, that the urgency of human rights as a narrative imaginary does not lie solely outside of the classroom where actions of speech receive political significance,[8] but in the very relations in classrooms themselves; second, that we need to shift the focus in social justice education away from *what* is represented in terms of difference and equality, towards *how* pedagogical relations create spaces where students feel that they can share their narratives, even though these may serve as counternarratives to the dominant understanding of the human rights subject.

CONCLUSION

The political dimensions of how different narratives on human rights are negotiated in a relational context point to the acknowledgement of human rights education as being far from politically neutral. It is, rather, socially constrained and framed by identity politics. Can we argue that human rights education is politically neutral if it is conflated with a certain outlook on the world in the national context in which it is taught? Does this national inflection of human rights silence difference in the name of political correctness? Nationally driven education on human rights passes through a national curriculum containing dominant (and generally patriarchal) narratives on religion, on geography, on history, on society, on philosophy—all of these dominant narratives overshadow alternative, particular narratives that might have other, different implications for identity shaping and the creation of a sense of self for the learners.

A relational approach to learning about human rights that focuses on relations *in* classrooms is, I argue, essential in understanding *how* human rights can become more than empty words when the political implications of human rights learning are acknowledged. What I prob-lematise is the danger that arises when the educator's perception of human rights learning is understood as politically neutral and intrinsi-cally good. Educators then risk reifying oppressive perceptions of 'who is the subject of human rights' by categorising unique human beings into group collectives that are characterised as either perpetrators of human rights violations, victims of human rights violations, or so called 'human rights defenders'.[9] These three distinctions may stand in the way of a more radical political imaginary of human rights, if received and interpreted by human rights learners as pacifying, as estranging/ excluding and as containing within them the burden of unequal power relations coloured by charity and aid. Critical analysis of HRE in terms of asymmetric practices may raise an awareness of the political impli-cations of how our words, speech and actions are relational rather than isolated actions for which we need not take political responsibility. Our experiences of human rights violations receive their political signifi-cance through the narratives in which they are stored—narratives that recount parts of and sequences in our own life stories.

NOTES

1. The concept of counter-narratives has been developed by Peters and Lankshear (1996) and will be discussed later in the chapter.
2. In Chapter 4 Sharon Todd explores the in-between human beings she calls the *liminality* of pedagogical relations, which is neither words nor body language, and hence hard to grasp in words.
3. See Kristeva (2001) on this theme in her reading of Arendt.
4. For further reading on HRE and inclusion of otherness as non-discrimination see Andreopoulos, 2002; Becker, 2012; Claude, 1996; Cole, 2006; Ellis and Forrest, 2000; Forrest, 2006; Kelly, 2006; Osler and Leung, 2011; Osler and Starkey, 2005.
5. See Andreopoulos and Claude, 1997; Douglas *et al.*, 1994; Huaman and Koenig, 2008; Kaufman, 1997; Claude, 1997) on HRE, which is focused on content and instuction, rather than critically examining the pedagogical relations in HRE.
6. In her later work, Martha Nussbaum moves away from this position towards notions of nationalism and patriotism. See for example Nussbaum, 2008.
7. Along similar lines, Ruth Cigman (in Chapter 9) argues that ethical learning comes about by turning to literature where moral philosophy is explicated rather than exercised.
8. The political significance of speech and actions in school education is something that Arendt asserts, but warns against, since she sees the loss of responsibility by adults as a loss of authority. Authority is here to be understood in the absence of violence or force. That loss is simultaneously a loss of secure guidance that can balance tradition and renewal.
9. The UN Declaration on the Right and Responsibility of Individuals, Groups and Organs of Society to Promote and Protect Universally Recognised Human Rights and Fundamental Freedoms is frequently abbreviated to and called 'the Declaration on Human Rights Defend-ers' and especially addresses individuals and NGOs working for the promotion and protec-tion of human rights: people who in some way 'help' victims of human rights violations.

REFERENCES

Ackerly, B. A. (2008) *Universal Human Rights in a World of Difference* (Cambridge, Cambridge University Press).

Adami, R. (2012) Reconciling Universality and Particularity through a Cosmopolitan Outlook on Human Rights, *Cosmopolitan Civil Societies Journal*, 4.2, pp. 22–37.

Adami, R. and Schumann, C. (2013) Towards a Critical Cosmopolitanism in Human Rights Learning: The Vienna Conference in 1993, in: T. Strand and M. Papastephano (eds) *Philosophy as Lived Experience. Navigating through Dichotomies of Thought and Action* (Berlin, VDM Verlag).

Andreopoulos, G. J. (2002) *Concepts and Strategies in International Human Rights* (New York, Peter Lang).

Andreopoulos, G. J. and Claude, R. P. (1997) *Human Rights Education for the Twenty-First Century.* (Philadelphia, PA, University of Pennsylvania Press).

Arendt, H. (1958) *The Human Condition* (Chicago, IL, University of Chicago Press).

Arendt, H. (1973) *The Origins of Totalitarianism* (New York, Harcourt, Brace, Jovanovich).

Arendt, H. (2005) *The Promise of Politics* (New York, Schocken Books).

Arendt, H. (2006) *Between Past and Future: Eight Exercises in Political Thought* (Harmondsworth, Penguin Books).

Becker, A. (2012) Identity Premised on Equality of Difference as a Fundamental Human Right, in: C. Roux (ed.) *Safe Spaces. Human Rights Education in Diverse Contexts* (Rotterdam, Sense Publishers), pp. 83–96.

Bucar, E. M. and Barnett, B. (eds) (2005) *Does Human Rights Need God?* (Grand Rapids, MI, Eerdmans).

Cavarero, A. (2000) *Relating Narratives: Storytelling and Selfhood* (London, Routledge).

Claude, R. P. (1996) *Educating for Human Rights?: The Philippines and Beyond* (Quezon City, University of the Philippines Press).

Claude, R. P. (1997) Global Human Rights Education: The Challenges for Nongovernmental Organizations, in: G. Andreopoulos, *Human Rights Education for the Twenty-first Century* (Philadelphia, PA, University of Pennsylvania Press), pp. 394–415.

Cole, M. (2006) *Education, Equality and Human Rights?: Issues of Gender, 'Race', Sexuality, Disability and Social Class* (London, Routledge)

Dembour, M-B. (2006) *Who Believes in Human Rights?: Reflections on the European Convention* (Cambridge, Cambridge University Press).

Donnelly, J. (2003) *Universal Human Rights in Theory and Practice* (Ithaca, NY, Cornell University Press).

Dooley, M. (2007) Truth, Ethics, and Narrative Imagination: Kearney and the Postmodern Challenge, in: R. Kearney (ed.) *Traversing the Imaginary* (Evanston, IL, Northwestern University Press), pp. 165–179.

Douglas R. *et al.* (1994) *Education for Human Rights: An International Perspective* (Paris, International Bureau of Education and UNESCO).

Dworkin, R. (1977) *Taking Rights Seriously* (Cambridge, MA, Harvard University Press).

Ellis, V. and Forrest, S. (2006) One of Them or One of Us? Sexuality, Identity and Equality, in: M. Cole (ed.) *Education, Equality and Human Rights* (New York, RoutledgeFalmer), pp. 78–99.

Forrest, S. (2006) Difficult Loves: Learning About Sexuality and Homophobia in Schools, in: M. Cole (ed.) *Education, Equality and Human Rights* (New York, RoutledgeFalmer), pp. 99–118.

Halme, M. (2008) *Human Rights in Action* (Helsinki, Helsinki University Printing House).

Hansen, D. T. (2008) Curriculum and the Idea of a Cosmopolitan Inheritance, *Journal of Curriculum Studies*, 40.3, pp. 289–312.

Hayden, P. (ed.) (2001) *The Philosophy of Human Rights* (New York, Paragon House).

Horsdal, M. (2012) *Telling Lives: Exploring Dimensions of Narratives* (Abingdon, Routledge).

Huaman, H. S. and Koenig, S. (2008) A Call and Response. Human Rights as a Tool of Dignity and Transformation, in: G. Andreopoulos (ed.) *Educating for Human Rights and Global Citizenship* (Albany, NY, State University of New York Press), pp. 11–23.

Ignatieff, M. (2003) *Human Rights as Politics and Idolatry*, A. Gutmann, ed. and intro. (Princeton, NJ, Princeton University Press).

Kaufman, E. (1997) Human Rights Education for Law Enforcement, in: G. Andreopoulos (ed.) *Human Rights Education for the Twenty-first Century* (Philadelphia, PA, University of Pennsylvania Press), pp. 278–295.

Kelly, J. (2006) Gender and Equality: One Hand Tied Behind Us, in: M. Cole (ed.) *Education, Equality and Human Rights* (New York, RoutledgeFalmer), pp. 6–21.

Kristeva, J. (2001) *Hannah Arendt?: Life is a Narrative* (Toronto, University of Toronto Press).

Langlois, A. (2001) *The Politics of Justice and Human Rights: Southeast Asia and Universalist Theory* (Cambridge, Cambridge University Press).

Morsink, J. (1999) *The Universal Declaration of Human Rights?: Origins, Drafting, and Intent* (Philadelphia, PA, University of Pennsylvania Press).

Nussbaum, M. C. (1998) *Cultivating Humanity?: A Classical Defense of Reform in Liberal Education* (Cambridge, MA, Harvard University Press).

Nussbaum, M. C. (2006) *Frontiers of Justice?: Disability, Nationality, Species Membership* (Cambridge, MA, Harvard University Press).

Nussbaum, M. (2008) Nationalism and Development: Can There Be a Decent Patriotism?, *Indian Journal of Human Development*, 2.II.

Osler, A. and Leung, Y. W. (2011) Human Rights Education, Politics and Power, *Education, Citizenship and Social Justice*, 6.3, pp. 199–203.

Osler, A. and Starkey, H. (2005) *Changing Citizenship: Democracy and Inclusion in Education* (Maidenhead, Open University Press).

Panigrahi, L. K. (2007) *New Directions in Education* (Chandigarh, Global Media).

Peters, M. (2013) Problematizing Cosmopolitan Citizenship Education: A Social Theory of Right and the Juridical Construction of the Subject, in his: *Citizenship, Human Rights and Identity: Prospects of a Liberal Cosmopolitan Order* (New York, Addleton Academic Publishers).

Peters, M. and Lankshear, C. (1996) Postmodern Counternarratives, in: H. Giroux, C. Lankshear, P. McLaren and M. Peters (eds) *Counternarratives: Cultural Studies and Critical Pedagogies in Postmodern Spaces* (New York, Routledge), pp. 1–39.

Rizvi, F. (2008) Epistemic Virtues and Cosmopolitan Learning, *The Australian Educational Researcher*, 35.1, pp. 17–35.

Tesón, F. R. (1985) International Human Rights and Cultural Relativism, *Virginia Journal of International Law*, 25.4, pp. 869–898.

Todd, S. (2003) *Learning from the Other?: Levinas, Psychoanalysis, and Ethical Possibilities in Education* (Albany, NY, State University of New York Press).

Todd, S. (2007) Teachers Judging Without Scripts, or Thinking Cosmopolitan, *Ethics and Education*, 2.1, pp. 25–38.

Todd, S. (2010) *Toward an Imperfect Education: Facing Humanity, Rethinking Cosmopolitanism* (Boulder, CO, Paradigm Publishers).

Todd, S. (2011) Educating Beyond Cultural Diversity: Redrawing the Boundaries of a Democratic Plurality, *Studies in Philosophy and Education*, 30.2, pp. 101–111.

9
Happiness Rich and Poor: Lessons From Philosophy and Literature

RUTH CIGMAN

> If we really wanted to be happier, what would we do differently?
> We do not yet know the answers . . . but we have a lot of evidence
> . . . The main evidence comes from the new psychology of hap-
> piness . . . (Layard, 2005, p. 3).

Happiness is a large idea. It looms enticingly before us when we are
young, delivers verdicts on our lives when we are old, and seems to
inform a responsible engagement with children. It may be a force for
good or ill. We want it for ourselves and others—it may be all we
want—but we do not know what it is. It turns some into hedonists,
others into philosophers, and it generates mountains of cliché. Happiness, as Sara Ahmed (2010) says, does things. Do we want to do the
things happiness makes us do?

One of the things happiness does is expose attitudes to life: cynicism, scepticism, sentimentality, optimism, seriousness, frivolity. My
hope for this chapter is that it takes happiness seriously, as its
largeness—including its large history—deserves. The recent happiness turn, evident in the ubiquity of the idea in educational policy,
economics, psychology, the media and elsewhere, has been met by a
kind of philosophical u-turn. It is the business of philosophers to be
sceptical, and large ideas can be grandiosely small. I have been
uneasy, however, about the sceptical target. At one level, happiness is
rightly mocked, and much of the philosophy surrounding it deserves
the same fate. Utilitarianism, for example, offers what I call a poor
conception of happiness, as unreflective, unconditionally desirable
and conveniently quantifiable (cf. Mill, 1962). Despite numerous
refinements, I believe the science of happiness also lacks the richness
we need if we are to claim and retain this large idea. Whether we want

Re-Imagining Relationships in Education: Ethics, Politics and Practices, First Edition. Edited by Morwenna
Griffiths, Marit Honerød Hoveid, Sharon Todd and Christine Winter. Chapters © 2015 The Authors. Editorial
organization © 2015 Philosophy of Education Society of Great Britain. Published 2015 by John Wiley & Sons Ltd.

to do so should be seen as an open question, requiring in the first instance a distinction between rich and poor conceptions.

My aim in this chapter is to explore what a rich conception might look like. To consign the idea of happiness to the flames, suggesting we are somehow better off without it, would be a serious step. I am not ready to say that parents and teachers should u-turn the traditional wish for children to be happy *in some sense*. I do not know what it would be to educate or raise children in responsible indifference to this wish. My thought is that if happiness is to receive its teleological due, recognised in rather the way Aristotle saw it, as a final end that crucially lacks specificity, it needs to be richly conceived without denying the significance of unhappiness or despair. It is an ethical idea; whatever else it turns out to mean or do, it must refer in some way to what is worth having. As such, it is vulnerable to impoverishment and corruption.

In this chapter, I pursue the idea that Aristotle's *Nicomachean Ethics* is 'completed' in a distinctively Aristotelian sense by certain works of literature. George Eliot, for example, *exemplifies* some of its key ideas in ways that 'complete' their meaning and (if we grapple with this meaning) bring about ethical learning. Virginia Woolf 'completes' ideas that are less Aristotelian than Wittgensteinian and Tolstoian, about the 'joy of living'. From such works, I believe we learn much about a rich conception of happiness.

These 'lessons from philosophy and literature' have a crucial place in everyday life, in the classroom and in the practice of philosophy itself. They exemplify what I call, following Margalit, an 'e.g.' as opposed to 'i.e.' style of thinking (Margalit, 2002; see also Cigman, 2014). Some philosophers, but not all, see examples as ineliminable reference points in their thinking. They are willing to learn from them, trust their illumination, without seeking a firmer footing in principles or definitions. Happiness scientists and many philosophers do not think or trust this way; they exemplify the i.e. style of thinking, and to see this as 'incomplete' is to open up a new way of imagining relationships in education. On the view I am presenting here, we attend communally, conversationally and often argumentatively to the dramas of human life. We move beyond the abstractions of the poor conception, and take a metaphorical trip with our friends, fellow students or teachers to the theatre. Side-by-side, we laugh or are frozen with terror, and we emerge into the night tingling with sensation, eager to talk. It is in such talk, passed around the pub or the classroom, that we (begin to) learn what kinds of happiness are worth having. From a classroom point of view, the literary examples discussed in this chapter could form the basis of lesson plans, but it is important to understand their purpose.[1] Novels, in the words of philosopher Cora Diamond, teach us 'how to think about human nature by making us think about it and not by giving us *what* to think' (1996a, p. 371). This is the difference between e.g. and i.e. styles of thinking, and it is crucial for our topic.

I HAPPINESS SCEPTICISM

What we want for children eludes our attempts to grasp it and pin it down. It is always beyond us, something we seem dimly to perceive, and it disappears as we approach it. It is nameless, and it is unmanageable (Smeyers, Smith and Standish, 2007).

There are good reasons to be sceptical about happiness as a focus of personal, philosophical and educational attention. The past decade has seen inflated claims and an extraordinary amount of muddle on this topic. We are familiar with the key narratives: we are richer but no happier than we were 50 years ago, we can master unhappiness, we have a duty/right to be happy etc. What concerns me here is a kind of counter narrative that disdains a connection between happiness and education or personal aspiration. A recent book (Smeyers, Smith and Standish, 2007) argues that we should seek:

> . . . a closer reconciliation with the ordinary human unhappiness that Freud, foregoing any fantasies of personal beatitude, took to be the real advance on human misery (p. 236).

This passage belongs to a critique of the culture that promises rapid, painless access to the holy grail of perfect happiness, and I agree with its main tenets. The phrase 'fantasies of beatitude' expresses a cynicism, however, that Freud did not share. Freud's remarks about 'common unhappiness' were about the proper aims of psychoanalysis: it will have succeeded (he reticently suggested) if the patient progresses from 'hysterical misery' to 'common unhappiness'. This is a pointedly uninflated claim: psychoanalysis does not aim to make people happy, but there is no disparagement of the quest for happiness as such. Freud was fascinated by those who seek happiness in the 'enjoyment of beauty', and seemed to regret his inability to say much of interest on this topic[2] (Freud, 1985).

The quest for happiness can be sentimental and naive, but some suppose it can be no other way. Ahmed also presents herself as a kind of happiness sceptic, placing a poor conception at the heart of her critique. She says, 'we could describe happiness quite simply as a convention, such that to deviate from the paths of happiness is to challenge convention' (p. 64). This is obviously *conventional happiness*, contained, as she notes, in the phrase 'happy housewife'. Such happiness involves 'the comfort of repetition, of following lines that have already been given in advance'. Sceptically though she positions herself, Ahmed also recognises a distinction, as I am suggesting we must. The problem with conventional happiness is that it forecloses richer and deeper possibilities that need to be opened up. 'If we think of happiness as a possibility that does not exhaust what is possible, if we lighten the load of happiness, then we can open things up. . . . When I think of what makes happiness "happy" I think of moments. Moments of happiness create texture, shared impressions: a sense of lightness in possibility' (p. 219). This is a rich conception that emerges, interestingly, through Ahmed's discussion of *Mrs Dalloway*. I turn to this novel now.

II THE JOY OF LIVING

The delight I take in my thoughts is delight in my own strange life. Is this joy of living? (Wittgenstein, 1980, p. 22e).

Mrs Dalloway (Woolf, 1976) is about a day in the life of a 53-year-old woman who does nothing much. She is privileged and indolent; she throws a party, but others do most of the work. She reminisces, she encounters people from her present life and distant past, and she experiences a variety of emotions that she appears powerless to refine or control.

Like Virginia Woolf, however, Clarissa Dalloway loves walking, and her errand to buy flowers for the party takes her through the streets of Westminster:

> For Heaven only knows why one loves it so, how one sees it so, making it up, building it round one, tumbling it, creating it every moment afresh . . . In people's eyes, in the swing, tramp, and trudge; in the bellow and the uproar; the carriages, motor cars, omnibuses, vans, sandwich men shuffling and swinging; brass bands; barrel organs; in the triumph and the jingle and the strange high singing of some aeroplane overhead was what she loved; life; London; this moment of June (1976, p. 6).

Mrs Dalloway loves, not goodness or beauty, but omnibuses, sandwich men, the sound of an aeroplane, and other ordinary details of a

London street. These form the *texture* of happiness for Mrs Dalloway at a particular moment on a particular day in June. Towards the end of the book, as the day too draws to a close, her happiness reaches a peak:

> Odd, incredible: she had never been so happy. Nothing could be slow enough; nothing could last too long. No pleasure could equal, she thought, straightening the chairs, pushing in one book on a shelf, this having done with the triumphs of youth, lost herself in the process of living, to find it, with a shock of delight, as the sun rose, as the day sank (p. 164).

Mrs Dalloway is not an educated woman, but she is receptive to what Dunne calls (referring to Aristotle's particularist account of moral education) 'the uncircumscribable range of potentially noticeable features' (Dunne, 1993, p. 312) within which we live and make choices.

Ahmed calls *Mrs Dalloway* a sad book, and it is. Privileged and depressed as she is, Clarissa Dalloway is ripe for education in Whitehead's sense: 'There is only one subject matter for education, and that is Life in all its manifestations.' She is not ripe for the kind of education that, as Whitehead goes on, inflicts 'airy generalizations' from which 'nothing follows' (Whitehead, 1967, pp. 6–7). She may not be ripe, either, in the sense of being inclined to engage in: 'a patient process of the mastery of details, minute by minute, hour by hour, day by day' (ibid.). What she exemplifies is the rapturous and intimate connection with objects that we hope to find and engender in children.

Mrs Dalloway is a disappointed woman, who at one level has given up 'life' for the promise of happiness: conventional happiness, as wife and mother. But she also rejoices in life, and we see this on the streets of London, in her rapturous responses to happenings around her that carry no promise of happiness, no risk of disappointment. No one ever promised rapture from omnibuses, vans or sandwich men, yet Mrs Dalloway experiences this. To love life in this way is to enjoy a kind of happiness that the novel makes us feel is well worth having. As Ahmed says: 'When I think of what makes happiness "happy" I think of moments.' I would put this by saying that 'light moments', moments of possibility, must have a place in what I call a rich conception of happiness.

The word happiness is related to happening, originating in the old Norse hap, meaning chance. We are all vulnerable to luck in countless ways, but education offers an opportunity, not to control the hand of fate, but to foster forms of awareness that can bring delight. The novel *Mrs Dalloway* delights us, not through the story it tells, but through the poetic rendition of the story. It makes us *feel* Clarissa Dalloway's delight, sensing that its real object, dispersed amongst objects that individually promise nothing at all, is life itself. This is nowhere more obvious than in the following passage, which appears near the start of the novel (also the start of the day), when doors are being 'taken off their hinges':

> And then, thought Clarissa Dalloway, what a morning—fresh as if issued to children on a beach.
>
> What a lark! What a plunge! For so it had always seemed to her, when, with a little squeak of the hinges, which she could hear now, she had burst open the French windows and plunged at Bourton into the open air. How fresh, how calm, stiller than this of course, the air was in the early morning; like the flap of a wave; the kiss of a wave . . . (p. 5).

This is 'life', and it is no accident that, like her excursion on the streets, it is experienced in the 'open air', the world beyond her confined domestic existence. We may think of Plato's prisoners here: those whose souls, like their bodies, are condemned to obscurity, far from the heat and light of the sun. This is a potent image of suffering, and Woolf presents an alternative: not the ravings of a mad woman who is obsessed with sandwich men and omnibuses, but the genuine happiness that issues from a sense of these as manifestations of life itself.

We are familiar with the ancient quarrel between optimists and pessimists. William James rebukes Schopenhauer for gloomily characterising 'life on the largest scale' as 'the same recurrent inanities, the same dog barking, the same fly buzzing, forevermore' (1960, p. 19). Literature helps to liberate us from the familiar iterations of this quarrel by engaging our attention at a deeper level. It is not Mrs Dalloway's story but the story poetically told that persuades us that 'life on the largest scale' is worth loving and living to the full. The extraordinary language *works on our senses*: we *hear* the 'strange high singing' of the aeroplane; we *smell* the morning, 'fresh as if issued to children on a beach'; we *feel* it on our bodies, like the 'flap of a wave . . . the kiss of a wave'.

We share Mrs Dalloway's pleasure, not only mentally but also bodily, and this makes us more receptive, more engaged, more captivated, more entranced, more susceptible to what I called moments of grace. Tolstoy saw it as his task—and the aim of art—to make people receptive in this way, and one could say as much about the aim of a teacher or parent. It is not to 'solve the problem' of what children should know and how they should live, but to bring about a joyous engagement with life. Happiness in this form comes unbidden in the form of moments—or maybe minutes, hours or longer—of grace, but we can go further than Mrs Dalloway by *putting ourselves in its way*. We may read novels, listen to music, take walks in natural or urban environments. We may sit in classrooms and, under the guidance of good teachers, make fascinating discoveries about the world of which we are a part. In these ways, we prepare ourselves to receive a kind of happiness that is worth having.

III THE LIMITS OF WORTHWHILE HAPPINESS

There is also the figure, rarer perhaps than Callicles supposed, but real, who is horrible enough and not miserable at all but, by any ethological standard of the bright eye and gleaming coat, dangerously flourishing (Williams, 1985, p. 46).

Can a tyrant be happy? This is one of philosophy's oldest questions, and Bernard Williams answers affirmatively. I think he misses the point, fundamental for both Plato and Aristotle, that the flourishing of such a person has a deep instability. There is the possibility of regret, remorse or sheer disgust, especially when we bear in mind that Aristotle's *eudaimonia* was not merely an object of aspiration, but an object of retrospective reflection. 'Call no man happy until he's dead' said Solon, and Aristotle quotes him approvingly. The tyrant is vulnerable, looking back, to the devastating discovery that his or her happiness was not worth having after all.[3]

George Eliot's *Mill on the Floss* (1998) takes us deep into this issue. Maggie Tulliver is clever, passionate and oppressed. We meet her as a child, misunderstood by her beloved brother and other small-minded relations, and we witness some heart-rending struggles before she develops into a beautiful young woman who, at age eighteen, is loved by two men. Maggie needs love: 'she was as dependent on kind or cold words as a daisy on the sunshine or the cloud; the need of being loved would always subdue her . . .' (p. 392) However one of her lovers is deformed; he is also a Montague to her Capulet, and her brother forbids her to see him. The other lover, Stephen, is handsome, tall and captivating, but all but engaged to her dear cousin Lucy.

The book's climax is the 'great temptation' in which Maggie and Stephen 'accidentally' find themselves marooned alone on the river. There is only one honourable option: to accept his ardent proposal of marriage. Not only for the sake of her reputation, Maggie is tempted;

she is 'in love' with Stephen. But what about the other man, Phillip, whom she also loves? What about the cousin?

It is a desperate struggle, but we sense from the start that she *cannot* accept the kind of happiness Stephen offers:

> We can't choose happiness either for ourselves or another: we can't tell where that will lie. We can only choose whether we will indulge ourselves in the present moment, or whether we will renounce that, for the sake of obeying the divine voice within us . . . (p. 477).

This passage, which could appear in a sermon, is the utterance of a person whose struggles we have shared over the space of almost 500 pages. If we are not by now moved by Maggie's story—I mean at the levels of thought, feeling *and* sensation—we may sit on our philosophical high horse and point out that sainthood is not reasonably required of a human being. Maggie's 'divine voice' sounds like a harsh Kantian imperative; she is unable to choose, in an Aristotelian spirit, the *best* possibility of action that inheres in her situation. Surely, we may feel, she is not obliged to choose (as she effectively does) her own destruction.

Eliot impresses on us the scale of Maggie's difficulty through poetry, drama and philosophy. It is, I would argue, not Kant but Aristotle who provides the 'lesson' of this particular book. The idea that Maggie 'should not' have chosen her own destruction is tempting, but it is a *general* idea, and in thinking this way, we, the readers, exemplify the generalizing tendency that Eliot has captured so strikingly in relation to Maggie's petty-minded relatives—people who live by 'maxims':

> All people of broad, strong sense have an instinctive repugnance to the men of maxims; because such people early discern that the mysterious complexity of our life is not to be embraced by maxims, and that to lace ourselves up in formulas of that sort is to repress all the divine promptings and inspirations that spring from growing insight and sympathy. And the man of maxims is the popular representative of the minds that are guided in their moral judgment solely by general rules, thinking that these will lead them to justice by a ready-made patent method, without the trouble of exerting patience, discrimination, impartiality,— without any care to assure themselves whether they have the insight that comes from a hardly earned estimate of temptation, or from a life vivid and intense enough to have created a wide fellow-feeling with all that is human (p. 498).

This is the key to Eliot's art: she aims to create in the reader a sense of 'fellow-feeling with all that is human'. We are tempted to accuse Maggie of failing to save her own skin, but are we sensitive to her anguish, her humanity?

Here is a literary-philosophical response to the happy tyrant problem. Maggie rejects Stephen because he offers a kind of happiness that could presumably be cultivated (a happiness scientist might offer some useful techniques), but is not worth having. Maggie, we understand, has no gift for tyranny, but those who are tempted to neglect the deep interests of others may be guided by this book to pose the question: is the happiness that I expect to achieve at others' expense ultimately worth having? *The Mill on the Floss* makes its readers *feel* an answer. The answer is not that Maggie should self-destruct; it is that you, the reader, should resist your presumed temptation to reach for lazy answers.

IV MAKING OTHERS HAPPY

> . . . there is no genuine *philia* between master and slave: the slave is 'something of' the master, an extension of the master's own good. He or she is not regarded as a separate seat of choice, whose *eudaimonia* it is the business of the relation to promote (Nussbaum, 2001, p. 355).

The science of happiness aims to be objective, and ethics hovers on its borders, patrolled by a kind of thought police. We should not, for a scientist, *reflect* on happiness, let alone learn from literature about its deeper meaning. Rather, we should define, survey and enhance it, working firmly within an evidence-base. Many happiness sceptics not only reject these ambitions; they resist the underlying idea of making, or trying to make, other people happy, in the belief that such ambitions are ethically shallow and conceptually arid.

As a generalised concern, I think this is wrong. It is not implied by my wish for your happiness that you should be protected from or endeavour to avoid unhappiness. What I reasonably want for you, as for myself, is *eudaimonia*, a kind of happiness that is worth having. This is embedded in a life, and is likely to contain many unhappy experiences. When I say that I want a person to be happy in a rich sense, I am not talking about experiences. What I mean, I think, are at least two things: one, I want her to be reasonably *lucky*, to have basic goods (reasonable health, wealth, friends etc.), without which happiness is hard or impossible to achieve; and two, that she should acquire a rich rather than a poor conception of happiness. Given basic goods, what I want most of all is that she should learn what happiness in its richest sense *means*, and aspire to achieve this and impart it to others.[4]

Indeed, achieving it and wanting it for others are deeply connected. Wishing for another's good brings *us* a kind of happiness: the happiness of loving another, joyous appreciation of their existence and qualities. It also it makes us vulnerable. I have spoken of happiness as a love of life, and we are now talking about it as a love of particular human beings. Placing love at the heart of a rich conception of happiness helps us to understand why this topic is so confusing. Love can bring earth-shattering grief and disappointment as well as euphoria.[5] It both matches and fails to match our idea of happiness as a state of pleasure, enjoyment or satisfaction. Happiness in a rich sense means loving 'wisely but not too well' and accepting grief when it comes. To love thus is something we can learn or hope to learn, and *Middlemarch* offers some pictures for our aid.

In Chapter 81, an encounter takes place between two unhappy young women. We see how one of them, Dorothea Brooke, brings a kind of happiness to the other, Rosamond Vincy, and there are two aspects to this. First she lifts her spirits, leaving her in a much more 'positive' frame of mind than the one she was in when Dorothea arrived. More fundamentally, she helps Rosamond to love.

Obviously, I can only sketch the broadest outlines of this relationship. We are by now 700 pages into the book, and are engaged, as I suggested earlier, on many levels. The immediate tension between them focuses on a man, Will Ladislaw. Will and Dorothea are in love, but their love is not yet, we are to suppose, known to each other. Dorothea is under the mistaken impression that Will loves Rosamond, but the reader has recently witnessed a scene in which Rosamond's fragile ego was shattered by Will when Rosamond complained that Will 'preferred' Dorothea. 'I never had a *preference* for her,' he replied bitterly, 'any more than I have a preference for breathing. No other woman exists by the side of her. I would rather touch her hand if it were dead, then I would touch any other woman's living' (Eliot, 1996, p. 732).

Dorothea has spent a night sobbing on her bedroom floor, in the belief that she witnessed a love scene between Will and Rosamond. She chooses to set her own pain aside, because she wishes to remove illusions in Rosamond's mind about the character and behaviour of her husband. Dorothea wants Rosamond to love and appreciate him as he deserves, and she deliberately ignores what she sees as Rosamond's illicit affair with Will, as though this is none of her business.

By the time this encounter takes place, the reader has grasped the point of the book's Prelude, in which Dorothea's passionate yearning to be good is anticipated.

Here and there is born a Saint Theresa, foundress of nothing, whose loving heart beats and sobs after an unattainable goodness tremble off and are dispersed among hindrances, instead of centring on some long-recognisable deed (p. 4).

As 'foundress of nothing', Dorothea is an unlauded saint, and her story gives us the opportunity to examine our doubtless ambivalent responses to the idea of sainthood. Rosamond, by contrast, is vain and self-absorbed, and we understand that her husband fell in love with her rather than Dorothea to his cost. He 'had taken the burthen of her life upon his arms. He must walk as he could, carrying that burthen pitifully' (p. 752). Dazzled by her beauty, he fell in love unwisely; he was in error about the path to happiness in his own life.

The encounter I am speaking of highlights on the one hand a *contrast* between the two women—Dorothea, selfless and loving, Rosamond, caring only for herself—and on the other, a *parity* between them. When Dorothea arrives, Rosamond is determined to 'meet every word with polite impassibility'. However the 'beam' of Dorothea's 'sweet openness' on Rosamond's 'painful confused vision' (p. 744) brings about a transformation. She 'delivered her soul [to Dorothea] under impulses which she had not known before' (p. 750), acting selflessly in a way we could never have anticipated. She returns Dorothea's love, saying what Dorothea needs to hear, though it is not what Rosamond wants to be true: Will cares only for Dorothea. It is a pivotal moment in the book, and when Rosamond's husband returns, we understand that happiness is now a possibility for them both.

Dorothea acted with exquisite love and generosity, and Rosamond emulates her. Aristotle would, I believe, have described Dorothea's action as *to kalon*. Usually translated 'noble' or 'fine', Joe Sachs insists on 'beautiful' for this term, as in 'that was a beautiful thing you did'. Sachs goes on: '. . . such a thing can be recognised only by sense-perception . . . The beautiful is what makes an action right, in the same sense in which a painting or poem or musical composition might get everything exactly right' (Aristotle, 2002, pp. 201–2).

We learn from Aristotle that beautiful actions are appreciated through the senses, and bound up with the kind of happiness that is worth having and imparting to others. Like Woolf, Eliot places beauty before us, not as a concept or set of claims, but as a picture for us to contemplate and be moved by. Dorothea acts beautifully, but she does not think of herself as an educator any more than she thinks of herself as a saint. She exemplifies what Buber calls the 'living tact' of the educator, who works within:

> . . . a realm of life which is entrusted to us for our influence but not our interference . . . [It] can be truly carried out only in the system of a reliable counterpoint . . . of giving and withholding oneself, intimacy and distance . . . (Buber, 2002, p. 112).

I believe that it is within this 'system of counterpoint' that we properly aim, as educators, to help others to lead richly happy lives. We do not interfere, in the manner of science; we open up the possibility of happiness as a kind of grace. *Middlemarch* shows us how this 'opening up' might look in everyday life.

V LESSONS FROM PHILOSOPHY AND LITERATURE

The poor conception of happiness is polarised: it hives happiness off from unhappiness and conducts a kind of witch-hunt against the latter. Nothing could have been further from Aristotle's intentions; *eudaimonia* is polarised only in the sense in which good lives differ from bad lives: not as fixed, polar opposites, but as objects of practical reflection.

We should resist polarisation *except* in ethics, where the difference between wishing for someone's good and wishing for their harm is obviously crucial. It is the difference between virtue and vice, love and hatred, generosity and meanness or envy. We need to polarise these; Aristotle instructs us to do so *contextually*, alert to fine and subtle distinctions. Literature guides us here, vicariously thrusting us into situations by which are bewitched, charmed, startled, frightened, moved, prompted to learn. We *practice* ethical thinking through a kind of Buberian counterpoint, which I take to mean a restless movement back and forth between stories, examples, pictures, ideas, and our practical and emotional responses. Aristotle characterises this process as aiming for the 'mean': this is not a doctrine of moderation, but an image reminding us how easy it is to go wrong, how hard it is to go right. 'It is work,' he says, 'to be of serious moral stature, since in each kind of thing it is work to get hold of the mean.' (2002, 1109a 24) Such work, I have been suggesting, usefully includes learning from literature; but personal testimony may also play a part.

In *A Common Humanity*, Raimond Gaita discusses an encounter he had with a nun when he was a young man working in a psychiatric hospital. She made a powerful impression on him, he says, by responding to severely afflicted patients without 'a trace of condescension' (Gaita, 2002, p. 2). These patients appeared to have lost all dignity, and although Gaita and the psychiatrists with whom he worked believed that they treated them with unconditional respect, the nun's behaviour showed (according to Gaita) that they were wrong. It was not they but she who treated them with unconditional respect, thereby revealing the patients' preciousness or dignity. 'Love,' says Gaita, 'is the name we give to such behaviour' (p. 20).

It is a fascinating testimony, much discussed by philosophers in recent years. What struck Gaita was a subtle but crucial distinction between those who hold an ideal of equality and believe they serve it, and those rare individuals for whom the question of equality does not arise because it is absorbed in the experience of love. Of particular interest here are Gaita's epistemological claims about this situation, which I think are excessive. I discuss this example because I think it helps us to appreciate the place of literature in relation to ethics, which is different from the place of testimony.

Gaita insists that the nun's 'behaviour was directly shaped by the reality which it revealed . . . There is no clear application here for the concept of a mistake' (p. 20). He means, I think, that to know or appreciate the nun's love is to foreclose the question whether its objects are truly lovable. I accept this interesting idea, but there is a further question that we must be permitted to ask: did he see the nun accurately? To this question we will doubtless never receive an answer, and although I am saying we must be *permitted* to ask it, it may be entirely unimportant that we do so. Precisely because the nun was a real person, belonging to Gaita's personal history, it is in a sense immaterial whether he perceived her accurately or inaccurately. What matters for our *reflections* on this topic is the *distinction* to which Gaita adverts, between love and sincere egalitarianism.

When we read novels, we enter a different kind of domain. Precisely because characters are fictional, rather than friends or acquaintances from our private lives, our experiences may be shared with other readers. We can approach the question of reality with curiosity, interest and all sorts of emotions, exactly as reality is ordinarily approached. We can compare and discuss our emotional responses to the characters. We can *scrutinise* the characters' behaviour (and often their uncommunicated thoughts and feelings), looking for clues, trying to understand their motives, considering *this* behaviour in Chapter X in the light of *that* behaviour in Chapter Y, etc. We may read and re-read, wondering whether we were biased or inattentive or for some other reason mistaken in our initial responses. The 'reality' of the characters is not inaccessible, like the 'reality' of Gaita's nun; it is there between the covers of the book, and assuming the book is a substantial one, it is available for endless viewing and reviewing, thinking and re-thinking, communally and alone. Serious literature demands an effort of understanding, just like everyday life, and it offers an arena in which we can engage in this together.

Anything does not go in this arena. We cannot reject Jane Austen's characterisation of Mr Darcy as 'too proud' at the beginning but not the end of *Pride and Prejudice*, for to do so would be to misunderstand the book. Austen's novels offer what Gilbert Ryle calls 'rational tutelage', guiding readers towards a proper or reasonable emotional response. Other novels are less instructive, and intentionally so. But they still offer what might be called a canvas on which a picture of reality is presented for our scrutiny and emotional response.

By 'literature', I mean, poetry, drama and film, as well as novels. 'The success of any set of abstractions,' says Gordon Bearn, 'rides oceans of repressed sensual energy' (2013, pp. 93–4). Such energy surges through all these forms, moulding our impressions and sensations in accordance with a vision, but leaving us optimally free to explore *alternative* visions, and hence to reflect and disagree. This, I have argued, is moral education, though it is not the only kind. In the hands of a gifted teacher, its power to bring about ethical learning—from the author, from her characters and from each other—is immeasurable.

The *Nicomachean Ethics* has an educative purpose, though its ambitions in this direction are limited. Like Wittgenstein, Aristotle directs us away from an i.e. style of thinking: a style that idealises reason over the experience of everyday. He tells us a great deal about the difficulties of becoming happy in a rich sense: the difficulties of making choices, our tendencies to err in one direction or another, our temptations towards pleasure and ease. He is a teleologist, concerned about the way one thing 'completes' another, as the formation of good habits (*ethos*) and active dispositions (*hexis*) 'complete' our natural capacity for virtue. But he does not go as far as Wittgenstein, who championed and indeed exemplified an e.g. style of thinking. This sees examples—literary, testimonial, everyday, imaginary— as ineliminable reference points in our thinking. Aristotle gestured towards the everyday; Wittgenstein placed it at the heart of our thinking (cf. Wittgenstein, 1953, 1980).

For an e.g. philosopher, ethical thinking is 'incomplete' independently of examples. The tendency of most philosophers is towards i.e., and for an e.g. philosopher, reading such work is rather like reading music criticism without having heard the music. It is a pointless exercise, for the music 'completes' the critical text, the text is 'incomplete' without it. In this chapter I have tried to *exemplify* e.g. philosophy: exemplify what it means for philosophy to 'complete' *its* meaning and *our* learning through literary examples. What we learn through this route may be as much about a rich conception of unhappiness as a rich conception of happiness; but this is a topic for another chapter.

VI CONCLUDING REMARKS

We do not become happy in a rich sense by practicing gratitude and appreciation in the manner recommended by scientists of happiness. At most, such practices (such as writing grateful letters to people) bring one to a threshold from which we can develop George Eliot's 'fellow-feeling with all that is human'. One only has to watch a TV dating show to see how far most young people are from appreciating this idea. 'Love' is a 'buzz' that 'happens' or 'fails to happen' within minutes of meeting a stranger. This is a fragile basis for an intimate relationship with another human being.

'Is it a kind of happiness worth having?' is a question we ask in the company of authors, characters, teachers, fellow readers, but are discouraged by many philosophers and scientists from asking. 'Happiness education', as it is currently conceived, reinforces this discouragement. Ian Morris, for example, urges us to 'systematically teach [children] the skills of how to be successful as human beings' (Morris, 2009, p. 4). At its simplest level, this means occupying the realm of the third person, the empirical study, rather than the realm of the first and second person, the conversation. A teacher who aims systematically to enhance children's 'skills for becoming successful' *differs from* a teacher who appreciates the complexity of a rich conception of happiness. This difference may be subtle, and it may slip through the net of an inspector's checklist. It may manifest itself in gestures, eye contact, or uneasy pauses, as the teacher finds herself unable to respond authoritatively to a thoughtful student as the 'systematic' or 'theoretical' approach requires. In such pauses, important learning may take place: students learn that happiness is no simple matter.

Teachers who conceive happiness richly invite children to think about an idea that they can put to work in their own lives. The *form* this invitation takes needs to be considered and reflected upon by example. We know that it is not focused on targets and outcomes. We know that it does not involve, as Cora Diamond says, 'giving us *what* to think' (1996a, p. 371). We know that ideas like 'making people happy' are easily corrupted, and I have discussed the kind of material that can help us to reflect on what this means. It is implied by the arguments of this chapter that the pedagogy of happiness rich and poor rests finally on exemplification. I cannot append a novel or even a short story to this chapter, but I hope I have drawn tellingly on excerpts. My aim was not to tell you, the reader, what to think and it was certainly not to recommend that teachers do this. The excerpts *make* us think without giving us *what* to think. This is not coercion; it is education, aimed at enlarging and enriching human lives.

Happiness is a general term, and its vagueness of meaning is legendary. To scientists and philosophers of a theoretical ilk, it seems to cry out for explication, and Bentham, Layard and Seligman are just some of those who have obliged. I have taken a different route, unsatisfying to those who are tempted to press questions like: what precisely is happiness? To defend a theory of happiness, I have supposed, is to attempt to tell people '*what* to think' about a matter that properly belongs to first person enquiry[6] and conversation. This chapter is an exploration into what is for a philosophy of happiness, untypically, to avoid doing this. Philosophers like Wittgenstein and Diamond have paved the way for this enquiry, and I have attempted to engage with what Diamond (1996b, p. 233) calls a 'secondary use of "meaning" '. She says: 'A . . . striking example is provided by Ruskin, who describes in detail the place and events by which he was moved to say "And then I learned—what till then I had not known— the real meaning of the word beautiful" '. I have discussed examples that I see as capable of *moving people to acquire a rich conception of* happiness, relating this to Sachs' Aristotelian comment, '[a beautiful action] can be recognised only by sense perception.' If the aspiration to be and make others happy makes any sense at all, it must be thoroughly contextual, and even sensual. We should focus on the thought that happiness in a rich sense looks, feels, sounds, smells *like this*. . . . Such a thought may turn out to be misguided in particular cases, but it is ripe for ethical reflection.

NOTES

1. Also compare Rebecca Adami on individual narratives, Christine Winter on making a curriculum your own, in relation, and the emphasis Morwenna Griffiths places on relationships between students as well as teacher and individual teacher (all this book).
2. Also see Aislinn O'Donnell (Chapter 6) on conceptions of educational success and failure.
3. I hope it is clear that my remarks in this paragraph are not intended as a prudential argument for a virtuous life.
4. It may seem circular to suggest that, in order to be richly happy, one needs to acquire a rich conception of happiness. I mean that there must be an ability to differentiate (or a desire to

do so) between forms of happiness that are and are not worth having. One needs, at least at moments of crisis or conflict, to be able to reflect on the distinction between what I am calling happiness rich and poor. This is done, not cognitively, but by reference to human life, as discovered in everyday experiences, in rich, evocative writing, in reflection with others.

5. See Marit Hoveid and Arnhild Finne (Chapter 5) on love in educational relations.
6. See Williams, 1985, ch. 1.

REFERENCES

Ahmed, S. (2010) *The Promise of Happiness* (Durham and London: Duke University Press).

Aristotle (2002) *The Nicomachean Ethics*, J. Sachs, trans. (Newburyport, MA, Focus Publishing).

Bearn, G. (2013) Sensual Schooling: On the Aesthetic Education of Grown-Ups, in: N. Saito and P. Standish (eds) *Stanley Cavell and the Education of Grown-Ups* (New York, Fordham University Press).

Buber, M. (2002) Education, in his: *Between Man and Man* (London, Routledge).

Cigman, R. (2014) Education without Condescension: Philosophy, Personhood and Cognitive Disability, in: L. Florian (ed.) *Handbook of Special Education*, 2nd edn. (London, SAGE).

Diamond, C. (1996a) Having a Rough Story About What Moral Philosophy Is, in her: *The Realistic Spirit: Wittgenstein, Philosophy, and the Mind* (Cambridge, MA, MIT Press).

Diamond, C. (1996b) Secondary Sense, in her: *The Realistic Spirit: Wittgenstein, Philosophy, and the Mind* (Cambridge, MA, MIT Press).

Dunne, J. (1993) *Back to the Rough Ground: Practical Judgement and the Lure of Technique* (Notre Dame, IN, University of Notre Dame Press).

Eliot, G. (1996) *Middlemarch* (Oxford, Oxford University Press).

Eliot, G. (1998) *The Mill on the Floss* (Oxford, Oxford University Press).

Freud, S. (1985) *Civilisation and its Discontents* (Harmondsworth, Penguin).

Gaita, R. (2002) *A Common Humanity: Thinking About Love and Truth and Justice* (London, Routledge).

James, W. (1960) *The Varieties of Religious Experience* (London, Fontana).

Layard, R (2005), *Happiness: Lessons from a New Science* (Harmondsworth, Penguin).

Margalit, A. (2002), *The Ethics of Memory* (Cambridge, MA, Harvard University Press).

Mill, J. S. (1962) *Utilitarianism*, M. Warnock, ed. (London, Fontana).

Morris, I. (2009) *Teaching Happiness and Well-Being in Schools: Learning to Ride Elephants* (Camarthen, Network Continuum).

Nussbaum, M. (2001) *The Fragility of Goodness*, rev. edn. (Cambridge, Cambridge University Press).

Smeyers, P., Smith, R. and Standish, P. (2007) *The Therapy of Education* (Basingstoke, Palgrave Macmillan).

Whitehead, A. N. (1967) *The Aims of Education* (New York, Free Press).

Williams, B. (1985), *Ethics and the Limits of Philosophy* (London, Fontana).

Wittgenstein, L. (1953) *Philosophical investigations* (Oxford, Basil Blackwell).

Wittgenstein, L. (1980) *Culture and Value* (Oxford, Basil Blackwell).

Woolf, V. (1976), *Mrs Dalloway* (London, Grafton Books).

10
Guattari's Ecosophy and Implications for Pedagogy

HEATHER GREENHALGH-SPENCER

At the start of *The Three Ecologies*, Felix Guattari (2008) reminds us of the 'ecological disequilibrium' that threatens 'the continuation of life on the planet's surface. Alongside these upheavals, human modes of life, both individual and collective, are progressively deteriorating' (p. 19). Guattari (2008) points to the 'relationship between subjectivity and its exteriority—be it social, animal, vegetable, or Cosmic— that is compromised . . . in a sort of general movement of implosion and regressive infantalisation' (p. 19). He catalogues the degradation of the soil, water, and air, the massive economic crises, the increasing gaps between the wealthy and poor, the unfettered racism and sexism, and he argues that we need a new type of theory, a new philosophy, that can help us grapple with all of these overlapping problems. Guattari writes, 'political groupings and executive authorities appear to be totally incapable of understanding the full implications of these issues . . . only an ethico-political articulation—which I call *ecosophy* . . . would be likely to clarify these questions' (2008, pp. 19–20).

Guattari advocates ecosophy as an 'articulation' that foregrounds overlapping spheres of reality, and the ways these overlapping spheres can be articulated in new ways toward transformation. He highlights both mentalities and materialities as he advocates for an ecosophy that engages with the material, social, and ideological 'registers' of life (Guattari, 2008, p. 19). According to Guattari (2008), our social problems are interdependent and spread through multiple registers or fields of existence, so we need a theory capable of engaging with these overlaps and inter-dependencies. He argues that we need to enunciate new assemblages of existence; we need collective assemblages of human-nonhuman that 'assemble' to form spaces and modes of being that subvert capitalist trajectories of destruction.

Guattari is calling for a more radical way of understanding and engaging with economics, social development, and environmental

Re-Imagining Relationships in Education: Ethics, Politics and Practices, First Edition. Edited by Morwenna Griffiths, Marit Honerød Hoveid, Sharon Todd and Christine Winter. Chapters © 2015 The Authors. Editorial organization © 2015 Philosophy of Education Society of Great Britain. Published 2015 by John Wiley & Sons Ltd.

damage. His call for more radical change is not new, but he adds something new with his insightful discussion of the interactions, relationality, and also dynamism of the ways that the material, social, and ideological fields interact and shape each other.

Guattari's incitement to more radical and encompassing engagement with the various registers of existence deserves particular exploration in light of the ways that it can illuminate pedagogical practice—and not just pedagogical practices devoted to environmental sustainability. Guattari's ecosophy has implications for many types of pedagogy practiced in the school. While, to my knowledge, Guattari never explicitly advocated the educational use of ecosophy, ecosophy can be used as a lens to 'read' pedagogy in nuanced ways, highlighting oppressive premises and practices. In this chapter, I first discuss Guattari's ecosophy, placing his work within the extant literature on environmental education and science and technology studies; defining key terms and examining ecosophy as a philosophy radical and encompassing enough to make intelligible the dynamic connections between various fields of existence. I then offer a 'reading' of two different pedagogical strategies that have achieved a wide following in the last few decades: direct instruction, and critical pedagogy. Reading these pedagogies through ecosophy allows us to name more fully the troubling assumptions and lacunae of these pedagogical strategies.

As one more note of preface, I would like to situate this chapter within this book. This chapter, like others, explores connections between individuals, communities, practices, and the nonhuman (material) world. This book explicitly argues that connections are integral to education, and should be brought to the fore as part of the process of becoming educated. Many of the authors in book focus on human-to-human connections (see Hoveid and Finne in Chapter 5), or connections within a specific community (see Shuffelton in Chapter 3). For my part, I argue not only that education is a matter of connection to people and communities, but also that education involves an exploration and reimagagining of our connections to things, processes, and living systems. In fact, I contend that to privilege the connections between humans is to elide the shaping and transformative power of the nonhuman.

GUATTARI'S ECOSOPHY

Ecosophy, as a term, has not only been used by Guattari. For example, the term 'ecosophy' was first coined by Arne Naess

(1973/2010). However, as John Tinnell (2011) points out, Naess's conception of ecosophy is quite different from that put forward by Guattari. Writes Tinnell: 'At a fundamental level, the mission of Naess's ecosophy is to expand the sphere of objects with which people identify' (2011, para. 2). In other words, for Naess, ecosophy is about a deep personal commitment to and responsibility for the environment. One comes to identify with nature in order to preserve it. For Guattari, ecosophy instead involves a subjectivity instantiated as a process of coming together with other parts of nature (human and nonhuman) that create assemblages of identity, materiality, and practice. Guattari is concerned with remaking ontology as an assemblage of materiality, social practices, and the ideological or mental capacities.

One of the positions that marks Guattari as different from Naess—and from other scholars concerned with sustainability or environmental preservation—is the desire to avoid privileging any one position or stance. According to Tinnell, Guattari's ecosophy insists that the world is 'a dance between chaos and complexity—a multitude of productive syntheses between nomadic parts that exist independent of any fixed structure or transcendental whole' (Tinnell, 2011, para. 7). For Guattari, not only is there a push against hierarchy, but there is also a foregrounding of dynamism. There are times when materiality and the nonhuman are privileged as shaping powers within the world, but also times when human and global politics are pinpointed as shaping powers. That is to say, Guattari's ecosophy positions both the human and nonhuman as actants; both have the capacity to act as subjects, objects, and somewhere in-between. Guattari's ecosophy aims toward instability—instability of identity, of relationships, of connections, of 'knowns'—in order to create space for something new and, hopefully, less enmeshed within a predatory capitalism that has already colonized many current forms of life.

Guattari argues that all registers of life are interconnected; that the production of material artefacts are connected with social and cultural production; that our world is produced through the interaction of discourse, human practice, and materialities. In this way, Guattari's work finds affinity with philosophers like Walter Benjamin (1968), Martin Heidegger (1971 and 1962) and Henri Lefebvre (1992), who also examine the connections between culture, practice, and materialities. Ecosophy insists on valuing and examining the material world, technology, artefacts, and the ways that *things* can both shape and be shaped by humans. Akin to the work of scholars such as Donna Haraway (1991), Katherine Hales (1999), and Roseanne Alcuquere (Sandy) Stone (2001), Guattari's ecosophy advocates for an analysis of the blurred lines between humans and machines, people and their environments. The relationships of human and machine have bearing on the wider natural world and institutional environments in which we live.

Ecosophy takes a broad and dynamic view of nature, humans, materiality, and identity. Ecosophy resists privileging the human, and for this reason, pushes against the work of scholars such as Chet Bowers (2008) who views humans as being the primary agents of change. For Guattari, humans are not the only part of the equation, and not the only entities capable of action or subjectivity. Ecosophy also resists preference for nature—resists ecocentricity—and this places ecosophy apart from the work of philosophers such as Helen Kopnina (2011, 2012, 2013), who argues for an ecocentric view of activism, education and the world. Guattari is not advocating for environmental activism or ecological sustainability *per se*, but for a more encompassing change in how we understand and act in our world; a change that would involve more than just personal commitments or government policies aimed at saving the environment. Ecosophy highlights the nonhuman, but also highlights the human, the processual, the systematic, the parts, the whole: a holism of multiple shifting flexible wholes, that is always and never simply made up of the whole and its parts.

Ecosophy is political and calls for a new politics, a new subjectivity, a new vision, and yet also resists saying or showing what that new vision, subjectivity, or politics might look like. In this way, Guattari's ecosophy contrasts with the scholarship of Andrew Stables and William Scott (2001) as well as Christine Winter (2007) who, like Guattari, contend that ecological disaster is linked to consumerism and capitalist forces. However, Guattari also insists that capitalism is not the only 'force' that has the power to shape the way we understand and practice identity, social institutions, processes, and 'making' of all sorts. Guattari resists calls to activism that are already pre-determined in what they would look like; he avoids the programmatic. Guattari's work is difficult to apply, and one of the main critiques of his political philosophy is that it is, perhaps, not concrete enough, or invested enough in a particular form of action.

On this view, ecosophical politics, activism, attitudes, and education are dynamic and multiple, attentive to time and place, and also mutating, continuous, and flexible. Both the human and nonhuman are linked and centred to become a bi-polarity of agency. The need for dynamism in how we think about activism and change finds resonance with many philosophers of education who have tried to draw attention to environmental issues and the complex interaction of politics, discourse, policy, and materiality. Michael Bonnett (1999, 2002), for one, has argued extensively for an environmental education that draws attention to the ways that identity formation and our sense of ourselves is bound up in our relationships with nature. Bonnett (2002) has also called for an understanding of ecology that neither privileges the anthropocentric nor the ecocentric, and that advocates for a dynamism in how we act toward making our world better. Guattari's ecosophy also finds resonance with Bob Jickling's (2003) argument that activism and education can and should involve a focus on the nonhuman, but should also be different in different spaces; there is always an insistence on multiplicity.

While Guattari's ecosophy tends to resist 'application', there are implications for pedagogy that deserve further exploration. Ecosophy allows us to engage critically with some pedagogical strategies that have, perhaps, become a little too taken-for-granted. Ecosophy pushes against the formulaic and technocratic tendencies that appear to be so rampant in schooling at the moment. And, unlike much of the literature in philosophy of education, it refuses to privilege environmental concerns, identity concerns, race, class, gender, individual action, social action, and material production and destruction. Ecosophy resists the idea of 'centring' any one issue or concern, and advocates for 'molecular change' in all of these areas. Rather than creating 'recipes for emancipation', 'learning objectives' or 'learning outcomes', Guattari's ecosophy is more organic, rhizomatic, and relational in its sense of reality and of transformation. This makes it a powerful counter-discourse to many pedagogical strategies—even progressive ones. It is also a powerful lens through which we can view pedagogical strategies and educational discourses that have become all too familiar; it is a lens that can push us toward re-thinking our own relationships in the classroom as well as our identities and actions in the larger world.

In order to argue that Guattari's ecosophy has profound implications for pedagogy, I first map out in more depth some key ideas in Guattari's ecosophy and explore in further detail what Guattari means by ecosophy, assemblage, the human-nonhuman, and the transformative project of enunciating new assemblages. All of these concepts are interwoven into Guattari's conception of reality and change. The concepts lean on and mutually-define each other; so my attempt to parse out these terms should be seen as an attempt to weave multiple threads together simultaneously, rather than defining one concept as hierarchically premised on another concept.

Guattari's definition of ecosophy specifically involves a broader understanding of ecology; ecology becomes reframed in reference to relationships with a wider range of processes, machines, people, the biological, the material, the sociological, and the ideological. He argues, 'The ecological crisis can be traced to a more general crisis of the social, political and existential', which 'involve[s] changes in production, ways of living and axes of value' (Guattari, 1995, p. 119 and p. 134). Guattari (1997) centres the interconnectivity of the material, social, and ideological/mental spheres when he writes:

> Ecological disasters, famine, unemployment, the escalation of racism and xenophobia, hunt, like so many threats, the end of this millennium . . . humanity . . . passively contributes to the pollution of water and the air, to the destruction of forests, to the disturbance of climates, to the disappearance of a multitude of living species, to the impoverishment of the genetic capital of the biosphere, to the destruction of natural landscapes, to the suffocation of its cities, and to the progressive abandonment of cultural values and moral references in the areas of human solidarity and fraternity (para. 1).

He explicitly connects environmental catastrophes, socio-economic problems, and mentalities. Guattari not only outlines what he sees to be mounting global problems, but he also argues for a change in how we characterise—and then contend with—these problems. Guattari continues:

> By what means, in the current climate of passivity, could we unleash a mass awakening, a new renaissance? . . . Emphasis must be placed, above all, on the reconstruction of a collective dialogue capable of producing innovative practices. Without a change in mentalities, . . . there can be no enduring hold over the environment. Yet, without modifications to the social and material environment, there can be no change in mentalities. Here, we are in the presence of a circle that leads me to postulate the necessity of founding an 'ecosophy' that would link environmental ecology to social ecology and to mental ecology (1997, para. 8).

Guattari (1997) argues that we need transformation in the material, the social, and the ideological fields. From these connections emerge the necessity of positing an ecosophy that enunciates—and calls for new enunciations—of the assemblages of the material, social, and mental spheres. Changes must be made that address all 'registers' of existence.

Guattari's notion of ecosophy comes into sharper focus when we reflect on his notion of 'assemblage'. Ecosophy regards humans, nonhumans, structures, ideologies, practices, and beliefs as 'parts' that can form an integrated constellation. For Guattari, 'assemblage' is not necessarily meant to participate in discourses linked in with machinery—although Guattari finds benefit in the non-hierarchic nature of machinic assemblages—but for Guattari the idea of assemblage is meant to draw attention to relationality and to the multiplicity of identity, where human and nonhuman can be synchronously subjects, objects, and somewhere in-between within larger wholes, and where these positionalities can change, overlap, and interact.

For example, when humans harness the power of wind—through the use of wind turbines—the wind becomes the object and the humans subjects who are using wind power toward particular ends. However, as a person who lives in an area where tornadoes are common, I can also attest to the fact that humans can become objects at the mercy of the wind. And even that example is not quite right because it participates in binaries where subject positionality is posited against object positionality.

Ecosophy instead subverts old binaries in which one must be identified, and perhaps reified, as *either* subject *or* object. The human-nonhuman, the whole-part, the subject-object, the individual-society, the social-material, the discursive-real—all are old binaries that Guattari (2008) rejects in favour of the argument that identity, in all of its forms, is always on the move, and can always break out into something new. The point of ecosophy is to re-think the old stable categories of identity, and so the term 'assemblage' is meant to call attention to the dynamism of life and materiality. Thus, even when Guattari uses terms such as 'human' and 'nonhuman', the idea is not to validate a binary, but to call attention to other 'parts' of our world that we do not normally consider—as we do not normally consider the nonhuman—in order to then push against the binary relationships in which we traditionally hold humans and nonhumans. Guattari (2008) advocates for a modularity where subjects and objects (and whatever lies in-between) can be named and described, but are never stable, reified, or completely known.

Guattari uses the idea of 'assemblage' to move away from such binaries, to promote multiplicity, and to draw attention to immanent context. For example, in *The Three Ecologies*, he posits the problem of analysing and critiquing the practice of hospital/clinic-based psychotherapy. In order to fully articulate and then change this practice, one must enunciate all of the various parts at play: 'the institutional context, its constraints, organizations, practices, etc., all those things and relations which normally exist in the background; in short, the group is how one gets at the institution' (Guattari, 2008, p. 50). Each 'part' plays into the assemblage. Each part is dynamic and is never fully stable. Transformation involves new enunciations of assemblage; and more than that, a process of continual enunciation and re-enunciation. Guattari prompts us to ask: What assemblage must be in place for this moment to happen? How can 'parts' come to form an assemblage in a different way to enact change? How can we continue to re-enunciate parts in new ways?

Integral to the concepts of both ecosophy and assemblage is the human-nonhuman connection. While Guattari rejects binaries, he argues for increased focus on the ways that things, locations, spaces, materialities (the nonhuman) are part of assemblages. Much like Griffith's work in Chapter 11—which focuses on the need to reflect on and engage with the 'more than human'—Guattari insists that what he terms the 'nonhuman' needs to be highlighted as a powerful 'part' of any assemblage. This is not to suggest that the nonhuman has more force or precedent than the human, but points to the fact that the nonhuman is usually elided in favour of 'human' considerations. Guattari continually brings our focus to the nonhuman as a way of reminding us of its equal importance to human processes.

In her own theorizations of Deleuze and Guattari, Jane Bennett (2010) argues that Guattari's focus on the human-nonhuman assemblage allows us to engage better with the 'force' of nonhuman parts. Bennett contends that the 'nonhuman' involves 'the capacity of things—edibles, commodities, storms, metals—not only to impede or block the will and designs of humans but also to act as quasi agents or forces with trajectories, propensities, or tendencies of their own' (2010, p, viii). Bennett asks: 'how analyses of political events might change if we gave the force of things more due' (2010, p. viii). Drawing on Guattari's concept of the nonhuman, Bennett poses the question:

> How, for example, would patterns of consumption change if we faced not litter, rubbish, trash, or 'the recycling', but an accumulating pile of lively and potentially dangerous matter? . . . What difference would it make to the course of energy policy were electricity to be figured not simply as a resource, commodity, or instrumentality but also and more radically as an 'actant'? (2010, p. viii).

As Guattari (2008) argues, it is often through the practice of focusing on the nonhuman that the assemblages of human-nonhuman become intelligible, and this begins the process of enunciating new assemblages.

Enunciating new assemblages transforms both mental and material spheres and creates the possibility for change and transformation. Guattari (2008) contends that the process of 'enunciating new assemblages' consists of reworking, reimagining, and re-experimenting with collectives of human-nonhuman parts. This 'enunciation of the new' does not point to projects of individualism or even liberation. Enunciating new assemblages is always an experimentation because assemblages are composed of various human-nonhuman parts that are co-variably and invariably agentic in the shaping of the political landscape. Still, these new assemblages can themselves be shaped through the rejection of capitalist values that exist in multiple registers. As Bennett puts it, new anti-capitalist assemblages can emerge or can be 'provoked into existence by shared experience of harm' (2010, p. xix).

For Guattari (2008), the enunciation of new assemblages should at least aim toward a newness that rejects capitalistic values. Pinder and Sutton (2008) argue that Guattari's ecosophy rejects capitalism because 'a capitalism that does not exploit resources . . . is as yet unthinkable. A capitalism that is symbiotic rather than parasitic may never be possible' (p. 15). Rather than trying to coerce capitalistic systems into the support of nature, materiality, society, and equity, Guattari (2008) argues that there needs to be a new and global politics of heterogenesis, where there is a continual process of enunciation that both unifies and makes politics, action, and identity, increasingly different and divergent. He champions enunciative processes and interventions that push away from the homogenization of global capitalism, and that instead create new venues for nascent subjectivity—an ongoing process of creating new subject positionalities that are always in flux toward the new—as well as creating a constantly mutating social landscape and an environment always in the process of being reinvented (Guattari, 2008). Ecosophy is anti-capitalist, but is very different in its forms of political intervention and activism when compared with many emancipatory projects.

The process of enunciating the new—new assemblages of material fields, social fields, and ideological fields—is not a directed process; neither is it something that is 'given' in advance. Guattari offers the following example as a way of defining what it means to enunciate new assemblages:

The best artists don't repeat themselves, they start over and over again from scratch, uncertain with each new attempt precisely where their new experiment will take them, but then suddenly, spontaneously and unaccountably, as the painter Francis Bacon has observed, 'there comes something which your instinct seizes on as being for a moment the thing which you could begin to develop' (2008, p. 8).

Enunciating new assemblages is a process that is immanent, that develops organically and in the moment. While Guattari insists that new assemblages will *de facto* consist of multiple parts, both human and nonhuman, there is no sense that these parts must stay together. The immanence and dynamism of 'parts' subvert the practice of creating a 'recipe' for emancipation or empowerment. There is an urge toward dynamism, cybernetic connection, and viral flow. Pinder and Sutton contend that, for Guattari, 'social activism involves *dissensus*' (2008, p. 9). There should be a proliferation of spontaneously-organizing groups: groups that spontaneously organise themselves, or that are organised from a spontaneous and organic moment. Again, Guattari resists the desire to turn activism into a program or project. This will lead to short-lived 'affinity groups', 'unified disunity' and 'pragmatic solidarity' (Pinder and Sutton, 2008, p. 10). Transformation is here both organic and dynamic.

All of these components of Guattari's ecosophy have implications for pedagogy. In many ways, ecosophy offers a direct challenge to several pedagogical strategies that have gained credence in the past twenty years. In the next section, I offer a reading of these pedagogical strategies through ecosophy, focusing specifically on the pedagogical practices of direct instruction and critical pedagogy.

READING 'DIRECT INSTRUCTION' THROUGH ECOSOPHY

Direct instruction is a model of teaching that has gained currency throughout the last several decades. It was born out the social efficiency movements of the earl 20th Century, and is a derivation of the technocratic curricula championed by Franklin Bobbitt (1913/1918) and Ralph Tyler (1949). It has its modern adherents in Stockard (2011), Ganz and Flores (2009), Vitale and Joseph (2008) and others. Direct Instruction (DI) is premised on the notion that education involves the breakdown of knowledge into discrete tasks and skills that can be memorised and then re-produced on tests. As one pre-service teacher educational handbook argues regarding DI, 'When teachers explain exactly what students are expected to learn, and demonstrate the steps needed to accomplish a particular academic task, students learn more' (Vockell, 1988, sec. 3.2). Note the following description of DI from this same handbook:

Direct instruction rejects (or at least sets aside) the assumption that students will spontaneously develop insights on their own. Rather, direct instruction takes learners through the steps of learning systematically, helping them see both the purpose and the result of each step (Vockell, 1988, sec. 3.2).

Yet another handbook for pre-service teachers contends that DI is one of the best ways to prepare students for tests because this pedagogical strategy gets the information across to students through: 'structured overview, lecture, explicit teaching, drill and practice, compare and contrast, and didactic questions' (Instructional Strategies Online, 2013). This pedagogical strategy moves away from problem-posing and problem-solving toward the dispersal of information, preparing students to memorise and recreate that information on tests. It is a method that tends to trust neither the teachers nor the students as learners. Nowhere can this be seen more readily than in the *Success for All* program.

Success for All (SFA) was developed by Robert Slavin of Johns Hopkins University as a pedagogical method 'designed to ensure that all students, from all backgrounds, achieve at the highest levels' (Lunnenberg, 2011, p. 1). According to many proponents of the method, 'SFA is a turnaround/transformational blueprint' for how schools should be run (Lunnenberg, 2011, p. 1). In this way, SFA is positioned as emancipatory because it can narrow achievement gaps on high-stakes tests.

SFA is built around the premise that all school lessons should be scripted. The goal is to reduce variance from one teacher to another such that—supposedly—all students will learn the same things. Teachers receive manuals outlining all of the lessons they should cover. Each lesson is scripted out with the exact language the teacher should use, and the exact responses that students should have. Students get workbooks that contain the lines that they are supposed to say. Teachers are not supposed to vary from the script and students are taught to say their 'lines' over and over again. In practice, SFA becomes a performance of 'drill and kill' methods.

On YouTube, there are countless examples of SFA and other DI methods being practiced in the classroom. In one of the more illustrative videos[1] you can watch as teachers read their scripts, without even looking up to make eye contact with any of the students, banging on their manuals, signalling to the students that it is now their turn to repeat the information just delivered by the teacher. And the kids do it with mostly one voice. The teacher proclaims, 'Spell sliced.' And the students unite in one chorus of 'S-L-I-C-E-D.' 'Again', the teacher says. 'S-L-I-C-E-D', the students chant back. These drills are not done at the whim or will of the teacher. Each drill is scripted as part of the daily activities that teachers must complete. Teachers are not supposed to take the time to engage with any questions or issues outside of the ones covered in the manual. If teachers get behind or go 'off script', then they are seen as doing a disservice to their students; they are seen as hindering student progress because they are not keeping up with the program. Teachers can be penalised by their principals and other district leaders for going off-script. There is also the force of parental concern; once parents have bought into the program, teachers who do not practice the program as it is scripted can be subject to complaints from parents.

In many ways, Guattari's ecosophy acts a counter-discourse to SFA and other DI pedagogies. At its core, ecosophy looks at the ideological, social and environmental problems in the world, sees the current assemblages in place that create those problems, and then argues that transformations can be made through processes of enunciating assemblages differently—through exploring new assemblages, new parts, and new ways of being that affect both mentalities and materialities. This is a continuous process, as assemblages—including the ones that validate predatory capitalism—are always changing. However, the changes do not often move toward new ways of being, but toward a re-enforcement of capitalist values and practices. Guattari's ecosophy argues for a re-enunciation of assemblages that aim to push against capitalism on multiple fronts or in multiple registers of existence in order to create possibilities for existence to be different. In DI, social and environmental problems are not seen as being connected to discourses, practices, and material objects; they are seen as a set of facts that should be memorised for later recitation. There is no acknowledgment of human-nonhuman parts. This means that students are not able to engage critically with the ways that the natural world, the world of things, and the world of humans, of social processes, interact with and shape each other for better or for worse. Students are not seen as even a 'part' of a locus of knowledge, action, or transformation into the new. In fact, if students—or teachers—try to enunciate newness, they can be reprimanded for going off script by their principals or other supervisors.

Through ecosophy, we can read DI as a failed pedagogy that focuses on tests rather than on being, reality, world problems, and transformation. This reading of DI, likely, comes as no shock to most of us within philosophy of education. Direct instruction is a fairly easy target if we value pedagogical strategies that aim to change human, environmental, and material conditions. But how would ecosophy help us 'read' a pedagogy explicitly devoted to change and empowerment? In this next section I focus on critical pedagogy—underpinned by Freire's *Pedagogy of the Oppressed* and his commitment to dialogue and problem-posing education—as also worthy of ecosophic critique.

READING CRITICAL PEDAGOGY THROUGH ECOSOPHY

In the past few decades, and often as a subversion of DI pedagogies, critical pedagogy has emerged as a strategy toward empowerment and transformation. Educational theorists and pedagogues such as Ira Shor and Caroline Pari (1999), Peter McLaren (1995), Patrick Finn (1999), and many others have touted critical pedagogy as a way to see and engage critically with the world around us, make connections between politics, ideologies, and oppressive practices, and—eventually— change the world and the plight of the people in it toward more egalitarian ways of being. Either explicitly or implicitly, these scholars invoke the work of Paulo Freire (1997) and his pedagogical strategies. While scholars such as Elizabeth Ellsworth (1989) have critiqued Freirean pedagogy for creating false binaries, there are many pedagogues who still use and advocate for some version of Freirean pedagogy in the classroom. In my own work with pre-service and in-service teachers, I am always struck by how many of these teachers (many of them white and upper-class) feel transformed by Freire's writings and consciously endeavour to employ his pedagogical strategies in their classrooms.

To my mind, Freire's work is profound, appealing, and aims in a positive direction. However, Guattari's ecosophy allows us to read Freire's work in a more nuanced way, to see its gaps and find alternative assemblages of parts.

Freire posits his pedagogy of the oppressed as 'the practice of freedom' (1997, p. 8). He writes:

[A] pedagogy that must be forged *with*, not *for*, the oppressed (whether individuals or peoples) in the incessant struggle to regain their humanity. This pedagogy makes oppression and its causes objects of reflection by the oppressed, and from that reflection will come their necessary engagement in the struggle for their liberation . . . The pedagogy of the oppressed is an instrument for their critical discovery that both they and their oppressors are manifestations of dehumanization (1997, p. 30).

Freire likens the project of liberation to that of birth, and suggests that there are allies and teachers who can act as midwives to this birth;

teachers engage students in a process of dialogue that results in *con-scientization* of the oppressed, which then leads to action toward liberation (1997, p. 30). The teachers are supposed to 'organize' the oppressed students into moments for this critical reflection (1997, p. 36).

While Freire's project aims at a pedagogy of transformation, there are two main critiques that ecosophy can make against Freire's version of transformation. The first has to do with Freire's framing of his project as one that pits the human against the nonhuman. Freire contends that the pedagogy of the oppressed enables people to 'change their weakness into a transforming force with which they can re-create the world and make it more human' (1997, p. 126). It is the goal of this pedagogy to move toward becoming more fully human; this pedagogy places humanness at its centre (1997, p. 65). In fact, Freire (1997) explicitly marks humans as separate from (and more important than) the world of animals, living systems, and material things. Freire points to the human capacity for thought and argues that 'this capacity distinguishes him from the animals' (1997, p. 78). Freire goes on to argue that animals and other living and nonliving systems exist ahistorically, and this 'ahistorical condition does not permit them to 'take on' life' (1997, p. 79). He contends that only humans are capable of reflective thought, and thus they exist as 'separate from the world' (1997, p. 80).

Freire's pedagogy, and most critical pedagogies that rely on Freire's work, frame humans and human interaction as the only important relationship worthy of critical reflection; interactions between and among humans are made the pinnacle of educative practice, to the elision of any other relationships and connections. As Freire argues, 'human beings emerge from the world, objectify it, and in so doing can understand it and transform it with their labor' (1997, p. 106). He positions humans as outside of the world and the only 'actants' within the world.

Guattari's ecosophy pushes against this pedagogical practice. Instead, ecosophy foregrounds the assemblages of the human-nonhuman relation. Ecosophy makes explicit the idea that human interaction is only one component of how we exist in the world. *Things* also have the ability to shape our world. Our relationships with living systems, material objects, geographical spaces—as well as social institutions and practices—need enunciation and re-enunciation in order to move toward transformation. Ecosophy prompts us to see the interactions of *all of the parts*, and invites a very different kind of pedagogical strategy than the one employed by Freire.

For example, while Freire's work in Brazil focused on socio-economic relationships between the peasant class and the upper class, ecosophy would reframe the moment as one that included not only upper class members of society (one part in the assemblage) as being in conflict with peasant members of society (another part in the assemblage), but would also include other parts that makeup the dynamic assemblage shaping these relationships: the tensions of the rural areas of the Amazon in conflict with the urbanised areas of Sao Paulo; the shaping power of global interests in Brazil's iron ore, petroleum, sugar, and coffee exports, which push against local concerns around food production; and the unique and situated inflections to the global discourse on entitlement and job creation.

Furthermore, ecosophy offers a more open and potentially radical notion of transformation. This brings me to the second critique ecosophy could make against critical pedagogy: that critical pedagogy is too didactic and scripted to lead to something really 'new.' Thinking with Guattari (1997), one could say that critical pedagogy may lead to a remodelling of the world, but not to transformation. For Guattari, transformation emerges in the spaces where people, collections, individuals, communities, materialities, places, and practices are enunciated (and enmeshed in the process of enunciating) toward difference, toward something new that does not already rely on current ways of being as either the foundation or the foil. Again, Guattari aims to thwart binary thinking; even as he first names the binaries—of capitalism and anti-capitalism for example—that need to undergo a process of re-enunciation, he also invites us to think and act apart from that binary. Transformation is developmental, but not didactic or directed. This type of transformation is in contrast to Freire's more directed project of liberation.

While Freire (1997) insists that true dialogue and emancipatory pedagogy consist of a breaking-down of hierarchy (the student becomes the teacher and vice versa), he is also quite clear that there are leaders and objectives. Freire's program for liberation involves certain steps that must be followed, and guides who are supposed to make sure that those steps are followed. Note the language as Freire describes the initial work of the teachers/investigators as they begin to interact with the students/oppressed:

> Once the investigators have determined the area in which they will work and have acquired a preliminary acquaintance with the area through secondary sources, they initiate the first stage of the investigation . . . In this first contact, the investigators need to get a significant number of persons to agree to an informal meeting

during which they can talk about the objectives of their presence in the area. In this meeting they explain the reason for the investigation, how it is to be carried out, and to what use it will be put; they further explain that the investigation will be impossible without a relation of mutual understanding and trust (1997, p. 91).

This quote shows that the teachers are always/already positioned as instructors of the people. The teachers have a set program, and are in charge of teaching the students how to carry it out. These investigators are also positioned as surveyors of their students or of the people-to-be-conscientised; it is their job to investigate and report on what the local people are doing or not doing. Freire writes: 'After each observation visit, the investigator should draw up a brief report to be discussed by the entire team, in order to evaluate the preliminary findings of both the professional investigators and the local assistants' (1997, p. 93). After all, 'the fact that the leaders who organize the people do not have the right to arbitrarily impose their word does not mean that they must therefore take the liberalist position which would encourage license among the people, who are accustomed to oppression' (1997, p. 159).

Teachers are positioned as knowers and governors of truth. Freire's project is to get the oppressed to see the truth of their oppression—the true reality. And it is the teacher who is positioned as the arbiter of what counts as that truth and reality. Conscientisation involves a 'process in which individuals analysing their own reality become aware of their prior, distorted perceptions and thereby come to have a new perception of that reality' (1997, p. 95). 'It is assumed' that the teachers will have the necessary 'critical perception of the world, which implies a correct method of approaching reality in order to unveil it' (1997, p. 92). Thus, the teachers decide what counts as a critical perception of the world as opposed to distorted perceptions of the world.

Ecosophy counters the more didactic tendencies of critical pedagogy by insisting that transformation—and any real change in the world that subverts capitalist tendencies and other oppressive systems—emerges in moments of experimentation where the end cannot be completely known and the process cannot be completely figured beforehand. Transformation comes about through new assemblages—collectives of all sorts. Whereas critical pedagogy consists of a program focused on coming to a 'truth', and on dyadic relationships (teacher/student, oppressor/oppressed, human/not-human, reality/distorted reality), ecosophy focuses on experimentation, organic exploration, and multiplicity of parts and possibilities. As we read critical pedagogy through ecosophy we can see the didactic practices and scripted moments that work against more radical change.

CONCLUSION

As Bennett (2010) argues, while ecosophy neither privileges the eco-centric nor the anthropocentric, it nevertheless creates a necessary emphasis on 'the agentic contributions of nonhuman forces (operating in nature, in the human body, and in human artefacts) in an attempt to counter the narcissistic reflex of human language and thought' (p. xvi). Ecosophy enunciates and enunciates-differently the assemblages of materialities, social institutions and practices, and ideologies, and also provides a critical lens on current practices in the school which tend to elide the variable and connected assemblages at play. Ecosophy focuses on newness; the creation of newness that happens—and needs to happen—in all registers of life. It focuses on a new type of politics, identity formation, and activism that articulates both unity and difference toward newness, experimentation away from capitalism and other consumeristic tendencies.

Ecosophy makes a particularly salient intervention in that it pushes against both neoliberalism's focus on the responsibility of the individual, and current educational policy's championing of an economistic and technocratic view of education. Where neoliberalism focuses on the individual, ecosophy focuses on the interconnections, tensions, and overlaps of assemblages that create and re-create never-fully-created wholes. Where current educational policy advocates for measurement, known strategies, and scripts, ecosophy advocates for experimentation and newness. Ecosophy makes a critical case for being sceptical and even pushing against current discourses around creating 'efficient' and monetarily independent schooling entities. Ecosophy moves toward new subjectivities, assemblages, de- and re-territorialisations that are flexible, dynamic, open, rhizomatic, and multiple.

Ecosophy resists becoming a 'recipe' for 'correct' pedagogical practice, but it still can offer us a more radical understanding of problems, inter-dependencies, and the possibility for change when compared to many of the pedagogies in use in schools. More can be done to use ecosophy as a way to understand the world in all of its dynamic and connected assemblages, and more can be done, perhaps, to use ecosophy—even if only as a critical lens focused on current pedagogies—within the site of the school.

NOTE

1. http://www.youtube.com/watch?v=3cwODCQ9BnU

REFERENCES

Benjamin, W. (1968) *Illuminations: Essays and Reflections* (New York, Random House).
Bennett, J. (2010) *Vibrant Matter* (Durham, NC, Duke University Press).
Bobbitt, J. F. (1913/ 1918) *The Curriculum* (New York, Houghton-Mifflin Company).
Bonnett, M. (1999) Education for Sustainable Development: A Coherent Philosophy for Environmental Education?, *Cambridge Journal of Education*, 29.3, pp. 313–324.
Bonnett, M. (2002) Education for Sustainability as a Frame of Mind, *Environmental Education Research*, 8.1, pp. 9–20.
Bowers, C. (2008) Why a Critical Pedagogy of Place is an Oxymoron, *Environmental Education Research*, 14.3, pp. 325–335.
Ellsworth, E. (1989) Why Doesn't This Feel More Empowering?: Working Through the Repressive Myths of Critical Pedagogy, *Harvard Educational Review*, 59.3, pp. 297–325.
Finn, P. J. (1999) *Literacy with an Attitude* (Albany, NY, State University of New York Press).
Freire, P. (1997) *Pedagogy of the Oppressed* (New York, Continuum Publishing Company).
Ganz, J. and Flores, M. (2009) The Effectiveness of Direct Instruction for Teaching Language to Children with Autism Spectrum Disorder, *Journal of Autism and Developmental Disorders*, 39.1, pp. 75–83.
Guattari, F. (1995) *Chaosmosis*, P. Bains and J. Pefanis, trans. (Bloomington, IN, Indiana University Press).
Guattari, F. (1997) *Remaking Social Practices*. Online at: http://www.nettime.org/Lists-Archives/nettime-l-9710/msg00015.html
Guattari, F. (2008) *The Three Ecologies*, I. Pinder and P. Sutton, trans. (London, Continuum)
Hales, N. K. (1999) *How We Became Posthuman* (Chicago, IL, University of Chicago Press).
Haraway, D. (1991) *Simians, Cyborgs, and Women: The Reinvention of Nature* (New York, Routledge).
Heidegger, M. (1962) *Being and Time*, T. Carmon, trans. (New York, Harper and Rowe Publishing).
Heidegger, M. (1971) The Thing, in his *Poetry, Language, Thought*, A. Hofstadter, trans. (New York, Harper and Rowe Publishing).
Instructional Strategies Online (2013) Online at: http://olc.spsd.sk.ca/DE/PD/instr/direct.html
Jickling, B. (2003) Environmental Education and Environmental Advocacy: Revisited, *The Journal of Environmental Education*, 34.2, pp. 20–27.
Kopnina, H. (2011) Revisiting Education for Sustainable Development (ESD): Examining Anthropocentric Bias Through the Transition of Environmental Education to ESD, *Sustainable Development*, doi:10.1002/sd.529.
Kopnina, H. (2012) Education for Sustainable Development (ESD): The Turn Away from 'Environment' in Environmental Education?, *Environmental Education Research*, 18.5, pp. 699–717.
Kopnina, H. (2013) Forsaking Nature? Contesting 'Biodiversity' Through Competing Discourses of Sustainability, *Journal of Education for Sustainable Development*, 7.1, pp. 51–63.
Lefebvre, H. (1992) *The Production of Space*, D. Nicholson-Smith, trans. (Oxford, Wiley-Blackwell).

Lunnenberg, F. (2011) A System-WideTurnaround/Transformational Blueprint for Closing the Achievement Gap, *Schooling*, 2.1, pp. 1–9.

McLaren, P. (1995) *Critical Pedagogy and Predatory Culture* (New York, Routledge).

Naess, A. (1973 / 2010) *The Ecology of Wisdom* (New York, Counterpoint).

Pinder, I. and Sutton, P. (2008) Translators Notes, for *The Three Ecologies* (London, Continuum).

Shor, I. and Pari, C. (1999) *Education is Politics* (Portsmouth, NH, Boynton/Cook Publishers).

Stables, A. and Scott, W. (2001) Post-Humanist Liberal Pragmatism? Environmental Education Out of Modernity, *Journal of Philosophy of Education*, 35.2, pp. 269–279.

Stockard, J. (2011) Direct Instruction and First Grade Reading Achievement: The Role of Technical Support and Time of Implementation, *Journal of Direct Instruction*, 11.1, pp. 31–50.

Stone, A. R. (Sandy) (2001) *The War of Desire and Technology at the Close of the Mechanical Age* (Cambridge, MA, MIT Press)

Tinnell, J. (2011) Transversalising the Ecological Turn: Four Components of Felix Guattari's Ecosophical Perspective, *The Fibreculture Journal* (18). Online at: http://eighteen .fibreculturejournal.org/2011/10/09/fcj-121-transversalising-the-ecological-turn-four -components-of-felix-guattari%E2%80%99s-ecosophical-perspective/

Tyler, R. (1949) *Basic Principles of Curriculum and Instruction* (Chicago, IL, University of Chicago Press).

Vitale, M. and Joseph, B. (2008) Broadening the Institutional Value of Direct Instruction in a Low-SES Elementary School: Implications for Scale-Up and School Reform, *Journal of Direct Instruction*, 8.1, pp. 1–18.

Vockell, E. (1988) *Computer in the Classroom* (New York, McGraw-Hill).

Winter, C. (2007) Education for Sustainable Development and the Secondary Curriculum in English Schools: Rhetoric or Reality?, *Cambridge Journal of Education*, 37.3, pp. 337–354.

11
Educational Relationships: Rousseau, Wollstonecraft and Social Justice

MORWENNA GRIFFITHS

INTRODUCTION

> A wild wish has just flown from my heart to my head, and I will not stifle it though it may excite a horse-laugh.—I do earnestly wish to see the distinction of sex confounded in society, unless where love animates the behaviour (Wollstonecraft, [1792] 1994, p. 126).

I consider educational relationships as found in Rousseau's *Émile* (and elsewhere in his writing) and the critique of his views in Wollstonecraft's *A Vindication of the Rights of Women*. I argue that we can benefit not only from her critique of Rousseau but also from her alternative approach. Rousseau and Wollstonecraft discuss educational relationships which contribute to a more socially just world: between human beings now and in the future, between teacher and students (individually and as a group), and between human beings and the rest of the natural world, the more-than-human. I argue that their educational approaches point to a significant difference in their understanding of social justice i.e. of how to live well, here, now, and in the future, as individuals always in relation with their human and more-than-human contexts.[1] This difference is connected to their conceptions of how human beings become who and what they are. I begin by placing the two authors in their historical contexts and then go on to outline how their views of educational relationships differ, starting with how they see education as contributing to a more just future and moving on to a consideration of relationships between teacher and students with regard to freedom and to individualised learning. Finally, I consider relationships between human beings and the

Re-Imagining Relationships in Education: Ethics, Politics and Practices, First Edition. Edited by Morwenna Griffiths, Marit Honerød Hoveid, Sharon Todd and Christine Winter. Chapters © 2015 The Authors. Editorial organization © 2015 Philosophy of Education Society of Great Britain. Published 2015 by John Wiley & Sons Ltd.

more-than-human. These relationships are seldom recognised as con-tributing to a more socially just education,[2] so I consider them at a little more length, drawing from observations by Kathleen Jamie (2005, 2012) and using an example from outdoor education to suggest possible implications for educational practices.

ROUSSEAU'S *ÉMILE* AND WOLLESTONECRAFT'S *VINDICATION*

Rousseau's book *Émile* published in 1762 reads as something between a manual and a (very long) fervent letter about how to educate a boy, Émile, and also a girl, Sophie, so they grow up to be ideal citizens of an ideal republic. Very briefly, the book takes the following form. The boy is removed from his family from the age of two, and put under the guidance of a tutor who ensures that the child's education matches his natural stages of development. He is taught on his own, being allowed only the occasional social event with other children, so that he does not get contaminated by contact with the imperfect, over-mannered, social world around him. He then moves through more stages of learning, all of which are tightly controlled, until he becomes a man, at which point he meets and marries Sophie. She, meanwhile, has been carefully taught, at home, by her mother, to be dependent, obedient and pretty because these are qualities which are all natural to her and which need to be encouraged for Émile's sake and also for the sake of the citizenry as a whole (Martin, 1985, 1986). The adult Émile has the virtues of a man: an autonomous, rational citizen in control of his emotions. The adult Sophie has the virtues of a woman: a dependent, obedient, loving partner.

Émile was immensely influential at the time, as well as being extremely controversial. Many of Rousseau's educational ideas draw on some of those found in other significant authors, such as Comenius and Locke, but the way he brought them together with his political commitments electrified his generation. The book was soon being discussed throughout Europe, having been translated into a number of languages. His influence on Kant's philosophy is well known, for instance (Bloom, 1979; Steinkraus, 1974). At the same time, the book was found to be so deeply offensive, especially in relation to his criticism of religion, most clearly evident in the character of the Savoyard priest who appears in Book IV, that Rousseau had to flee the mob.

After Rousseau's death, *Émile* caught the imagination of future educators, many of them influential in their own right: Pestalozzi, Froebel, Steiner, Montessori and Dewey are just a few of them.

Darling and Nordenbo trace the history of progressivism and emphasise the significance of Rousseau, stating that Comenius is 'nothing more than an overture to the first of the classics in the history of progressivism: Rousseau' (2004, p. 290). As Darling and Nordenbo argue, the main strands of progressivism are easily traceable to Rousseau but are primarily pedagogical rather than broadly political in intent. They argue that the main features of progressivism are a consideration of the child's nature, personal growth, creativity, and natural motivations. I would add to this list the importance attached to children learning by experience, through activities with physical objects, especially natural ones. All of this is now so commonplace that it has become part of so-called 'best practice' for much primary (and some secondary) education. Rousseau's pedagogical ideas no longer seem radical to a modern reader.

Mary Wollstonecraft was three when Rousseau's book was published; as a young adult she had been persuaded and excited by many of his educational ideas. However, she also denounced many of his educational ideas in her extended polemic, *A Vindication of the Rights of Woman*. Her polemic was primarily directed at his proposals for girls' education. This is not surprising. Not only was she female and so likely to notice Sophie—as generations of male commentators have not—but also she was herself far from fitting Rousseau's ideal of a submissive, unintelligent, modest, flirtatious, virtuous woman trying to be pretty. Not for nothing was she called a 'hyena in petticoats' by Robert Walpole.

Wollstonecraft was like Rousseau in that she had a difficult childhood and grew up to be a charismatic, difficult, often personally unhappy misfit in society. Like Rousseau, she stirred up controversy by writing best-selling books that were both widely admired and widely vilified. Also like him, she is difficult to categorise as straightforwardly 'Enlightenment' or 'Romantic'. She asserts her adherence to reason, and her two *Vindications*, first of the rights of men, and then later of the rights of woman were thought to be masculine in approach. (In what follows, all references to the *Vindication* refer to *A Vindication of the Rights of Woman*.) Other books, especially her *Letters written in Sweden, Norway and Denmark*, were praised for their female sensibility. She appeals to reason throughout the *Vindication*, but does so with 'energetic emotions', (rather than with 'pretty feminine phrases'). In spite of these similarities Wollstonecraft's ideas were soon forgotten, while Rousseau's lived on.[3]

Wollstonecraft's polemic in the *Vindication* is fun to read—and usually apposite—and the book could be read simply as an indignant response to contemporary statements about the inferior position of women, including Rousseau's view of Sophie as naturally dependent and lacking in reason. To do so would be to miss what is more significant for current educational practices. I turn to Wollstonecraft because she provides a (now submerged) response to *Émile* that suggests an educational approach which, in my view, would be productive of more socially just educational relationships than those proposed by Rousseau. Her proposals form an implicit critique of many of Rousseau's basic assumptions in *Émile* as well as constructing an alternative approach. Education had been a continuing preoccupation for her, and she had written several successful books on the subject, grounded in her own experiences of teaching in school and as a governess. In the *Vindication* she suggests alternative approaches and makes some concrete, constructive proposals about education in general. Some of these appear in the penultimate chapter, 'On national education'. However the chapter is not a summary of her approaches and proposals. These can also be found scattered throughout the book in the form of comments on educational practices, as she considers the harm she thinks they do to both boys and girls.

It is important to note that there is no simple polarised difference between Rousseau and Wollstonecraft. Her proposals demonstrate that there are significant similarities between them. Both of them not only pay attention to the place of education in creating a just society, but also to the happiness of children during their education. Unlike most writers on education at the time (and since) each considers the implications of the education of *both* boys *and* girls for the future shape of society.[4] Further, they share a critique of society as corrupt and unequal, and disliked the refined manners of polite society. They both explicitly say they want to be honest and straightforward in expressing their views. Finally, they each express a wish for a more equal world of smallholders/tradesmen to replace class divisions between the aristocracy, the middle classes and, to some extent, the poor.

Wollstonecraft's critique is a significant one, precisely because of her partial agreement with Rousseau. She demonstrates that there is a different way of approaching the good things to be found in Rousseau, while avoiding some of the unfortunate implications of his system. The different threads of Rousseau's educational thinking in *Émile* weave together into a whole cloth that has been found to be attractive down the centuries. Wollstonecraft suggests a way of using many of these threads while discarding others, in order to weave a different cloth that would serve education better. In other words, both thinkers understand how details of pedagogy must cohere with its wider purpose educationally and politically. Like Rousseau, her concern is less to do with particular pedagogical techniques or even approaches, more to do with the full complexity of educational relationships. The educational relationships they consider include those between human beings now and in the future, between teacher and students, between students, and between human beings and the rest of the natural world, the more-than-human.

Educational Relationships in the Present Affecting Relationships in the Future

The education of the young is always concerned with the future as well as with the present, since the relationships cultivated in young people will affect the kinds of relationships they are able and willing to form in adulthood. Hence education is looked to as a way of producing a better future. It is hoped that the future may be, variously, happier, healthier, more productive, more democratic, more prosperous, more dynamic, more peaceful and/or more just. It is the last of these that most concerned both Rousseau and Wollstonecraft. Both of them wanted education to produce social justice in the future as well as being a benefit to young people in the present. Their different understanding of how to achieve it is reflected in the kinds of educational relationships each of them favours.

One view of social justice, dating back at least to Plato's *Republic*, takes the form of a blueprint for a perfect society. In this view, we know what it would be to live well, and what conditions would be needed to allow it. Rousseau took this view. He was an admirer of the *Republic* and was self-consciously and explicitly emulating it. His aim was to devise a blueprint for a socially just republic in which education is as key as it was for Plato. Once a blueprint has been drawn, all that remains is to construct it accurately, at least as far as possible. His educational proposals for Émile and Sophie are designed so that as adults they would inhabit an ideal republic.[5]

Wollstonecraft appears to have held an alternative view: that social justice is always in the making, and necessarily responsive to changing conditions, especially those conditions which are themselves the result of a struggle for social justice. It is probably relevant that the *Vindication* was written against the tumultuous background of the French Revolution. So while Wollstonecraft agreed with Rousseau that education could lead to a more socially just society, her aims remained at the level of general principle rather than providing specific proposals about what such a society would be. Her proposals seek to change contemporary educational practices so that it would be possible to create a more socially just society but she is content not to see beyond the horizon, knowing that at the horizon somebody else may be able to see further:

It is difficult for us purblind mortals to say to what height human discoveries and improvements may yet arrive when the gloom of despotism subsides, which makes us stumble at every step . . . ([1792] 1994, p. 102).

Wollstonecraft has been described as reformist rather than radical, but as Ferguson (1999) argues, it is right to call her radical even though she stopped short of challenging either the class basis of society, or the assumption that mothers had the primary responsibility for children.[6]

Indeed the contradictions at the heart of her wish that women should both be employed in the professions, and also take responsibility for the home, are ones that she could hope would be resolved when the first principle of sex equality was put into practice. In other words, she wanted the society 'reasonably organised' but had no blueprint for what it might look like.[7]

Between Teacher and Student(s)

Rousseau intends that Émile will learn personal autonomy and independence through the experience of exercising them. But this is a strange kind of personal autonomy, perhaps not surprisingly given Rousseau's felt tension between harmony and individual freedom, something which appears and reappears in his various books (Rorty, 1998). It is a personal autonomy that is entirely controlled by the tutor, though intended to be felt as a rugged, individual independence. The tutor knows precisely what Émile should learn as he grows through various broad stages of development. Each learning objective is controlled by the tutor. However, the child himself thinks that he is freely choosing what he does and attending to the consequences. This pedagogic approach is described by Rousseau as 'purely negative' (1979, p. 93). The tutor is never to demand obedience either through force or reason. Rather, he makes sure the boy's education is one of 'well-regulated freedom . . . One enchains, pushes, and restrains him with the bond of necessity alone without his letting out a peep' (1979, p. 92). Meanwhile, Sophie is being made well aware that she must do as she is told by her mother. That is how she is to learn a proper docility. Rousseau says that little girls must become accustomed to being interrupted in the midst of their games without grumbling. They must feel their dependence. They must not be allowed, ever, to know themselves free of restraint (1979, p. 370).

Wollstonecraft does not describe the details of pedagogy, since she focuses on the students and their perspectives rather than on teaching. However, her few remarks intimate an approach in which the teacher makes space for students' ideas to influence the direction of the lessons. She speaks of the business of education as conducting 'the shooting tendrils to a proper pole' (p. 190). But she is also keen that children are encouraged to work out their ideas in conversation with each other, without too much interference from an adult.

> In order to open their faculties they should be excited to think for themselves; and this can only be done by mixing a number of children together, and making them jointly pursue the same objects ([1792] 1994, p. 241).

She seems to be advocating a social pedagogy of principles rather than objectives, and in which children learn from each other in social groups rather than individually on their own.

Gender relations are key to understanding these differences. Rousseau's proposal requires single sex education; Wollstonecraft's requires co-education. Émile's education is intended to make him hardy and tough. He is to be guided by reason not emotion, while Sophie learns to be soft and to express emotion, though not to exercise her reason. In adulthood, the two sexes and their different capacities would be perfectly combined to create a just republic governed by reason in public and by appropriate emotions in private. Wollstonecraft wanted all children to learn both reason and affection. That would lead, she hoped, to a more just society in which the understanding had enlarged the heart of all men and women (p. 281). For this, social relations between children and within the family are key.

> To make men citizens two natural steps might be taken, which seem directly to lead to the desired point; for the domestic affections, that first open the heart to the various modifications of humanity, would be cultivated, whilst the children were nevertheless allowed to spend great part (*sic.*) of their time, on terms of equality with other children ([1792] 1994, p. 242).

She sees independence as coming not from solitary living or self-sufficiency but from everyone being able to make a living: 'to earn their own subsistence' (p. 250).

Rousseau has a dualist, tightly-linked set of assumptions in which naturally manly characteristics (independence, strength, rugged self-sufficiency and action) are in opposition to naturally womanly ones (dependence, weakness, tenderness towards others and a concern with personal appearance). He thought:

> A perfect woman and a perfect man ought not to resemble each other in mind any more than in looks . . . woman is made to please and to be subjugated . . . there arises . . . the audacity of one sex and the timidity of the other, and finally the modesty and the shame with which nature armed the weak in order to enslave the strong ([1762] 1979, p. 358).

Wollstonecraft, on the other hand, draws no dualistic links like the ones for Rousseau:

> Yet thus to give a sex to mind was not very consistent with the principles of a man who argued so warmly, and so well, for the immortality of the soul—But what a weak barrier is truth when it stands in the way of an hypothesis ([1792] 1994, p. 110).

She was not alone among philosophers or educationists in proposing the radical view that the sexes were intellectually and morally equal. Rousseau's contemporaries, Voltaire and Diderot, both thought so too (Clinton, 1975).[8] Wollstonecraft herself cites *The History of Sandford and Merton*, a didactic children's book published in the 1780s, which advocates that girls as well as boys should be educated in reason and philosophy (p. 108). Her contribution, similar to Rousseau's, is to draw together these current ideas and knit them into a structure, in which connections are made between an educational present and the good of a future society.

Feminist theory over the last 40 years has drawn attention to the ways that Rousseau's kind of dualism is embedded in the structures of much modern thinking in a way that distorts what it is possible to think and to do. Feminists have long argued that the existence of dualism in thinking is associated with the binary of sex (Irigaray, 1985; Fox Keller, 1986; Whitford, 1991; Langton, 2005). Dualistic thinking goes beyond the more obviously gendered concepts such as mind/body, nature/reason, subject/object or emotion/reason. Its implicit gendering extends to many of the concepts used in everyday educational life to describe young people: boy/girl, active/passive, strong/weak, clever/diligent, autonomous/dependent and so on. Dualism lives, for example in current stereotypes of big strong boys playing football and taking up most of the playground, and the neat and tidy groups of girls chatting round its edges. This dualism has been given a recent impetus from some neuroscientists. The feminist neuroscientist, Cordelia Fine usefully presents a critique of their attempts to give a rationale for gender duality in spite of evidence to the contrary (Fine, 2010). I am reminded of previous feminist scientists' struggles with gender determinism in biology (Sayers, 1982), psychoanalysis (Bernheimer and Kahane, 1985) and sociobiology (Haraway, 1991).

An alternative to dualism, equally problematic, is the phallogocentric imaginary which assumes a worthwhile humanity to be masculine, if not actually male. Perhaps it is not surprising that many commentators have not really noticed Sophie or have thought of her as an anomaly.[9] They think Émile is just a child, which is to miss one of Rousseau's main arguments, as pointed out by Martin (1985, 1986). As mentioned earlier, Rousseau's utopia depended as much on the existence of an adult Sophie, domestic, emotional and obedient as it did on an adult Émile, citizenly, reasonable and autonomous. Inattention to Sophie means that the Rousseau's ideal boy becomes the ideal child: who 'climbs trees, fires catapults, swims in streams' and who appears in fiction as:

> Tom Brown, Just William and Huckleberry Finn, and includes such honorary boys as Tarzan, Richard Hannay and Alan Quatermain (Griffiths and Smith, 1989, pp. 286–7).

The effects in current educational thinking are to make a stereotypical masculine life desirable for all human beings, forgetting the dependence of this life on the physical and emotional work of women.[10] So it is taken for granted that girls should do as well as boys in 'boys' subjects' (though when they do better, then it seems to be a matter of concern). But boys are not expected to do well in 'girls' subjects'. The ideal pupil is still masculine—even if the high attaining one is a girl.

In our own time, education largely remains caught between new dualisms (that look much like the old ones), either in which women know their place as supportive to men, or in which the ideal citizen is masculine and nobody is left to do what has been traditionally women's work (at least in a society of equals). Wollstonecraft offers an alternative. She wants both men and women to have the same virtues: both the domestic ones and the citizenly ones.

The significance attached to this masculinist autonomy by educators remains strong. Yet, as my dialogue with Richard Smith (Griffiths and Smith, 1989) shows, the concepts of autonomy, dependence and independence in educational settings are multiple, and often mutually incoherent while remaining enmeshed in a Rousseau-like disdain for dependence.[11] We point out:

Most teachers take friendship patterns very seriously, and attach importance to their own personal relationships with the children in their class. They are also likely to pay a lot of attention to the importance of the home, community and culture as an influence on the child. The importance of other people in the development of children remains, however, insufficiently acknowledged as far as the development of self and of knowledge are concerned. In literature, whether with a psychological or philosophical flavour, it is far more common to find 'autonomy' and its cognates posited as the end to which development tends than any recognition that most of us gladly choose a world in which our autonomy is constrained by personal relationships (Griffiths and Smith, 1989, p. 286).

Current calls for individualism, 'personalisation' and also, at the same time, team-work or group-work, are, arguably, tensions inherited from Rousseau.

Between Human Beings and the More-Than-Human

Rousseau uses 'nature' or 'natural' in more than one way, for instance describing the more-than-human world, the physical and psychological development of human beings and in distinguishing artifice from what is authentic. However, as Wain points out:

These are not, however, contradictory or inconsistent uses but complex ways of using the same term in different contexts of meaning. It is neither necessary nor usual for a word to carry one constant meaning whenever it is used, provided that the different uses are clearly signalled by the context (2011, p. 47).

In short, Rousseau's view of nature is Romantic. He re-theorizes nature as good, against views of his time that the rationality or spirituality of human beings is manifested in a transcendence of nature. Rousseau's view, radical at the time, was significant because, if nature is the source of our goodness, then a natural man can trust his conscience which will not have been corrupted by society. Nature has a double use. It is needed to allow a boy to develop into a man. Then, as a man, he can return to Nature as a source of sublime feelings and restoration. Taylor describes Rousseau's approach:

We return to nature because it brings out strong and noble feelings in us … Nature is like a great keyboard on which our highest sentiments are played out. We turn to it, as we might turn to music, to evoke and strengthen the best in us (1989, p. 297).

Rousseau sees nature as something that draws a response from the solitary individual of sublime appreciation. Nature requires him to be able to deal with its challenges with rugged strength, endurance and courage. All of this is evidently a nature that is always, and necessarily, other than human except for the natural boy or man who experiences it. This nature, at least as found in man, is perfected by civilization (as is made clear both in *Émile* and in the *Discourse on Inequality*). Ironically, this understanding is reminiscent of a rational, scientific Enlightenment that Rousseau rejects. It could be argued that he advocates using nature, just as a rationalist like Bacon wanted to use it for the benefit of men. In both cases the preservation of nature can be understood as enlightened self-interest. For followers of Rousseau this means advocating outdoor education in order to experience a response to nature (Jickling, 2009; Bonnett, 2007); for followers of Bacon it means advocating Sustainable Development because the ecosystem needs to be preserved if human beings are to survive at all (Kopnina, 2013a,b).

Wollstonecraft offers a different approach from either of these. For her, nature nourishes the spirit in several ways, all of which are to be found through a proper education. In her pedagogical proposals she does not impose a sharp demarcation between what is inside walls and what is outside them, neither does she distinguish a wild nature from one influenced by human beings. The sublime is significant, as is also clear throughout her *Letters written in Sweden, Norway and Denmark* where she describes the Scandinavian landscape. However she is also attentive to the (more social) pastoral landscape as well as the (non-human) sublime. For Wollstonecraft, nature is both good and bad, restorative and dulling. The outdoors provides the pleasures of being in shady lanes or sitting on stiles, and the nuisance of muddy lanes and wet weather—and the pleasure of returning home, out of it.

I still recollect with pleasure, the country day school; where a boy trudged in the morning, wet or dry . . . [to] return alone in the evening to recount the feats of the day close at the parental knee . . . I appeal to many superiour men, who were educated in this manner, whether the recollection of some shady lane where they conned their lesson: or, of some stile, where they sat making a kite, or mending a bat, has not endeared their country to them ([1796] 2009, pp. 242–3).

She writes of her spirits being restored by lakes, fir groves and rocks, but she also writes of being 'bastilled by nature' ([1796] 2009, p. 69) in a place where rocks and sea shut people out from finer sentiments.

Nothing genial, in fact, appears around this place, or within the circle of its rocks. And, now I recollect, it seems to me that the most genial and humane characters I have met with in life, were most alive to the sentiments inspired by tranquil country scenes ([1796] 2009, pp. 69–70).

Sublime nature can be enhanced by human additions. She mentions with approval a carefully placed stone seat ([1796] 2009, p. 21). She remarks how the place 'bastilled by nature' becomes 'extremely fine' when viewed from the sea: 'In a recess of the rocks was a clump of pines, amongst which a steeple rose picturesquely beautiful' ([1796] 2009, p. 70). But the non-human is not there simply for our exploitation. Kindness to animals is a significant virtue for her, partly, though only partly, because it connects with the treatment of one human being by another.

Humanity to animals should be particularly inculcated as a part of national education, for it is not at present one of our national virtues. Tenderness for their humble dumb domestics, amongst the lower class, is oftener to be found in a savage than a civilized state . . . where they are trodden under foot by the rich, to domineer over them to revenge the insults that they are obliged to bear from their superiors ([1792] 1994, p. 258).

She wants book learning and the real things to be integrated with play in the outdoors, valued not only for itself, but also because:

These relaxations might all be rendered part of elementary education, for many things improve and amuse the senses . . . to the principles of which, dryly laid down, children would turn a deaf ear ([1792] 1994, p. 253).

These relaxations also allow natural animal spirits to improve body and mind:

With what disgust have I heard sensible women, for girls are more restrained and cowed than boys, speak of the wearisome confinement, which they endured at school. Not allowed, perhaps, to step out of one broad walk in a superb garden, and obliged to pace with steady deportment stupidly backwards and forwards, holding up their heads and turning out their toes, with shoulders braced back, instead of bounding, as nature directs to complete her own design, in the various attitudes so conducive to health. The animal spirits, which make both mind and body shoot out, and unfold the tender blossoms of hope, are turned sour and vented in vain wishes or pert repinings, that contract the faculties and spoil the temper ([1792] 1994, pp. 248–9).

Wollstonecraft's educational proposals suggest the relevance of the more-than-human in the education of children in ways that are neither in the long shadow of Rousseau's Romantic conception, nor in its converse of rationalist instrumentalism.

OUTDOOR EDUCATION AS AN EXAMPLE

I have been discussing different approaches and proposals about educational relationships: between human beings now and in the future, between teacher and student(s) (who also have relationships with each other), and between human beings and the rest of the natural world, the more-than-human. All of these are significant because they concern the social justice issue that faces all human beings: how to live well, here, now, and in the future. In this section I focus on one of these sets of relationships: the more-than-human.

Wilderness and the Outdoors. Human Beings in Relationship with the More-Than-Human

In this section I draw attention to how the world can be described using the terms which do not fall easily on one side or another of Rousseau's dualist distinctions between Nature and what is natural, on the one hand, and what is social and civilized, on the other hand. There is an alternative to seeing ourselves as distinct from an innocent, good, wild, non-human nature; instead, like Wollstonecraft, we need to employ no sharp demarcations between what is indoors and outdoors, what is wild from what is social. Kathleen Jamie's two recent books of essays (2005, 2012) demonstrate a way of understanding our natural selves that is much closer to Wollstonecraft's perceptions than to Rousseau's. As Jamie puts it in her trenchant critique of Macfarlane's *The Wild Places* (2008), the dominant imaginary in the Romantic tradition of nature writing is, following Rousseau, a 'lone enraptured male' in search of the spiritual resources of remote places seen as 'wild' (2008). Her work asks us to notice that nature is more complex. It is all of: organic, inorganic, indoors, outdoors, and both; of our bodies, in our bodies and beyond them; made/created/formed by people; growing, inanimate; beautiful, grim; huge, minute, and all sizes between; mysterious, wild, ordinary, unspoilt, worked over, innocent and a force to be struggled with. Like Wollstonecraft, she thinks that what we term 'nature' is not there to be exploited, though it is to be engaged with; that it can seem benign or malign; and that it demands an ethical response from us.

Jamie's essays may seem to be just simple, careful, attentive descriptions of her observations. But each of them is an implicit criticism of the dominant, Romantic approach to descriptions of nature. She challenges the usual distinctions made between indoors and outdoors; the wild and the common place; the wild and the domestic; attention to what is non-human and attention to human beings. For instance, in her essay, 'Peregrines, Ospreys, Cranes' she does all of this. She begins by noting the call of a peregrine both outside and inside the house:

> The sound enters my attic room through its window, and if I turn from my desk to glance out of that window I see the hill (2005, p. 29).

Later, on a bike ride she discusses the peregrines with a grumpy old man:

> 'Ach—the young ones have no interestit,' he'll say, shaking his head (2005, p. 31).

Later still, she comes across a young mechanic at the garage who is concealing a telescope on a dirty oil drum so he could watch them. She writes:

> Between the laundry and the fetching kids from school, that's how birds enter my life. I listen (2005, p. 39).

In 'Skylines', she demonstrates the artificiality of Rousseau's dualism. The outdoors is linked to buildings, people, passers-by, her own everyday working life, the weather, geology, history and, most of all, to looking with attention. She starts an article about looking at Edinburgh skylines through a telescope on Calton Hill, by saying:

> One afternoon last November I was crossing Charlotte Square and, happening to glance up, saw a comet. . . . this beautiful

brass comet, a shining ball towing a deeply forked tail (2005, p. 147).

In her essay, 'Pathologies', Jamie blurs another set of distinctions; the wild and the outdoors, the wild and ourselves. When her mother dies, somebody uses a phrase about nature taking its course. Shortly after, she attends a conference where people are pontificating about humanity's relationship with other species, and how we have to 'reconnect with nature', as if, she notes, we are not bodily, mortal beings, using vaccinations and eating meat. She thinks more about this issue, and gets permission to attend some biopsies. She looks at bacteria grazing on a stomach lining:

> It was an image you might find in a Sunday-night wildlife documentary. Pastoral but wild, too. . . . in the wilderness of our stomachs (2012, p. 35).

The Outdoors in Educational Practice

The influence of Rousseau on education in the outdoors is clear. Orthodox educational approaches see the outdoors as providing real experiences in order to meet the pre-defined objectives of the science, geography or history curriculum. Alternatively, it provides adventure and a chance to develop physical skills in response to risk. Or it allows children to find the spiritual resources missing when they are suffering from 'nature deficit disorder' (Louv, 2008; Moss, 2012). The critique presented by Wollstonecraft and Jamie suggests that a better approach would be to acknowledge the rich complexity of human life in and of the world. It would be to acknowledge that nature is not only 'out there' but also 'in here' and 'around here'. Within education an approach like this would mean asking students to pay attention and then reflect using various forms of symbolisation and expression. However, as Haluza-Delay (2001) argues, this needs to be done in familiar places and in the midst of ordinary social events, acknowledging them, not bracketing them. Attention and reflection can be done alone or in a group, but in either case it thrives on conversations whether in the moment or remembered, and then on collaborative reflections, learning with peers as well as with tutors, in order to come to independent, unforced ways of understanding ourselves, in and of the world.

It is possible to find such an approach in some practices of 'outdoor education'. Higgins and Wattchow (2013) describe how a canoe journey down the Spey can be the occasion for students coming to attend reflexively to the many ways in which they are connected to the canoes, to the river, to its past, to present inhabitants, and to each other. I suggest that if this approach were more integrated into an understanding of education then the ethics—the social justice—of living a good life together with each other and the rest of the world (benign and malign) would permeate education and give more hope for the future. With such an education, we may hope with Wollstonecraft that the next generation and the next one after that will be able to imagine a more ethical—a more socially just—world than any we are able to imagine today:

These would be schools of morality—and happiness of man, allowed to flow from the pure springs of duty and affection, what advances might not the human mind make? ([1792] 1994, p. 254).

NOTES

1. Social justice is, as Michael Walzer (1994) argued, a thin concept. This sentence thickens the concept a little, expressing the most recent result of my evolving understanding of social justice over the last two decades (see Griffiths, 2013; Griffiths forthcoming, 2014).
2. There are notable exceptions. See, for instance, work by Michael Bonnett (2007, 2009, 2012), Bob Jickling (2009), Helen Kopnina (2013a, 2013b), and Andrew Stables (2010) on aspects of ethics and social justice in relation to the outdoors, to sustainability and to the environment. See also Heather Greenhalgh-Spencer (Chapter 10).
3. The canon of progressive educational thought includes hardly any women: in Darling and Nordenbo (2004), only Montessori makes it into the list.
4. Rachel Jones and Caroline Wilson discuss the significance of there being two sexes in education (Chapters 1 and 2, respectively).
5. Also see Jones, Chapter 1.
6. This assumption should be seen in the context of there being no reliable form of contraception.
7. Christine Winter (Chapter 7) contrasts Gove's policy of providing a blueprint for curriculum by prescribing 'core knowledge' with more flexible and open relationships with the subject matter to be learnt.
8. Also see Voltaire's marginal note on the *Discourse on Inequality*, at the point Rousseau asserts that women as a sex ought to obey men: 'Ought to obey? Why?' (Rousseau, [1755] 1983, p. 179n).
9. These commentators have failed to listen to what Rousseau was saying, in the sense of 'listen' put forward by Marit Hoveid and Arnhild Finne (Chapter 5). They appropriate what he says to their own politics while also appropriating the female into the male ideal. See Jones (Chapter 1).
10. See Shuffelton (Chapter 3).
11. The significance of dependence is further discussed by Shuffelton, Jones and Wilson (all this book, Chapters 3, 4 and 1 respectively).

REFERENCES

Bernheimer, C. and Kahane, C. (eds) (1985) *In Dora's Case* (London, Virago).

Bloom, A. (1979) Introduction, in: J-J. Rousseau, *Émile or On Education* (New York, Basic Books).

Bonnett, M. (2007) Environmental Education and the Issue of Nature, *Journal of Curriculum Studies*, 39.6, pp. 707–721.

Bonnett, M. (2009) Systemic Wisdom, the 'Selving' of Nature, and Knowledge Transformation: Education for the 'Greater Whole'. Special issue of *Studies in Philosophy and Education: Environmental Concern and the Transformation of Knowledge*, 28 pp. 39–49.

Bonnett, M. (2012) Environmental Concern, Moral Education, and Our Place in Nature, *Journal of Moral Education Special Issue: Moral Education and Environmental Concern*, 41.3, pp. 285–300.

Clinton, K. B. (1975) Femme et Philosophe: Enlightenment Origins of Feminism, *Eighteenth-Century Studies*, 8.3, pp. 283–299.

Darling, J. and Nordenbo, S. (2004) Progressivism, in: N. Blake, P. Smeyers, R. Smith and P. Standish (eds) *The Blackwell Guide to the Philosophy of Education* (Oxford, Blackwell).

Ferguson, S. (1999) The Radical Ideas of Mary Wollstonecraft, *Politics and Public Administration Publications and Research, Paper 2*. Online at http://digitalcommons.ryerson.ca/politics/2. Accessed 13 January 2014.

Fine, C. (2010) *Delusions of Gender: The Real Science behind Sex Differences* (London, Icon Books).

Fox Keller, E. (1986) *Reflections on Gender and Science* (New Haven, CT, Yale University Press).

Griffiths, M. (2013) Social Justice in Education: Joy in Education and Education for Joy, in: I. Bogotch and C. M. Shields (eds) *International Handbook of Educational Leadership and Social (In)Justice* (New York, Springer).

Griffiths, M. (2014) My Life as a Vixen, in: L. Waks (ed.) *Leaders in Philosophy of Education* Volume 2 (Rotterdam, Sense Publishers).

Griffiths, M. and Smith, R. (1989) Standing Alone: Dependence, Independence and Interdependence, *Journal of Philosophy of Education*, 23.2, pp. 283–294.

Haluza-Delay, R. (2001). Nothing Here to Care about: Participant Constructions of Nature Following a 12-day Wilderness Program, *The Journal of Environmental Education*, 32.4, pp. 43–48.

Haraway, D. (1991) *Simians Cyborgs and Women: The Reinvention of Nature* (London, Free Association Books).

Higgins, P. and Wattchow, B. (2013) The Water of Life: Creative Non-fiction and Lived Experience on an Interdisciplinary Canoe journey on Scotland's River Spey, *Journal of Adventure Education and Outdoor Learning*, 13.1 pp. 18–35.

Irigaray, L. (1985) *This Sex Which Is Not One* (Ithaca, NY, Cornell University Press).

Jamie, K. (2005) *Findings* (London, Sort Of Books).

Jamie, K. (2008) A Lone Enraptured Male. Review of *The Wild Places* by R. Macfarlane, *London Review of Books* [Online] 30.5 pp. 25–27. Online at: http://www.lrb.co.uk/v30/n05/kathleen-jamie/a-lone-enraptured-male. Accessed 13 January 2014.

Jamie, K. (2012) *Sightlines* (London, Sort Of Books).

Jickling, B. (2009). Sitting on an Old Grey Stone: Meditations on Emotional Understanding, in: M. McKenzie, H. Bai, P. Hart and B. Jickling (eds) *Fields of Green: Restorying Culture, Environment, and Education* (Cresskill, NJ, Hampton Press).

Kopnina, H. (2013a) Forsaking Nature? Contesting 'Biodiversity' Through Competing Discourses of Sustainability, *Journal of Education for Sustainable Development*, 7.1 pp. 47–59.

Kopnina, H. (2013b) Requiem for the Weeds: Reflections in Amsterdam City Park, *Sustainable Cities and Society*, 9, pp. 10–14.

Langton, R. (2005) Feminism in Philosophy, in: F. Jackson and M. Smith (eds) *The Oxford Handbook of Contemporary Analytic Philosophy* (Oxford, Oxford University Press).

Louv, R. (2008) *Last Child in the Woods: Saving Our Children from Nature-Deficit Disorder* (Chapel Hill, NC, Algonquin Books of Chapel Hill).

Martin, J. R. (1985) *Reclaiming a Conversation: The Ideal of an Educated Woman* (New Haven, CT, Yale University Press).

Martin, J. R. (1986) Redefining the Educated Person: Rethinking the Significance of Gender, *Educational Researcher*, 15.6, pp. 6–10.

Moss, S. (2012) *Natural Childhood* (Swindon, National Trust).

Rorty, A. (1998) Rousseau's Educational Experiments, in: A. Rorty (ed.) *Philosophers on Education: New Historical Perspectives* (London and New York, Routledge).

Rousseau, J-J. [1762] (1979) *Émile or On Education*, A. Bloom, ed., trans. and intro. (New York, Basic Books).

Rousseau, J-J. [1755] (1983) *A Discourse on Inequality*, M. Cranston, ed., trans. and notes (Harmondsworth, Penguin Books).

Sayers, J. (1982) *Biological Politics; Feminist and Anti-Feminist Perspectives* (London, Tavistock).

Stables, A. (2010) The Song of the Earth: A Pragmatic Rejoinder, *Educational Philosophy and Theory*, 42.7 pp. 796–807.

Steinkraus, W. E. (1974) Kant and Rousseau on Humanity, *The Southern Journal of Philosophy*, 12.2 pp. 265–270.

Taylor, C. (1989) *Sources of the Self* (Cambridge, Cambridge University Press).

Wain, K. (2011) *On Rousseau: An Introduction to his Radical Thinking on Education and Politics* (Rotterdam, Sense Publishers).

Walzer, M. (1994) *Thick and Thin. Moral Argument at Home and Abroad* (Notre Dame, IN, University of Notre Dame Press).

Whitford, M. (1991) *Luce Irrigaray: Philosophy in the Feminine* (London, Routledge).

Wollstonecraft, M. [1792] (1994) *A Vindication of the Rights of Woman and A Vindication of the Rights of Men*, J. Todd, ed. and intro. (Oxford, Oxford World Classics).

Wollstonecraft, M. [1796] (2009) *Letters written in Sweden, Norway, and Denmark*, T. Brekke and J. Mee, eds, intro. and notes (Oxford, Oxford University Press).

Index

Re-Imagining Relationships in Education: Ethics, Politics and Practices, First Edition. Edited by Morwenna
Griffiths, Marit Honerød Hoveid, Sharon Todd and ChristineWinter. Chapters © 2015 The Authors. Editorial
organization © 2015 Philosophy of Education Society of Great Britain. Published 2015 by JohnWiley & Sons Ltd.